Contemporary Welsh Plays

Contemporary Welsh Plays

Tonypandemonium
Rachel Trezise

The Radicalisation of Bradley Manning
Tim Price

Gardening: For the Unfulfilled and Alienated
Brad Birch

Llwyth*
Dafydd James
***(in Welsh)**

Parallel Lines
Katherine Chandler

Bruised
Matthew Trevannion

With a foreword by David Ian Rabey

General introduction by Tim Price and Kate Wasserberg

Introduction to 'Llwyth' by Arwel Gruffydd

Bloomsbury Methuen Drama
An imprint of Bloomsbury Publishing Plc

B L O O M S B U R Y
LONDON • NEW DELHI • NEW YORK • SYDNEY

Bloomsbury Methuen Drama
An imprint of Bloomsbury Publishing Plc

50 Bedford Square   1385 Broadway
London   New York
WC1B 3DP   NY 10018
UK   USA

www.bloomsbury.com

**BLOOMSBURY METHUEN DRAMA and the Diana logo are trademarks of
Bloomsbury Publishing Plc**

First published in 2015

Introduction, foreword and *Llwyth* introduction copyright © Bloomsbury Methuen Drama 2015

Tonypandemonium first published in 2014 by Parthian Books

First published by Bloomsbury Methuen Drama as part of this collection in 2015
Copyright © 2014, 2015 Rachel Trezise

The Radicalisation of Bradley Manning first published in 2012 by Bloomsbury Methuen Drama
First published as part of this collection in 2014
Copyright © 2012, 2013, 2015, Tim Price

Gardening: For the Unfulfilled and Alienated first published in 2014 as part of this collection by
Bloomsbury Methuen Drama
Copyright © 2015, Brad Birch

Llwyth first published by Sherman Cymru in 2010
First published by Bloomsbury Methuen Drama as part of this collection in 2015
Copyright © 2010, 2015, Dafydd James

Parallel Lines first published in 2015 as part of this collection by Bloomsbury Methuen Drama
Copyright © 2015, Katherine Chandler

Bruised first published in 2015 as part of this collection by Bloomsbury Methuen Drama
Copyright © 2015, Matthew Trevannion

British Library Cataloguing-in-Publication Data
A catalogue record for this book is available from the British Library.

ISBN PB: 978-1-4725-7658-3
EPUB: 978-1-4725-7661-3
EPDF: 978-1-4725-7659-0

Library of Congress Cataloging-in-Publication Data
A catalog record for this book is available from the Library of Congress.

Typeset by Fakenham Prepress Solutions, Fakenham, Norfolk NR21 8NN
Printed and bound in India

Contents

Chronology

1997 – elected Labour government promises to create a devolved institution in Wales. With the narrowest of margins – 50.3% – Wales votes in favour of its first national governing body since Owain Glyndwr's parliament in 1404.

1999 – The National Assembly for Wales opens as a consequence of the Governance of Wales Act 1998, with the power to decide how the government budget for Wales is spent.

1999 – The Millennium stadium – one of the few sporting arenas in the world located in the city centre – is opened to host the rugby World Cup. Wales is knocked out in the quarter finals by eventual winners Australia.

1999 – The rugby world cup coincides with the year dubbed 'Cool Cymru'. With chart-topping albums and singles from Catatonia, the Stereophonics and the Manic Street Preachers, Welsh popular culture is exported around the world.

2001 – Census trends for the previous century are bucked by results which show an increase in Welsh speakers from 19% to 21%. The rising popularity of Welsh-medium schools is credited for the rise in bilingualism in Wales.

2003 – Theatr Genedlaethol Cymru, a non-building-based touring national theatre for Wales in the Welsh language, is launched. The company's first season is opened by Meic Povey's Yn debyg iawn ati a fi (Very much like you and me) at Clwyd Theatr Cymru before touring Wales.

2004 – The Mike Ruddock-coached national rugby team wins the Grand Slam after a thrilling opening encounter with England, featuring a remarkable performance from Gavin Henson.

2006 – Rachel Trezise wins the inaugural Dylan Thomas prize, the world's richest literary prize, for her collection of short stories, *Fresh Apples*, describing life in the former mining valleys.

2007 – National new writing company Sgript Cymru is merged with

Cardiff producing house Sherman Theatre to form the Sherman Cymru as a bilingual, touring building-based new writing company.

2008 – The Welsh rugby team wins a second Grand Slam, this time coached by New Zealander Warren Gatland. The final game against France was played at the Millennium Stadium in front of ecstatic crowds, as the team won 26-19.

2008 – Deep Cut, produced by Sherman Cymru and written by Philip Ralph, premieres at the Edinburgh Festival and wins the Amnesty International Freedom of Expression Award. The play explores the death of four trainees at the Deep Cut Barracks in Surrey, based on first-hand testimonies.

2009 – The English language National Theatre Wales is launched with their first season of plays opening in 2010-2011. The company produces 13 plays in a map of Wales. The youngest national theatre in the UK, broke new ground with site-specific, community engaged, digitally enabled work.

The season ended with the extraordinary *Passion Play* in which Hollywood star Michael Sheen returned to his home town of Port Talbot to perform the Gospel story.

2010 – Submarine, an adaptation of the book with the same name, is released to critical and popular acclaim. The coming-of-age story set in Swansea was the first novel by Joe Dunthorne, and the film staring Craig Roberts as fifteen-year-old Oliver Tate was directed by Richard Ayoade.

2011 – A referendum to extend the law-making powers for the Assembly is passed with a majority of 63% meaning the Assembly can now pass laws on devolved matters known as Acts of Assembly, without the need for approval from Parliament.

2011 – The Welsh rugby team were widely seen as the in-form team at the 2011 Rugby World Cup, reaching the semi-final in seemingly unstoppable form, only for captain and talisman Sam Warburton to be red-carded in the 18th minute. A valiant effort from the Welsh team could not overcome the set-back and lost narrowly to France 9-8.

2011 – Welsh language musicians go on strike after a change in 2007 by the Performing Rights Society in how it collects money from Radio Cymru. The change resulted in an 85% drop in income Welsh language artists make from the BBC. Widespread protests ensued.

2012 – Under austerity measures, the UK Government forces the BBC to fund S4C from the licence fee, rather than the Department of Culture Media and Sport funding the channel directly. Despite protests, the merger goes ahead.

2012 – The Welsh rugby team completes its third Grand Slam in eight years in a tense 16-9 defeat of France at the Millennium Stadium. The result was sweet revenge for the team that lost to France in the World Cup semi-final.

2013 – EOS is launched to take the place of PRS in Wales, to represent Welsh musicians in all publishing rights and distribution negotiations with broadcasters.

2014 – Rough Guide readers vote Wales the best country to visit in the world, for its extraordinary range of mountains, coastlines and castles, in such a small land mass.

Editors

Tim Price is a Welsh playwright and screenwriter. His plays include *For Once, Salt, Root and Roe* (winner of Best English Language playwright at the Theatre Critics of Wales Award), *Demos, The Radicalisation of Bradley Manning* (winner of the James Tait Black Prize for Drama), *I'm With the Band, Protest Song* and *Teh Internet Is Serious Business*. He is associate playwright at the Traverse theatre and co-founder of Welsh new writing company Dirty Protest.

Kate Wasserberg is the Artistic Director of The Other Room, Cardiff's first pub theatre. She is the former Associate Director of Clwyd Theatr Cymru, where she was responsible for new writing and for programming the annual Celtic Festival. Directing at Clwyd includes *Aristocrats, Salt, Root and Roe, Glengarry Glen Ross, Last Christmas, Bruised, Roots, Gaslight, Dancing at Lughnasa, Pieces* (which went to New York as part of the Brits Off Broadway Festival), *The Glass Menagerie* (CTC and tour) and *A History of Falling Things* (CTC and the Sherman Theatre, Cardiff). Previous to this she was Associate Director of the Finborough Theatre, London, where she directed *The Man* (which also toured nationally), *Sons of York* and *Little Madam*, all by James Graham and *The Representative, I Wish to Die Singing* and *The New Morality*. Other directing includes *The Knowledge/1hr45minutes* (Royal Court), *Mirror Teeth* (Finborough Theatre), 2007 Schools Festival (Young Vic*), Switzerland* (Hightide Festival), *Doing Lines* (Pleasance), *Blue Velvet* (Gilded Balloon) and *The Firebird* (Exeter Phoenix). As an Assistant Director, Kate has worked at the Barbican, the Abbey Theatre Dublin, the Young Vic, Shakespeare's Globe and the Theatre Royal Bath.

David Ian Rabey is Professor of Drama and Theatre Studies at Aberystwyth University and Artistic Director of Lurking Truth/ Gwir sy'n Llechu Theatre Company. His critical publications include *English Drama Since 1940* (2003), *Howard Barker: Ecstasy and Death* (2009), and, forthcoming, *The Theatre and Films of Jez Butterworth* (Methuen Drama Critical Companions, 2015) and

Theatre and Time (Intellect, 2016). His plays include two volumes, *The Wye Plays* (2004) and *Lovefuries* (2008), and *Land of My Fathers* (awaiting production).

Arwel Gruffydd graduated from Bangor University, before training as an actor at Webber Douglas Drama College, London. He was Literary Manager with Sgript Cymru between 2006 and 2008, and Associate Director at Sherman Cymru from 2008 to 2011. He is now Artistic Director of Theatr Genedlaethol Cymru.

Playwrights

Rachel Trezise
Plays include: *Sing of a Maiden*; *Lemon Meringue Pie*; and *Tonypandemonium*. Literary works include: *In and Out of the Goldfish Bowl*; *Fresh Apples* (winner of the inaugural Dylan Thomas Prize in 2006); *Dial M for Merthyr*; *Sixteen Shades of Crazy*; and *Cosmic Latte*.

Brad Birch
Plays include: *Running on Empty*; *Milton*; *Light Arrested Between the Curtain and the Glass*; *Even Stillness Breathes Softly Against a Brick Wall* and *Gardening: For the Unfulfilled and Alienated* (Fringe First Award Winner 2013).

Dafydd James
Plays include: *Terrace*; *Heritage*; *The Village Social* (with Ben Lewis); *My Name is Sue* (with Ben Lewis, Total Theatre Award Winner, 2009); *Sue: The Second Coming* (with Ben Lewis); and *Llwyth* (winner of the Best Language Production at the Theatre Critics of Wales Awards, 2012).

Katherine Chandler
Plays include: *Before it Rains* (winner of the Writers Guild Playwright Award at the Theatre Critics of Wales Awards 2012 and finalist for the 2013 Susan Smith Blackburn Prize); *The Silly Kings*; *Bird* (Judges Prize, Bruntwood Prize 2013); and *Parallel Lines*.

Matthew Trevannion
Plays include: *All But Gone* and *Bruised*. Matthew studied Acting at Rose Bruford College. His first full-length play, *Bruised* was produced by Clwyd Theatr Cymru in 2012. Matthew is under commission from Sherman Cymru and National Theatre Wales.

Foreword

Though it is impossible to offer a fully inclusive snapshot of contemporary Welsh drama, theatre and performance in any introductory essay or indeed play collection, we can identify significant efforts, characteristics, concerns and achievements happening at this current time. Several of the plays featured in this volume show a younger generation struggling to make sense of their inheritance – often dramatically personified by fragile or regressive parents – and edging towards shocking outbursts of action which take, and locate, a responsibility, when those around them will not. A seething desperation at the failures of material consumerism, the promises of a culture of centralisation, takes the form of a resilient linguistic vitality (sometimes wry, often surreal) in appraising the ridiculousness of self and others, when strained by these social conditions.

In these respects, it is appropriate to identify the inspirational precedence of two earlier Welsh writers, both Thomases (Dylan and Ed). Dylan Thomas sensed and dramatised bizarre, surprising forms of thwarted longing in his dramatic work, *Under Milk Wood*, which probes beneath apparently banal surfaces to expose fantasies of murder and rhapsodic escape in the inner lives of his characters. The 1990s plays by Ed Thomas (whom I would propose as the most significant and influential Welsh dramatist since Dylan wrote his one play) constitute equally inventive, poignant and remarkable dramatisations of their chosen terrain, a post-industrial South Wales; plays which, through their mythic depth, reflect the worldwide disappointments and possibilities of globalisation: feeling stuck with a screaming soul; and/or being taken somewhere new. Ed Thomas avoids portrayals of linguistic restriction and enclosure (such as those searingly dramatised in Edward Bond's *Saved*) as part of his depictions of domestic and national desperation; rather, Thomas dramatises faith in survival through wild imaginative expression, even as he shows characters compulsively haunted by the returning ghosts of others, recurrent voices of residual presences, departed family members and their own (former or possible) selves. I detect similar objectives and keynotes in the works of all dramatists collected in this volume: these plays manifest a keen awareness of problems of negotiating the pressures and messages of gender identity, in the bids to construct a viable self.

Rachel Trezise's inspired title and coinage, the word 'Tonypandemonium', crystallises this mixed sense of exasperation at the loss of traditional forms, and the forced, grim cheer of determination to negotiate and swim the waves of anarchy, nevertheless. Trezise's protagonist, Danielle, senses her social and familial restrictions, which disarmingly promise structure, a congruence based on tradition. Significantly, Trezise depicts Danielle as fragmented, in order that she, and we, might see her self whole. *Tonypandemonium* unfolds a series of mutually informative dialogues which ultimately permit a self-acceptance.

Matthew Trevannion's *Bruised* continues the enquiry, how might people go beyond the terms and limits of their upbringing, and make a difference? Again, the central image of the family creates a dramatic tension, between the impulse to belong, and the will to independence. Trevannion's protagonist, Noah, discovers that the wider world represents a further series of economically driven confidence tricks (a chain which extends from a Japanese jeweller to local drug-dealing). Finally, a haunting remembrance of lost potential and courage prompts Noah to take startlingly decisive action.

Brad Birch's *Gardening: For the Unfulfilled and Alienated* offers a darkly comic meditation on envy, suffocation and the importance of a personal space and time. Indeed, one of the most arresting and engaging aspects of Birch's play is the way that the layout of his text artfully demands performer and audience take time, encounter 'breathing spaces' in which to entertain the protagonist's conjectures, and their implications: not the only intimations in this volume that surprising forms of life can break through shapes which are dead and broken.

My Aberystwyth Welsh-speaking colleague/*Cymraes*, Charmian Savill, Teaching Fellow in Drama and Theatre Studies at Aberystwyth University, adds her perspective on Dafydd James's *Llwyth*:

> *Llwyth's* cheeky poetic rhythms, speedy as a racer bike, spurt with interjections from all involved. Protagonist

Aneurin collides with London characters, with a splash of
acidic abuse, or a dash past, and a rant on the wing. Back
in the bay, he jousts playfully and dangerously with his gay
Cardiffian community, where *maswedd* (banter) blooms
with the help of the whizzing white stuff, and words whirl
as in an orgiastic 'Milk Wood'. Then the narrative spirals
into the dark, where flailing gay warriors are 'mashed' with
drugs and misery (a modern mock-heroic counterpart to the
sixth century epic poem by Aneirin, about the defeat of six
hundred Welsh soldiers), but characters move onwards to
jagged clarity, complete with choir on stage. Dada, an older
gay character, offers significant encouragement: 'Enjoy the
contradictions. Enjoy the mess'.

Katherine Chandler's *Parallel Lines* dramatises incisively how a
politics based on fear damages the lives and hopes of working-class
and middle-class characters alike, by demanding complicity and
silence. This even taints the expansive ideals of education, when
its institutions become hierarchies of systematic repression. The
character Steph raises the question of determinism: are you, or aren't
you, born into being 'fucked up'? Chandler's play, like others in
the volume, insists on the possibility and importance of action for
consequence: that damage persists, and accrues, when people choose
to turn aside, and do nothing to challenge the terms of dominance.

Issues of inheritance, independence, complicity, gender identity
and making a difference are perhaps most strikingly fused in Tim
Price's *The Radicalisation of Bradley Manning*. Described in the
text as 'a fictional account … inspired by a true story', with 'ficti-
tious characters and incidents' and words 'as imagined by the
author', Price's play has some affinities with documentary and testi-
monial drama; but this 'fictional account' deals with the prosecution
(ongoing at the times of first performances) and (current) prison
sentence of someone who seems to have done the opposite to the
'war crime' (whereby, for example, a serving Nazi officer cannot
maintain in retrospect that he was 'just following orders' as an
excuse for the murder of civilians).

Manning acts as a whistle-blower on military practice which is
both self-defeating and lethal, and is charged with compromising

military and national security – perhaps appropriately, in the literal sense, of military and nation needing to maintain that they feel *secure with* their actions and their consequences. In counterpoint, imagined scenes from Chelsea Manning's schooldays show how her burgeoning radicalism refuses to stay within confines, even the structures of her most compassionate (but inevitably not perfect) teacher. These intertwine with Manning's entanglements with repressive military authorities, who order killings on the basis of suspicion, leading to his resolution, 'The world can't be like this, or I can't be in it', and a gruelling odyssey of insistently consequential personal revolt, building to Scene 27, in which the isolated Bradley struggles, in solitary confinement, to reacquaint himself with the sound of his voice: building to the word, which is suddenly spoken, and heard, as a verb or process which is questioned: 'Manning'.

In Scene 29, Bradley takes action in a spirit of active self-acceptance: to the appropriate soundtrack of Lady Gaga's 'Born This Way', which suddenly gains a startling political and existential depth. Should this scene seem too romantically idealistic, Scene 30 presents us with personal repercussions in gruelling detail and duration, as Bradley is tortured with repetitive questioning, ironically professing concern about his welfare, triggering different renditions of the persistent word 'yes'. Price's final scene returns to Chelsea's schooldays in Milford Haven, 2004: Bradley is unrepentant about a first performance of defiance, which 'worked', brought personal 'clarity': nevertheless he plans to 'help people' by joining the army, with the naïve idealism: 'If I want to help people, make the world a better place, I can't think of anywhere better than the US army'. Indeed, joining the army has often been the recourse of people who maintain, like Bradley, that they 'don't have a choice' in their interpretation of their social circumstances: which accounts for some of the limits and problems of military intelligence, in terms of the results it is required to deliver and the theories it is required to support.

The plays in this volume contain notes of deep pain at human dismissal and marginalisation, but also demonstrations of wholehearted persistence, of an enthusiastic belief in human potential (including its *wilder*ness), despite the prevailing centralised presumptions and edicts. Indeed, all the Welsh theatre artists I mention re-present and re-vision a keen awareness of place, and how it nevertheless cannot and should not be divorced from its wider contexts. Their emphasis on location contains a distinctive strength and appeal in order to generate deeper (international) resonances, to counter globalisation's dissipatory tactics (and the potential dismissal, 'Why should what's happening over that border have anything to do with me … ?'). One of the deepest resonances occurs in the last scene of Price's play: Manning's words, 'I don't have a choice', remind us of the extent to which he is shaped by the social, political and national aspects of his upbringing, in both Wales and America; BUT they also suggest that her principles and refusal of compromise are, at least to some degree, an active response to a national tradition of honourable revolt, about which she is informed (as are the audience), and to which she is also encouraged to belong (as are the audience): reminding us all that history, and the fight against corrupt concentrations of power, are never over.

Introduction

This collection is intended as a celebration of all Welsh writers and those who support them, and the six plays it contains can only hope to be a snapshot of the fantastically diverse work currently being made in Wales. The plays are united by a confidence and authenticity that is indicative of the work being created in Wales today, specific to, but not bound by, its origins.

Since I began working in Wales six years ago, I have been humbled and delighted by the extraordinary writing to be found here. To choose only a small number of plays for this collection was an extremely difficult task, but I felt strongly that Tim Price's *The Radicalisation of Bradley Manning* should be included. I saw this thematically complex and passionately political play in Edinburgh and was blown away by its sharp and emotionally rooted dialogue. Price's trademark combination of acuity and emotional truth is the heart of a play that refracts and shatters traditional narrative in a hugely affecting delivery of content through dazzlingly original form. Produced by National Theatre Wales, *The Radicalisation of Bradley Manning* exploded the perceived boundaries of Welsh writing with international impact and a global perspective. It speaks volumes that Olivier-nominee Price came home to Wales to write this audacious and passionate play, and that from Wales it reached out to the world, winning the inaugural James Tait Black Prize for Drama and being re-mounted at the Edinburgh festival to critical acclaim.

The brilliant and hilarious *Gardening: For the Unfulfilled and Alienated* by Brad Birch explores the relationship between life and death through a blackly comic monologue about one man's quest to find some meaning in life and win back the respect of his family by turning a barren patch of land into a beautiful back garden. Politically astute and horribly funny, the play won a Fringe First Award in 2013 and is a fantastic early work where we can clearly see the beginnings of Birch's preoccupation with the modern displacement of the human soul and the forceful reclaiming of this through transgression and violence. As the land refuses to thrive, the chance death of a visiting pigeon reveals a possible way to transform the garden to a beautiful place – but what is the cost of such abundance?

When *Bruised* by Matthew Trevannion landed on my desk at Clwyd Theatr Cymru, I was awestruck. A debut play of such assurance is a rare thing and the wit and daring of the dialogue made it clear that this was a very special writer. Set in Trevannion's hometown of Pontypool, *Bruised* is the story of prodigal son Noah returning to the family home after ten years away to find his place usurped by Shane, an aggressive and controlling cocaine dealer. Trevannion mixes monologue and long, dramatically complex scenes with a confidence and deftness that draws on his experience as an actor and belies his newness to playwriting. The world Trevannion creates feels solid and real, the boundaries clear, but they are not. The tension is palpable as *Bruised* barrels towards a heart-breaking revelation that would only be possible on the stage. Plays such as *The Radicalisation of Bradley Manning*, *Gardening* and *Bruised* have made my time working on new writing in Wales thrilling and it is my privilege to share them with you.

Kate Wasserberg

For a lot of people in Wales, *Llwyth* by Dafydd James is a watershed play. The only Welsh language play in this collection, *Llwyth* ("Tribe"), was first produced by Sherman Cymru and Theatr Genedlaethol Cymru. Wales is a country often wrongly described as divided by language, but you only had to sit in one of the many sold-out shows for *Llwyth*, to see that Welsh-speakers, learners and those with barely a grasp of the language, could enjoy this show. I was lucky enough to see *Llwyth* in its reincarnation at the Sherman Cymru after a high-kicking triumph at the Edinburgh Festival Fringe and an all-conquering Taiwanese sojourn. It was like nothing I had seen before. Dafydd James charts the growing pains of a gang who find themselves divided by morality and shifting priorities, but unified by language and, ultimately, love. The story follows Aneurin and friends as they hit the gay night spots of Cardiff on the day Wales lose a rugby match. Capturing the modern bilingual experience, James explores how one tribe can learn from another. He depoliticises the language making it merely everyday and in doing so changed the landscape of Welsh language theatre forever.

Rachel Trezise is one of Wales' finest short story writers and it was National Theatre Wales who commissioned her first play, the semi-autobiographical *Tonypandemonium*. It tells the story of Danielle, a young tattoo artist running out of time to make peace with a destructive mother. Trezise's decision to play with timeframes and to have three actors playing the same role are bold decisions rarely seen in debut plays, but it is the mark of a confident storyteller working in a company and a community where risk-taking is encouraged. This freedom to experiment is one of the rare privileges that comes from a writing community unburdened by a historic canon of work. I saw *Tonypandemonium* at the Parc and Dare, Treorchy, in 2013, the centenary of that theatre. The themes of neglect and renewal fitted perfectly in a Valleys community coming to terms with its past and forging a new identity.

Katherine Chandler has quickly become one of Wales' most celebrated playwrights. Having won the inaugural Wales Drama Award for *Parallel Lines* and the inaugural Theatre Critics of Wales Award for Best Playwright for *Before It Rains,* she was also one of the Bruntwood playwriting prize winners in 2013. *Parallel Lines* is Chandler's most explicitly political play. A writer driven to explore class inequalities, Chandler interrogates these fault lines through the prism of a sexual assault. I first read *Parallel Lines* when Katherine sent it to me asking if Dirty Protest would support an Arts Council research and development grant for the play. Like all of Chandler's work, the play is incredibly accomplished, witty, fearless and burning with something to say. Like in *Tonypandemonium*, the protagonist in *Parallel Lines* is a teenage girl trying to make sense of her place in the world. It is a defining play for Wales, a snapshot of working-class life in 2012, capturing how the shifting parameters of class can do untold damage to the powerless in society. Dirty Protest's production of *Parallel Lines* went on to win Best Production in the English Language, at the Theatre Critics of Wales Award 2013.

For me, these plays capture the flourishing playwright movement that is taking place in Wales. It is a collegiate movement where playwrights help each other by reading, dramaturging, producing and acting in each other's work. In such a tightly knit creative group there is no room for rivalry or competition only encouragement and support. And so this collection is not just the work of individual playwrights, but of a community. And one I am very proud to be a part of.

Tim Price

Tonypandemonium

Rachel Trezise

Tonypandemonium received its world premiere on 10 October 2013 at Park and Dare Theatre, Treorchy with the following cast:

Danielle #1 (9 years old) / **Nurse**	Tamara Brabon
Danielle #2 (15 years old)	Molly Elson
Danielle #3 (18 years old)	Sarah Williams
Deborah	Siwan Morris
Craig/Mr Morgan	Berwyn Pearce
Jerry Davies/Leon	Dean Rehman
Tommy Simcox	Adam Redmore

Director	Mathilde Lopez
Designer	Jean Chan
Lighting director	Ceri James
Music designer	Gareth Evans
Casting director	Sam Jones
Emerging director	Rachel Louise Boulton
Production manager	Tom Reilly
Stage manager	Donna Reeves
Deputy stage manager	Gemma Thomas
Voice coach	Patricia Logue
Skateboarding instructor	Huw Caddy

Scene One: *Tattoo Parlour, Pontypridd, 1996*

Tommy   (*Embarrassed*) Oh, sorry lovely. (*Steps back behind the curtain.*)

Danielle #3   It's OK, I'm just finishing up. (*Starts bandaging the customer up. Sends him out to reception.*)
(*To* **Tommy**) Come in.

Tommy   Alright, love? Nice place you've got here. (*Looks around at the walls, intimidated.*) D'you think a tattoo would suit me, then? (*Shows* **Danielle** *his knuckles*) I could get **love** here on this hand, look, and **hate** here. All the things I did in my life, I never got a tattoo. Some of the boys did, on tour, y'know. I don't think I fancied the pain. (*Nervous laughter.*)

Danielle #3   (*Stern*) What? Just passing were you?

Tommy   (*Coughs*) Your mother, it is.

Danielle #3   (*Starts cleaning her tattoo machine*) What's she done now?

Tommy   Thing is, lovely – What it is – The hospital says she's only got about two weeks left.

Danielle #3   Two weeks? (*Confused*)

Tommy   To live, love. You're mother's dying. She's dying, Dan.

Danielle #3   Dying? Fuck off. She's mean enough to live forever. What's she after?

Tommy   I'm serious, love. Cirrhosis.

Danielle #3   Cirrhosis? I might have known

Tommy   Nothing they can do for her now. (*Shrugs sadly*) Ward 5, East Glam. It's not far from here.

Tommy   Will you go to see her, lovely?

Danielle #3   Has she asked?

Tommy *shakes his head.*

Danielle #3   Then why should I?

Tommy   She won't ask. You know what she's like – It doesn't mean she doesn't want to see you. She's dying, love. She knows she's dying. She doesn't know how long; she doesn't want to know. Two weeks. If she knew she'd ask.

Danielle #3   (*Angry*) She's only forty-four.

Tommy   I know.

Danielle #2   (*Shouting from off stage*) Next customer is in, Dan. Butterfly anklet?

Tommy   Time for me to go anyway, lovely. Shopping, I am. New nightie and Turkish Delights. Got a real thing for the chocolate these days, she has. Have a think. (*Pats* **Danielle***'s shoulder awkwardly.*) See you then, lovely. (*Exits*)

Receptionist   (*Shouting from off stage*) Yoo-hoo. Ready?

Scene Two: *Kitchen in a terraced house, Tonypandy, 1987*

Danielle #1: What's this?

Deborah   (*Nods at the empty chair*) Go on, I've made your breakfast. You need some substanance, don't you? Growing girl like you.

Danielle #1   Substanance isn't a word.

Deborah   Yes it is. Substanance. Like nutritions.

Danielle #1   Nutritions isn't either.

Deborah   Sit down.

Danielle #3   (*Chewing her Mars Bar. To* **Danielle #***1*) She wasn't much of a cook. It all came out of tins and packets. Don't think I'd tasted a real potato. She used the freeze dried stuff. I can't remember what we did before Tommy got the microwave for us, cheap from Bessemer Road. It was alright for her. Lived on Turkish Delight, she did. Like the ice queen of Narnia. My father tried to teach her but – (*Too tired to* *explain. Slumps into the empty chair between* **Danielle #1** *and* **Deborah**.)

Deborah   Think you can do me a favour now I've fed you up nice and full?

Danielle #1   (*Sighs*) I knew it! What now?

Deborah   Run down the big pine end house on the main road.

Danielle #1   Why? I've got combined science at nine o'clock with Mr Morgan. I'm making a grandfather clock out of a Weetabix box. With a pendulum in it and everything.

Deborah   Go on. It won't take you five minutes. I threw my shoes in the garden on my way home last night. My best ones. My leopard print ones.

Danielle #1   Why did you do that?

Deborah   My feet were tired.

Danielle #1   You could have carried them.

Tommy Simcox *enters.* **Deborah** *puts her leopard-print shoes on and joins him.*

Tommy   Well this happened back when I was working on the railways in London, see. I was on my way to meet my mucker in this pub we'd been going to. Myfanwy's, it was called; Welsh place off Holloway Road. They'd let you smoke a bit of wacky backy in the cubby, like. I was walking past this theatre and all the audience were spilling out onto the street, hundreds of people. All of a sudden, there's David Bowie. Right in front of me, in the flesh. The eyes, everything. So, I shook his hand, like. 'Alright, Dave? Nice to meet you, butt.' And he just sort of disappeared back into the crowd. Later on, me and this mate, we're coming out of Myfanwy's. Two o'clock in the morning. There's David Bowie again, stood in the middle of the road. He's just standing there on his own, whistling this tune, looking a bit lost, like. I swear to God. And that's when he started stalking me. The whole time I lived in London. I couldn't go to the shop to get milk without him turning up like a bad penny. Caught him once, up on the extension roof, staring through the bathroom window.

Deborah   Stupid bloody things. Killing me. (*Flings her shoes*)

Tommy   Watching me have a shower. Fucking Bowie, like.

Deborah *jumps on* **Tommy**'s *back.*

Tommy   (*Catches her*) Oh, bloody hell, love. I'm too old for this.

Deborah   What? I'm only light. (*Covers* **Tommy**'s *eyes.*)

Tommy   (*Walking unsteadily.*) Whoa! Whoa, you nutter. Can't see where I'm going. (**Deborah** *laughing, removes her hands.*) Good job I fancy you, aye. Banger short of a barbeque you are, love.

Deborah   **Fancy** me, do you?

Tommy   And the rest.

Danielle #1   (*Clicks her tongue*) You could have hurt yourself.

Deborah   (*Impatient*) It's only half past eight. Go on, sweetheart. They'll still be there.

Danielle #1   You go. They're **your** shoes. You threw them away. Why'd you throw them away?

Deborah   (*Shouts*) Because – (*Takes the breakfast to the bin, starts scraping the plate*)

Danielle #1   OK! But this is the last time. (*Under her breath*) Things you have to do around here for a quiet life. (*Exits*)

Deborah   (*Daydreaming and talking to herself*) 'And the rest.' Seven years younger than me, he is. See, I've still got it. Everywhere I go, men tripping over their toes to get a sniff of me.

Danielle #*1* *returns with a baby's sock, puts it down on the table.*

Danielle #1   They weren't there. All I could find was this, in the gutter.

Deborah   Well, did you have a proper look?

Danielle #1   (*Playing with the sock*) Yeah! And then I had to run away because the man came out shouting at me for being on 'private property' or something.

Deborah   They're my best shoes. The leopard-print ones from Oliver's. I paid for them myself!

Danielle #1   Someone must have taken them.

Craig:*(To **Danielle #3**)* Dan, what're you doing?

Danielle #1   Perhaps your boyfriend went back to get them. Present for his wife. Finders keepers.

Deborah   I'm only a size four! **That** woman's a size nine. Big boat feet like a man!

Scene Three: *Fast food restaurant, Pontypridd, 1992*

Jerry   So how's your mother then, love?

Danielle #2   (*Shrugs*) Y'know –

Jerry   What did you tell her?

Danielle #2   I told her I was ice-skating with Katie in Cardiff. Believe anything won't she?

Jerry   It's for the best, love. If she knew you were with me she'd have my knackers off. You know what she's like –

Danielle #2   Yeah, **I** know what she's like. I'm the one who has to live with her.

Jerry   She seeing anyone now then, love?

Danielle #2   Tommy Simcox.

Danielle #2   Off and on, like. She sends him home to his wife every other weekend, then, when she wants him back she gets all dressed up and goes looking for him round the pubs. Wears her best fur coat.

Jerry   Never satisfied, is she?

Danielle #2   I want to come and live with you, Dad.

Jerry   You know that's difficult, love. I'm with Margaret now. She's a stickler for a clean and tidy house. She drives me mad half the time.

Danielle #2 ⋅ Not a nutcase though, is she?

Jerry   Don't say that about your mother, love. She's got a heart of gold.

Deborah   Stop drawing on the furniture!

Jerry   Fragile, she is – It's hard to explain.

Danielle #2   She's mental, Dad. And you know it. She totalled your car. She had the injunction taken out. She ruins everything. Everything she touches she turns to shit. Everything she's had, she's pissed all over it.

Jerry   You shouldn't be so hard on her, love. She can't help it. Always been the same: selfish, self-centred. She cuts her nose off to spite her own face. She doesn't do it on purpose, love. She doesn't know any other way.

Danielle #2   It's not fair, Dad. She's pissed all the time. Thursday night she had Shirley Bassey on blaring 'til four in the morning. I had a maths test the next day. That's not right, is it? It's like she's the kid and I have to be the mother.

Jerry   I'll have to talk to Margaret, love. You have to see things from her point of view. She hasn't got any children. It's a lot to ask, a strange teenager in the house.

Danielle #2   I'm not a stranger, Dad. I'm your daughter.

Jerry   You know what I mean, love –

Danielle #2   She said you'd do this. She said you wouldn't want me. It's only her you care about. Every time I see you she's all you go on about. 'How's your mother? Who's she seeing?' Obsessed with her, you are. You don't even care about me.

Jerry   I'll talk to Margaret.

Danielle #2   It's not going to be for long. I'm nearly sixteen. I've got to do my exams, then I can get my own flat.

Jerry   It's the cleaning thing it is, love. She's awful strict.

Danielle #2   She won't even know I'm there. I can help her with the cleaning. Who do you think does the cleaning up there? It's not my mother, is it? It's not Tommy bloody Simcox.

Jerry   We'll see.

Danielle #2   That means yes.

Jerry   It means we'll see. Because you know there'll be trouble. You know she'll kick off.

Scene Four: *Bedroom, terraced house, Tonypandy, 1987*

Danielle #1/Danielle #2 (*joins on underlined*)   Uncle Tommy doesn't love you because you're a slut and a single mother. You stole your ex-husband's car and got away with it because you slept with the copper who arrested you. You're not right in the head, love. All fur coat and no knickers.

Danielle #1/Danielle #2 (*joins on underlined*)   Shut your mouth, you fat bitch. And guess what? He does love me. Because why would he love you? You've got three chins and enough fat on your arse to open a lipstick factory.

Danielle #1/ Danielle #3 (*joins on underlined*)   And you're ill, love. An alcoholic. You should be in Bridgend with your sister.

Danielle #1/ Danielle #2 (*joins on underlined*)   Oh, mind your own business. Jealous cow. I don't ask you to pay for my drinks, do I?

Danielle #1/ Danielle #3 (*joins on underlined*)   No, you ask my husband, darling. Anyway, let's ask Tommy who he loves. Who do you love, Uncle Tommy? Which one of us do you love?

Danielle #1/Action Man Figure   One woman man, I am. You know me mun, love. You're a bit confused aren't you, Debs? Had a bit too much to drink?

Danielle # 2/Danielle #3   You're a bloody liar, Tommy Simcox. A liar. You've always been full of shit, you. (*Cries*)

Danielle #1   Don't worry, Mammy. I love you. I love you more than Uncle Tommy. I love you more than anyone. No-one loves you more than me. I'll look after you, I will. I'll save you, Mammy.

Deborah   Don't you want to go out to play, sweetheart? Why don't you take your dolls up the park?

Danielle #1   I can't take my dolls up the park. The big girls'll steal them. It's raining anyway.

Deborah   I need the house to myself for a few hours, see. (*Pause*) I know! There's a fancy dress competition in the church hall this afternoon. I saw a poster for it in the pub. Why don't you go to that?

Danielle #1   I haven't got a fancy dress costume. I don't want to anyway. I'm playing house.

Deborah   What do you want to go as? We can make a fancy dress costume for you.

Danielle #1   I don't want to go to a fancy dress competition.

Deborah   Indian? Cowboy? I know! A Charleston girl! I've got a dress somewhere with fringes like the Charleston girls used to wear. And we'll put an ostrich feather in your hair? Yeah!

Danielle #1   What's a Charleston girl?

Deborah   (*Impatient*) Oh, it's these girls from the 1920s and they used to dance like this (*does the dance*). Come on, we'll get you all dressed up and when you go in you have to dance like this (*does the dance*) Bet you any money you'll win.

Danielle #1   I'm not dancing like that.

Deborah   But you'll win.

Danielle #1   I don't want to win. I'm playing house.

Deborah   Come on, sweetheart. Be a good girl now. Mammy's got things to do, see. Private things, grown up things. There you are, look. (*Turns **Danielle** to face the mirror.*)

Danielle #1   I look stupid. I've never seen one of these
Charleston girls before. Nobody'll know what I'm meant to be.

Deborah   You look brilliant! You do. Do the dance then.

Danielle #1   Nuh!

Deborah   Go on, do the dance. More chance of winning!

Danielle #1   No! (*Pulls the feather out of her hair*)

Deborah   (*Puts the feather back in*) Come on, sweetheart.
Please? I need the house for an hour, that's all. You can take your
dolls with you, mun. Go on, you might win.

Danielle #1   I'm not going to win. They won't even know what I
am. How's the vicar going to know what a Charleston girl is?

Deborah   He will. Go on. You won't know if you don't try. You
can have one of my Turkish Delights when you come back.

Danielle#1   This is stupid, this is.

Deborah   But you might win.

Danielle #1   I won't win.

Deborah   Go on. (*Waving her off*) Remember to do the dance.

Craig and **Leon** *cross the stage.* **Craig** *gives* **Leon** *a can of beer.*

Scene Five: *Living Room, terraced house, Tonypandy, 1992*

Tommy *arrives home from work carrying his hard hat and
lunchbox to find* **Deborah** *sitting on the settee drinking a glass of
vodka. She's quite slurry.*

Tommy   Started early haven't you, love?

Deborah   Not like I've got much else to do, is it? Not like I've
got any kids to look after.

Tommy   (*Exhausted*) So, are you hungry? I'll pop down Conti's
for chips again, is it?

Deborah   Whatever.

Scene Six: *Alleyway, Tonypandy, 1992*

Danielle #2   Let's have a can'en.

Leon   Blow job first.

Danielle #2   As if.

Leon   Your mother would.

Danielle #2   I'm not my mother, am I?

Leon   (*To* **Craig**) Danielle's mother was the kissogram in my cousin's thirtieth.

Danielle #3   (*To* **Danielle** *#2*) Better than poisoning rats for a living.

Leon   Is that what you're going to be, Dan? A stripper? (*Giggling*)

Danielle #3   Which is what he's going to end up doing.

Danielle #2   (*Glaring at* **Leon**) Least she's not a Jehovah's Witness. What are you having for Christmas, Lee?

Craig   Fucking hell, Dan. He can't choose what religion his parents are.

Danielle #2   Yeah, and I can choose who my mother is, can I?

Craig   Who would you choose though?

Danielle #2   Easy. Sally Field out of Steel Magnolias.

Danielle #3   Aww. (*Grimaces*) Too sweet.

Leon   Madonna.

Craig   For your mother? Weirdo. Leon's got his father's Malibu, Dan.

Danielle #2   Come on then, Lee.

Leon   Nah, get your own. You owe me half a bottle as it is.

Danielle #2   She's moved her stash, mun. I think she's onto me.

Craig   Try the toilet. You know, the cistern. I saw it on TV. It's an alkie's favourite place to hide their booze. (**Danielle** *looks at him, hurt.*)

Leon   Neck me for it.

Danielle #3   (*Looking up in disgust.*) Don't neck him.

Craig   Don't neck him, Dan.

Danielle #2   Go on then.

Danielle #2 *looks pointedly at* **Craig** *before moving in to kiss* **Leon***, stopping short at the last moment; meanwhile* **Craig** *takes the bottle of Malibu out of* **Leon***'s pocket.* **Danielle #2** *moves away again.* **Craig** *throws the bottle to her and she catches it. She stands up and starts drinking from it.*

Leon   (*Opening his eyes and getting up to chase* **Danielle**) Come on, Dan. It's mine.

Craig   That's the third time you've fallen for that. How gullible are you, mun?

Leon   (*Following* **Danielle** *around and around the stage*) You've had some now, Dan. Give it back. (*To* **Craig**) This is your fault, Craig. You'll do anything she tells you, because you fancy her. You're like her little puppy dog or something mun.

Craig   (*Embarrassed*) No I don't.

Leon   Yes you do. You told me you want to finger her.

(*To* **Danielle**) You want to neck me really. Just frigid.

Danielle #2   Yeah. Frigid when it comes to you, Lee. I'm scared of your little pencil dick, I am.

Leon   Why are you such a bitch, mun?

Danielle #2   You think I'm a bitch? You should meet my mother. Oh, you already have, haven't you? I almost forgot.

Danielle #3   You're turning into her.

Danielle #2   What?

Danielle #3   You're turning into your mother. She's teaching you how to manipulate people. She's teaching you how to manipulate men. You want Malibu? Buy it. Get a paper round or something. You don't kiss boys to get what you want. What does that make you?

Danielle #2   I didn't kiss him.

Danielle #3   So you're a tease as well?

Danielle #3   Go home. It's cold. You'll catch a cold. (*Pushes her off set. Takes a swig of the Malibu and makes a face*) Nah, I never did like rum. (*Throws the bottle back to* **Leon**. *Approaches* **Craig** *and holds his chin. Kisses him forcefully on the mouth. Exits*)

Craig   Dan!

Leon   She's got you wrapped around her little finger, butt. Fuckin' cock tease bitch.

Craig   (*Dazed*) She's alright, mun, Lee. Give her a break.

Leon   Hark at Prince fuckin' Charmin'. No chance, butt. She's a lesbian, I reckon, like her auntie. She's either a lesbian or a slag.

Craig   Which one?

Leon   I don't know, do I? Both.

Scene Seven: *Living Room, terraced house, Tonypandy, 1987*

Danielle #2   (*Not looking up from the magazine*) The thing with our mother; she was always trying to get us out of the house. (**Danielle #1** *turns to look at her*)

Deborah   (*Puts the phone down*) Don't you want to go out to play, sweetheart? Come on. I need the house to myself for a few hours. Don't you want to go up to the park to play? Take the skateboard Uncle Tommy got for you in the market?

Danielle #1   It's raining.

Deborah   Well there must be something you can do. Go on, I've got things to sort out here.

Danielle #1   What things?

Danielle #2   You don't want to know.

Danielle #1   It's raining, Mam. Morph'll be on now. I've only just come in.

Deborah   What about that St. John's Ambulance Club in the Legion? You're interested in First Aid, aren't you?

Danielle #2   Jesus wept.

Danielle #1   No!

Deborah   Come on, Danni. Don't make trouble for me tonight. I need the house to myself. Only for a couple of hours. I've got things to do. Private things. Grown-up things.

Go to the St. John's Ambulance Club. Just this once. For Mammy. You might like it.

Danielle #2   She won't like it! (*Pause*) You've got to be thirteen!

Danielle #1   You've got to be thirteen to join St. John's Ambulance. It's only for kids from the comp. And it costs a pound. I don't want to go anyway. I won't like it.

Deborah   (*Tips a jar of copper coins onto the table and begins to count them*) Go on, sweetheart. I'll give you a pound.

Danielle #1   I'm not paying in two pences. It's embarrassing.

Deborah   It's all I've got. It's just the same as a pound coin, but different. Seventy, eighty.

Danielle #1   I can't go to St John's Ambulance, Mam.

Deborah   (To Audience member) C'mon, can you lend me 10p love?

Danielle #1   You've got to be thirteen.

Deborah   Be a good girl for Mammy now.

Danielle #1   I'm only nine.

Danielle #2   She's only nine.

Deborah   Please, love. Go. Just this once. For me. Just this once. Mammy's got things to do, see. I've got a few things to sort out. Please, sweetheart. It's important. (*Hands the coins to* **Danielle #1**)

Danielle #1   (*Sniffing the coins*) Smell these do.

Deborah   It's all I've got.

Danielle #1   I can't go, Mam. They'll know I'm not thirteen. They'll know I'm lying. I'll stay in my bedroom. I won't come out.

Deborah   They won't know how old you are. You're tall for your age, aren't you? If they ask, all you've got to do is tell them your date of birth but with the year changed so it works out at thirteen.

Danielle #1   What is it?

Danielle #2   '75. 1975.

Danielle #1   (*To* **Deborah**) 1975.

Deborah   See, you're cleverer than half those kids from the comp, gul. Come on, sweetheart. Be a good girl.

Danielle #1   I can't believe you're making me do this.

Deborah   I can't believe you're being cheeky to your poor mother.

Danielle #1   (*Sniffing the coins*) Smell these do, like blood.

Craig   (*To* **Danielle #3**) How did it go Dan?

Deborah   It's all I've got. Be a good girl now.

Danielle #1   I am a good girl. It's you who's making me tell lies.

Deborah   Go on then sweetheart. You never know, you might like it.

Danielle #2   (*Shouts*) She won't like it!

Deborah   Go on, you might learn something. They'll teach you the discovery position, isn't it?

Danielle #2   (*Sighs*) Go on, it's only an hour.

Danielle #3 *draws furiously on the floor,* **Deborah** *jives from kitchen table into centre.*

Scene Eight: *Kitchen, terraced house, Tonypandy, 1992*

Deborah   Oh, I was the best jiver around when I was younger. Debbie rock 'n' roll they used to call me up the Polikoff's Club.

Tommy   (*Noticing* **Danielle**) Oh, where d'you come from, lovely?

Danielle #2   The front door.

Deborah   Don't be smart, girl.

Tommy   (*Lifts the towel from the basket, looking inside*) What's this, then?

Danielle #2   Rice and veg and stuff. It's called Risotto Primavera or somin'. Cookery teacher's from the Vale, thinks she's posh.

Tommy   Bloody hell, lovely. I know what it is. Practically lived off this stuff when I was working on the canals in Italy, I did. There was this little osteria around the corner from our hostel. All they served was risotto. Donkey risotto, mind. Look at that! Have this for tea tonight, is it?

Deborah   (*Eyeing* **Danielle** *jealously*) I'm making my corned beef pie tonight. May as well put that out for the birds.

Tommy   Corned beef pie? When's the last time you made corned beef pie, Debs? Thought I was going down Conti's for chips again. You can do pie anytime. (*To* **Danielle**) Put it in the oven, lovely.

Deborah   (*Moving to block the oven door.*) What's in it, then?

Danielle #2   Beans, carrots, onions, cheese, tomatoes –

Deborah   Well there you are. I can't eat that. I'm allergic to tomatoes. It's their skin, it irritates my throat. You know that. Chuck it out for the birds, gul. It'll only get left in the fridge, going off, cluttering up. I'm doing my corned beef pie. I've been planning it for days. (*Pause*) What? Don't look at me like that. I've bought all the ingredients.

Tommy   That's going to take ages, love. Stick a bowl of Danni's risotto in the oven for me while I'm waiting. I'm starving.

Deborah   No, I'm not having you spoiling my corned beef pie with that foreign rubbish, Tom.

Danielle #2   Jesus. It's not foreign. I made it in school. Llewellyn Street. Half a mile away.

Deborah   You know what I mean, sweetheart. It's too rich. He hasn't got the stomach for it.

Danielle #2   He likes risotto. He just said.

Deborah   Listen, I don't know who he was sleeping next to when he lived away but I'm not putting up with his rich food farts all night, alright?

Danielle #2   You think the whole world revolves around you, you do. You're jealous because I cooked a risotto. Pathetic. I didn't even want to do it. The school made me do it. Ain't my fault Tommy wants to eat it. Any normal mother would want to eat their daughter's food from cookery.

Deborah   (*Peeling potatoes, sipping vodka*) Me? Jealous of you? I don't know what you're talking about, Danielle. What have you got that I'd be jealous of? Duller than you look you are, girl. And pick up your drawings!

Danielle #2   Yeah, right. I'm going to change. (*Exits*)

Tommy   Corned beef pie? Vegetable Risotto? Do me a favour. I'd kill now for one of my ex-Mrs' beef Wellingtons. Debs, right? She wasn't my first choice. I got caught cheating, didn't I? Stuck with her. It's like walking on eggshells, mun. (*Looking back to the kitchen, slightly worried*) Last weekend she kicked me out for eating her chocolate. Turkish Delight. I don't even like the bastard stuff. (*Makes a face*) Sweet pink jelly, sickly as hell. Starvin', I was. And she flushed my signed Stones plectrum down the lav.

Keith Richards gave that to me, personally. Personally, mind. Richmond Athletic Ground 1964.

Knew she was trouble, first time I saw her. Debs was the kissogram at my stag do. My mate hired her for fifty quid. Couldn't resist, could I? Stunning. Only human, I am. Moth to a flame, like. So here I am. Happy bloody families. Daren't go back to the ex. I mean there's only so many times I can afford to put the car in for a respray.

Danielle #2 *enters wearing a Guns 'n' Roses T-shirt and a pair of clumpy motorbike boots.*

Tommy   (*Spying* **Danielle** *over the paper*) Nice boots, lovely.

Deborah   (*Shouting from the kitchen*) Don't encourage her, Tommy. Ugliest things I've had the displeasure of seeing on a human being's feet. Years ago I couldn't keep her away from my shoes. Now she wants to dress like a feller. Can't get a skirt on her for love nor money. People'll be thinking my daughter's a Lesbos.

Danielle #2   Lesbian! It's lesbian! Lesbos is an island. Off Greece. Fuck's sake.

Tommy   You like Thin Lizzy then, lovely?

Danielle #2   Prefer Metallica, Tom.

Tommy   Me 'n' Pete the papers were roadies for Thin Lizzy, see. Back in London, good few years ago. Those were the days, love. Touring with Slade. Me 'n' old Gary Moore were like that. (*Crosses fingers. Breaks into song and plays air guitar*) **Guess who just got back today** – Taught me a lot, that Phil Lynnott. Black kid growing up in 1940s Ireland. Can you imagine the stick he must have got? Never complained about it, not once. Gave me the strength to forgive all the shit I had to endure around here for having one arm longer than the other.

Deborah   (*Shouting*) Come on, it's ready.

Deborah   I didn't have any carrots. Or onions. Got everything else though. C'mon, tuck in.

Danielle #2   Got all the ingredients you said.

Tommy   Like corned beef hash then love, but in a pie? Nice one. (*Pats Debs' shoulder proudly.*)

Deborah   I'm good, aren't I? Creative, see. Cooking's creative. I'm awful creative. I can turn my hand to anything creative. They thought I was going to be a hairdresser. My father used to let me cut his hair from the time I was six. I'd just sit on his lap with a scissors doing whatever I wanted to him, soft old sod.

Danielle #2   Baking's a science.

Deborah   Remember, Dan? When I made a fancy dress costume for that competition in the church hall? Dressed her up as a flapper with my old fringed dress. Two minutes it took me. Couple of feathers. She only bloody won. First bloody prize.

Tommy   Never. What d'you win, lovely?

Danielle #2   Five pack of Mars Bars. Wish I had five Mars Bars here now. I'd eat them all, instead of this. Your potatoes are like rocks. How can you have a corned beef pie without onions, anyway? Baking is a science. You follow a recipe. There's no creativity in it. You couldn't bake a jam tart, Mam.

Deborah   Watch your mouth, girl. I didn't use a recipe. I did it from memory. You're not too big for a clout.

Danielle #2   Mam, you're lucky you can see me, you're that drunk. Hit the one in the middle, is it?

Deborah   I can see you alright, girl. (*Stands up*)

Tommy   Not tonight, ladies. C'mon. Calm down. Let's eat our tea in peace for once, is it?

Danielle #2   I'm not eating this. (*Picks her plate up*) Where's my risotto?

Deborah   You can't eat that now. I've put it out for the birds.

Danielle #2   Well, what d'you do that for?

Tommy   You shouldn't have put it out for the birds, love. Rice, see. It expands in their stomachs. It makes them spontaneously combust.

Danielle #2   She shouldn't have put it out for the birds because it's my fucking risotto. (*To* **Deborah**) You're not right in the head, you ain't. A normal person would not put a perfectly good risotto out for the birds. Let alone their own daughter's!

Tommy   Don't swear in front of your mother, lovely.

Danielle #2   She fuckin' swears in front of me.

Deborah   (*Shoving to get closer to* **Danielle**) I've had as much of your lip as I can take today, madam. I'll teach you a lesson now.

Danielle #2   I've had as much as I can take from you in a lifetime. Mental hospital you ought to be, with your sister.

Deborah   Don't talk about my sister.

Danielle #2   (*Exasperated*) Out for the birds? What have I ever done to you?

Deborah   Implored me, you have. For fifteen long years you've been imploring me. I tell you, I should have listened to that doctor!

Danielle #2   Imploring you? You don't even know what that means. Provoking you. Provoke, you stupid cow. I can't even have an argument with you. You're too thick.

Tommy   Love? Don't swear at your mother.

Danielle #2   Don't **you** tell me what to do either. You must be mental to stay with her. Going to live with my father, I am.

Deborah   Try it, Danielle. He doesn't want you. When was the last time you saw him? Twelve years ago. He doesn't want you.

Danielle #2   Why's that, Mam? Because you had an injunction taken out on him.

Deborah   Yes, because he beat me up.

Danielle #2   He didn't beat you up. Tommy's ex-wife beat you up. Then you used the photographs to say it was my father, because you're psychotic like that, aren't you? (*To* **Tommy**) That's a true story, that is. Bet she never told you that one.

Deborah   That's **it,** girl.

Danielle #2   I'm going anyway.

Tommy   Don't go, lovely. Where are you going to go? Sit down, mun. We can sort this out.

Danielle #2   We can't sort this out until she's stopped drinking. She won't even remember this tomorrow. I'm sick of her starting on me for nothing. Then she won't apologize because she can't even remember what she's done. She's going to give me a nervous breakdown. I'm trying to revise for my exams.

Deborah   Let her go. I'm sick of the sight of her and her stupid, ugly boots. Get out, you spoiled little bitch.

Danielle #2   Me a spoiled bitch? You should fucking see yourself. What kind of woman gives her own daughter's risotto to the birds? Wake up. You're not what you think you are. You're not a little girl competing with your sisters for your father's attention. You're a grown woman. You've got a fifteen-year-old daughter. Who's brainier than you.

Deborah   (*Upset*) Don't talk about my sisters.

Tommy   OK, lovely. Perhaps you'd better go out for an hour, cool down, like.

Danielle #2   I'm going. (*Exits carrying her plate.*) Watch the birds spontaneously combust after this shit. (*Smashes the dish off stage.*)

Scene Nine: *East Glamorgan Hospital, Ward 5, 1996*

Danielle #3   Mother?

Deborah   (*Disappointed*) You.

Danielle #3   Yeah me, Mam.

Deborah   How did you find out? Bloody Tommy, wasn't it? Couldn't keep his mouth shut. I don't want you coming here. I don't want your bloody sympathy.

Danielle #3   Who said anything about sympathy? Cirrhosis of the liver? It's your own fault.

Deborah   (*Turns her head away*) Anyway, it's not even visiting time. You'd better go before the nurses catch you. They're strict. (*Turns back, looking hesitantly at* **Danielle**.) I don't want them seeing you, truth be told. You look like a tramp off the street, gul. Ripped jeans? Come to see your mother in hospital and you can't even be bothered to wear a dress.

Danielle #3   (*Sarcastic*) And you look beautiful. Gorgeous as ever. Prettier than Elizabeth Taylor, you are.

Deborah   Shut it you. You've still got a mouth on you. I thought you might have grown up a bit by now. I can't help what I look like. I'm ill!

Danielle #3   (*Quietly*) Yeah. (*Looks down at her jeans.*) I came straight from work.

Deborah   Well you shouldn't have bothered. You know better than to listen to Tommy. You know he's full of shit. He's the one looking for sympathy, feeling sorry for himself because there's no-one there to cook for him when he gets in. It's not as bad as he's making out. I'll be OK. I always am. Have to be, don't I? The liver is the only organ capable of repairing itself. So actually it's a good job it's not cancer like the rest of them. Your grancha died of lung cancer. Terrible thing. They reckoned it was his smoking but it wasn't. It was the coalmines that killed him. Bloody NBC. I sat next to his bed watching him getting worse day after day, sinking into himself 'til there was nothing left of the poor dab.

Danielle #3   Well I thought you might have wanted some company. You hate hospitals, you always did. You wouldn't even go in to have me. Thought you might have been lonely.

Deborah   I'm not lonely, thank you very much. I've made hundreds of friends here. And I've got the nurses. At least they look after me. Not like you with your ripped jeans and your dirty boots. You told me you weren't going to look after me when I got old so I don't know why you've bothered coming now.

Danielle #3   You're not old. Anyway, you didn't look after me.

Deborah   I did my best.

Danielle #3   No you didn't.

Deborah   (*Stern*) I'm too ill to argue with you, Danielle. I'm tired. (*Shouts*) Nurse! Nurse! Intruder! Nurse!

Danielle #3   Don't be silly, Mam. Jesus Christ.

Nurse *(Danielle #1) enters carrying a kit, walks towards the bed.*

Nurse   It's not visiting time. It ended over an hour ago. Can you come back tomorrow?

Danielle #3   (*Stands up*) I'll come back tomorrow.

Nurse   Time for your bandages now, Mrs. Simcox. (*Begins bandaging*)

Danielle #3   Do you want me to come back tomorrow, Mam?

Nurse   I'm sorry young lady, you really have to go now. It's almost nine o'clock.

Danielle #3   Do you want me to bring anything?

Nurse   The hospital should be empty of visitors by now.

Deborah   (*Shouting after her*) Danni? Turkish Delight. Turkish Delight. And cranberry juice.

Craig, Danielle #2 *and* **Leon** *enter.* **Craig** *hands* **Leon** *and* **Danielle** *two cans.*

Scene Ten: *Terraced Street, Tonypandy, 1992*

Danielle #3   (*Looking around, making sure no-one's listening. To* **Danielle #2**) Hold your head up. Hold your head up. You've nothing to be ashamed of.

Danielle #2 (*Looking about, cross*) Nothing to be ashamed of? Are you real, or what?

Danielle #3 Yeah. (*Smiling*) Well, no.

Danielle #2 Stop fucking with my head. Why can't she just be normal? Why does it have to be *me* who gets the wino for a mother?

Danielle #3 Why not you? You're someone aren't you? Normal? No fucker's normal, babe. (*Pause*) You'll be alright, you know. You're not the first teenage daughter of a dipso to walk the bloody earth. Look at me! Come on, get yourself home. She worries.

Danielle #2 (*Incredulous*) She does not worry.

Danielle #3 She does though. And go easy on her or it'll end up being one of those nights. She's on the change: temperamental as fuck. And you're on your period. Hormonal teenager and alcoholic mother under one terraced roof? Daddy's got a word for it.

Leon Tonypandemonium.

Danielle #2 Fuck off! Bet she's through a bottle of vodka already, singing Shirley Bassey in the kitchen. (*Doing an impression of a drunken* **Deborah**, *singing*) **I, I who have nothing. I, I who have no-one.**

Danielle #3 (*Doing an impression of a drunken* **Deborah**, *singing*) **Diamonds are forever. They're all I need to please me. They can stimulate and tease me.**

Danielle #2 Don't you want to go out and play, sweetheart? Come on, I need the house to myself for a few hours. Things to do. Private things. Grown up things.

Danielle #3 Why couldn't you have a normal job? Work in a pub or something. Tattoos! On women as well! You've got to have a screw loose to want to mark your body like that, mun.

Danielle #2 I should have listened to that doctor! Party girl, I am!

Danielle #3 See, I've still got it. Everywhere I go, men tripping over themselves to get a good look at me. Prettier than Elizabeth Taylor, I was. She ain't got nothing on me. Fat Jewish tart.

Danielle #2   Oh, Danni, look at your big ugly shoes. People'll think you're a lesbos. A Lesbos, mun. You might find a nice boyfriend if you wear prettier shoes.

Danielle #3   (*Laughing*) Come on.

Craig, Leon and **Danielle #2** *are drinking beer.*

Scene Eleven: *Living room, terraced house, Tonypandy, 1987*

Deborah   (*Into the receiver, sighing*) Yes, this is the Jade Flower. How can I help you, sweetheart? (*Pause; winks at* **Danielle #1**.) Black bean sauce, yep – Egg fried rice, yep – Four poppadums, yep – And a bag of chips? Big or small? Ok no problem, I'll just pass you onto my colleague who can check your order.

Danielle #1   Ok so that's black bean sauce, egg fried rice, four poppadums and a small bag of chips? Are you sure you want a small bag? If you buy a big bag you can have a free Barbie with every chip …

Deborah   That'll teach them for dialling the wrong number again, silly buggers.

Scene Twelve: *Living room, terraced house, Tonypandy, 1992*

Deborah*'s in her nightdress, staring into space.* **Danielle** *#2 enters,* **Craig** *and* **Leon** *run away. Both of them are drunk and slurring.*

Deborah   You OK, sweetheart? Where've you been then?

Danielle #2   Out. You threw me out, remember?

Deborah   Did I? I didn't, did I?

Danielle #2   Huh. Yeah.

Deborah   No, I didn't, mun. I wouldn't do that. You're my favourite girl, you are. Do you know when I was having you the doctor thought you were a virus? 'Funny bloody virus, doc,' I told him. A virus with arms and legs!

Deborah   See, I knew I was pregnant. I knew. One Sunday I walked into my mother's house and she was cooking the dinner, and I loved her Sunday dinner. But ych-y-fi, the smell of it. Like something dead and rotting. 'I'm pregnant, I am,' I said to your father. 'Don't be silly,' he said. But I knew. And the doctor?

Deborah and **Danielle**   He told me to have an abortion.

Deborah   'If there's a baby there,' I said, 'It's staying there. It's staying put!'

Danielle #2   You wished you listened to that doctor. That's what you always tell me.

Tommy   (*Shouting from off stage*) Debs? You coming to bed? It's late. Come to bed. Debs?

Deborah   (*Shouting to* **Tommy**) Alright, I'm coming, Tom. I'll be there now. Keep your cock on. (*To* **Danielle***, quieter*) I don't mean that, sweetheart. You know the trouble I'm having with my hormones. I wouldn't abort a baby, I wouldn't. Not like that ex- of Tommy's. She's had abortions, she has. Calloused cow.

Danielle #2   Well maybe you should have. All you've done all my life is reject me, ignore me, humiliate me. Don't love me, do you?

Deborah   Do you remember that time –

Danielle #2   See, you can't say it. You can't even say it when you're pissed.

Deborah   Do you remember that time when you were little and I had to go to court?

Danielle #2   When you lied about my father beating you up?

Deborah   I didn't lie. You stayed with your grandparents.

Danielle #2   Yeah?

Deborah   Your grancha didn't –

Danielle #2   What?

Deborah   Your grancha didn't touch –

Danielle #2, *(without catching what* **Deborah** *has said), begins to retch.* **Deborah** *slides a waste paper bin over to her and smoothes* **Danielle**'s *hair to the side while* **Danielle** *vomits.*

Deborah   There, there, sweetheart. Get it up. Come on. (*Rubbing* **Danielle**'s *back*) Get it all up. I know you've been drinking. I know my vodka's been going missing. Your poor young body can't take it see, love.

Tommy   (*Shouting from off stage*) Debs? Debs, you coming to bed, or what?

Danielle #2   (*Pushing Debs off and wiping her mouth on her sleeve*) You? Of all people? **You're** going to lecture me about drinking? It's not the drink, Mam. It's not the drink that's made me sick. It's you! You and your corned beef pie. Your joke of a fucking corned beef pie!

Danielle #3 Shittest mother ever, you are the shittest mother ever, you the shittest mother ever, ever in the world – *(to the tune of Diamonds are Forever).*

Scene Thirteen: *Living room, terraced house, Tonypandy, 1993*

Deborah   Danielle? Danielle?

Tommy   No, it's me, Debs.

Tommy   Bloody hell, love. How much have you had?

Deborah   What's it got to do with you? You're my husband not my father.

Tommy   I'm only saying, love.

Deborah   Well don't say, right? It's got piss all to do with you. You don't know what it's like to be me.

Tommy   (*Exhausted*) Are you hungry then, love? I'll get us some chips.

Deborah   Shove your chips up your arse, Tommy Simcox.

Danielle #1 *crosses the stage singing Big Spender*

Scene Fourteen: *Back garden, terraced house, Tonypandy, 1992*

Deborah *is lying on a sun lounger, wearing a bikini and sunglasses.* **Craig** *and* **Leon** *are in school uniform sitting around her with glasses of lemonade in their hands, looking slightly worried.*

Leon   How long do you think she'll be, Mrs Davies? See, we like to be up there early, by four or the boys from Dinas take up all the best swings.

Deborah   Oh, she won't be long now. Gone down the Wishing Well for new pencils or something. She's a glutton for that drawing of hers, isn't she? I used to go out with an artist once. Used to be his life model, I did. (*The boys giggle*) Hey, don't laugh, I was good at it. He did hundreds of sketches of me. Drink your lemonade now. I don't give my lemonade to anyone. I like to save it to go with my drinks. (*The boys drink their lemonade.* **Deborah** *adjusts her bikini.*)

Craig   Perhaps we should go, Mrs Davies. Tell Danielle to meet us up there. She'll know where we are.

Deborah   (*Sits up, pushes her sunglasses onto her head*) Oh, don't go yet. I'm enjoying your company, boys. She won't be long now. Tell you what; you couldn't give me a hand? (*Lifts a bottle of suntan lotion, passes it to* **Leon**.) See, I can't reach my back. (*Turns onto her stomach. The boys stare at each other*) Come on, sweetheart, or I'll be burnt to a crisp.

Leon *starts working haphazardly on her shoulders.*

Deborah   That smells nice, doesn't it? Like summer. Delicious. Coconut flavour. (*Craning her head to look at* **Craig**) Can someone do my legs too?

Craig   Not me, Mrs Davies. I have to go. (*Drinking his lemonade)*

Leon   Don't be chicken, Craig. (*Makes chicken noises under his breath*)

Deborah   I won't bite you, sweetheart. Hey, what's that? On your neck? Come here, let me have a look. (*Sits up and pats the lounger, beckoning* **Craig**. **Craig** *goes hesitantly.* **Deborah** *inspects his neck*) Blackhead. Let me get it. (*Puts her arms around him.*) This weather is brilliant for picking blackheads. See, your skin here, (*massaging his neck*) all hot and moist, it'll just slide right out in one go. Here. (*Starts squeezing.* **Leon** *is snorting with laughter*)

Danielle #2 *enters, walking towards them but looking down at her drawing pad.*

Danielle #2   Mam? Ma-am? They had them. A2, acid free. (*Looks up to see the boys*)

Craig   (*Jumps up. Picks his skateboard up*) We came to call for you, Dan. We're going boarding up Clydach Hill. Hang around the park for a bit?

Danielle #2   (*To her mother, screaming*) You fucking nymphomaniac slut. You can't keep your hands to yourself for one minute. You even have to try it on with my school friends. Find someone your own age. (*To* **Craig**) Fuck off. Just fuck off. (*Runs into house*)

The boys look at **Deborah**.

Deborah   (*Shrugging nonchalantly. To* **Craig**) Must be her time of the month or something, kiddo.

Chaz enters dragging **Tommy** *by the hair, slams his head against the microwave table. Morph enters and punches* **Deborah** *in the stomach.* **Wonder Woman** *enters, strangles* **Deborah** *with the cord of the iron and leaves. Slams iron down.*

Scene Fifteen: *Living room, terraced house, Tonypandy, 1992*

Deborah *and* **Tommy** *sit at opposite sides of the settee.*

Deborah's *drinking vodka,* **Tommy**'s *drinking beer. They're listening to loud music. (*In the Air Tonight *by Phil Collins)*

Tommy   (*Shouting over the music*) Know what this song's about? (*Pause.* **Deborah** *doesn't answer*) It's a true story, see, about when Phil Collins was at this party at this record executive's house in LA and everyone there's plastered out of their skulls on coke, like. Early in the morning when everyone's pretty much comatose, he looks out the window and sees one of these record execs holding this other guy down in the pool. One of them liver-shaped pools, like. Anyway the guy drowned, right, but the record exec made out like it was because the guy was out of it on drugs. Phil Collins never said anything. Probably didn't want to mess his contract up or whatever. Then, years later, Phil Collins sees this record exec in the crowd at one of his shows. And he starts singing the song to him. Straight into his eyes, like. Spotlight on him, everything. (*Singing*) **Well if you told me you were drowning, I would not lend a hand. I've seen your face before my friend, but I don't know if you know who I am. Well I was there and I saw what you did, I saw it with my own two eyes. So you can wipe off that grin, I know where you've been. It's all been a pack of lies.** (*Air drumming to the drum solo*)

Deborah *ignores him, unimpressed, and finishes her glass of vodka. She pours herself another.*

Tommy   Love? What's wrong? Why don't you talk to me about your sisters? What's the big secret? Problem shared problem halved. All that.

Deborah   Huh. What's there to say? Eating biscuits in Bridgend, she is. Tapped, see. Started off she had a thing about germs. She'd let the next-door neighbour in to use her phone but then afterwards she wouldn't touch it in case she caught some disease. She had to wait for her fella to come home to clean it. She'd leave it ringing all day, just ringing and ringing. Then she tried to strangle herself with the cord because she couldn't stand the ringing. Stupid cow. (**Tommy**'s *lost interest and is nodding again to the music.* **Deborah** *notices this but continues*) That's what happens when you open up. Couldn't keep it zipped, poor cow. Same with my other sister. Living on some estate in England somewhere, Lesbos man hater. (*Laughs bitterly*) You open Pandora's box and it all starts coming out. Then you can't get it all back in again. (*Shouts*) Tom! Put your bloody headphones on. This noise is getting on my tits! Worse than Danielle with your music, you are! Worse than a fifteen-year-old.

Tommy   (*Too loudly*) You don't know what you're missing, love. Better than Bassey any day.

Deborah   I was my father's favourite. Course I was. Wasn't my sister was it? Poor cow. Big fat legs and massive tits. Looked unnatural on a twelve-year-old. And not my little sister. Like a little boy she was. She had a thing about these shirts. Men's shirts with big pointy collars. The Lesbos in her probably. I was the pretty one, wasn't I? Turned heads, I did. I was my father's favourite. 'Til I married Jerry Davies. Lot of good that did me. He wanted me cooped up in the house all day, cooking. Party girl, I am. He kept accusing me of sleeping with the bank manager. Got bored of taking the rap for something I didn't do. So I had an affair with the electric meter bloke. Serves him right for banging on about Elizabeth bastard Taylor day in, day out. (*Shouts*) Fat Jewish tart.

Tommy   Love? You sure you're alright?

Deborah   I'm al-fucking-right, mun. Stop asking me that.

Tommy   Well, the risotto thing. That was a bit harsh, wasn't it? You know what she said, about you being jealou –

Deborah   Don't you fucking start now, Tommy.

Jealous? Course I'm fuckin' jealous. Skin like a peach. Waist like a bloody washboard. She doesn't even know the power she's got. I know. Eighteen-inch waist I had on my wedding day. They don't look at *me* anymore. They look at her. She doesn't even notice. She doesn't even know it yet.

Tommy   (*Pulls his headphones off excitedly, points at the noise coming from them*) Pink Floyd. Shine On You Crazy Diamond. Bloody amazing, this track. I met Syd Barrett once, see. Fucking nutter. It was in this little bar in Cambridge. (*Pause*) He was drinking a pint of his own piss.

Deborah   Never.

Tommy   Aye. His own bloody piss, mind. With a Rémy Martin chaser. Whatever the hell that is.

Scene Sixteen: *Kitchen, terraced house, Tonypandy, 1987*

Danielle #2   What're you doing?

Danielle #1   (*Defensive*) Drawing.

Danielle #2   You're drawing her?

Danielle #1   She's beautiful.

Danielle #2   You think?

Danielle #1   Yeah. She looks like a princess. Look at her.

Danielle #2   Why don't you draw me instead? I'll be your life model. (*Smiles, strikes a pose*)

Danielle #1   You're not the same.

Danielle #2   What? I'm not beautiful?

Danielle #1   Not like her.

Danielle #2   But I'm here though. Where's she? In the pub. She's always in the pub. You need that picture to remind yourself what she looks like. I'm always here though, just a step ahead of you. You going to draw a picture of me or what?

Danielle #1   It's not the same! She's got nice hair, and green eyes, and pretty shoes. You're – (*Gestures at* **Danielle #2***'s motorbike boots*) different.

Danielle #2   You know that being pretty isn't all it's cracked up to be, right? You don't have to be pretty to draw a good picture, do you?

Danielle #1   No, but you need to be pretty to get a husband.

Danielle #2   Who wants a husband?

Danielle #1   Everyone has to have a husband.

Danielle #2   Who told you that? You don't have to have a husband. Some women don't have husbands. Catwoman hasn't got a husband.

Danielle #1   She goes out with Batman.

Danielle #2   Batman hates Catwoman.

Danielle #1   He loves her sometimes.

Danielle #2   OK, bad example. Wonder Woman, then. Wonder Woman hasn't got a husband. She doesn't want a husband. What does Wonder Woman want with a husband? All he'd do is try to put his arm around her all the time, snap her bra strap, ask her what colour her knickers are.

Danielle #1   Is she a lesbos?

Danielle #2   No! And anyway, it doesn't matter. What I'm trying to tell you is that it isn't important to be pretty. There's other things you can be.

Danielle #1   Ugly.

Danielle #2   No. Nobody's ugly. You can be clever. You can have a nice personality and make people feel happy. See, if you listen to Mammy she'll tell you that all you need is good looks. A bit of charm. But that's not true, is it? She reckons she's prettier than Liz Taylor, that her fandooly drips pure liquid honey, but all she's got is Tommy Simcox, a liar with one arm longer than the other. Because she's not pretty on the inside. You only get pretty on the inside by not worrying too much about the outside. Get it? (*Stands up*) Come on, I want to show you something. (*Plugs an iron in*).

Danielle #1   What are you doing?

Danielle #2   I'm going to show you how to iron your school uniform.

Danielle #1   Why?

Danielle #2   Because you're getting to that age when you'll start to look around at your school friends' clothes and wonder why they're neat and tidy and yours aren't. (*Ironing a shirt together*) See, when I was your age I couldn't work out why all the girls had V-neck imprints on the backs of their jumpers. Turned out their mother's ironed their clothes. There you are. Cuffs and collars first. Then we do the sleeves and we're halfway there. Your turn.

Scene Seventeen: *Living room, terraced house, Tonypandy, 1994.*

Tommy   You alright, love?

Deborah   *Grunts*

Tommy   Oh, come on love. This isn't any good, is it? Sat in all day drinking on your own? If you're missing Danielle why don't you give her a ring? You know where she is.

Deborah   Does it look like I'm missing that little cow?

Tommy   Well –

Deborah   Having the time of my life, I am. No-one to have to wait on hand and foot. Look at me! I'm on cloud nine, mun. (*Sings*) I, I, sing with me, One, two, three, I …

Tommy   I, I Who Have Nothing, I, I Who Have No One.

Tommy *and* **Deborah** *sing I Who Have Nothing.* **Craig** *helps* **Danielle #3** *take her jeans off.*

Scene Eighteen: *Teenager's bedroom, terraced house, Tonypandy, 1992*

A suitcase is open on **Danielle #2***'s bed, half-filled with clothes.* **Deborah** *and* **Danielle #2** *are running around the bed, screaming at one another. As* **Deborah** *tries to empty the suitcase,* **Danielle #2** *keeps trying to refill it.*

Deborah   (*Screaming*) You've got no idea the heartache that man caused me. You wouldn't believe it. Burned me with cigarettes, he did. He broke my dog's leg because he was so jealous of it. That man is evil, Danielle. He is evil. (*Rolling her sleeves up to show her the cigarette burns*)

Danielle #2   (*Screaming*) You're lying, Mam. There's nothing there. (*Looking at her arms and pushing her away*) There's nothing there. You've told the lies so many times you've started to believe them yourself. Stop lying. It's degrading. I'm going to live with him. You can't stop me.

Deborah   (*Screaming*) Don't you understand? You don't understand, Danielle. I've been trying to protect you. All these years I've been trying to protect you. From him. He never cared about you, Danielle. It's only me he wanted. I'm all he cared about. Trying to protect you and this is the thanks I get.

Danielle #2   (*Screaming*) I don't want protecting. Fifteen, I am. I can make my own mind up. I've been looking after myself since he went anyway. Where've you been? Hiding in a bottle of vodka. Don't try to put one of your guilt trips on me. It won't work. Can't you see? I'm all grown up. I can see right through you, mother. You're pathetic. I wish you were dead.

Deborah   (*Screaming*) You can't see anything. You're too much like him. Too bloody soft. If you leave now I won't have you back. And you'll be sorry, Danielle. You mark my words, you'll be sorry.

Danielle #2   (*Screaming*) I'm not coming back. And don't come looking for me when you're old and lonely because I don't care what happens to you. You'll die lonely and alone and I won't care. I'll dance on your grave, I will. It's not like you ever loved me. You're a shit mother, you are. I should get you one of those mugs for Mother's Day. **Shittest Mother in the World. Ever.**

Danielle #3   That was it.

Deborah   How could I love you?

Danielle #3   That's when her head went.

Deborah   How could I love someone like you, so cruel and hell-bent on putting me in an early grave?

Danielle #3   That was the ultimate betrayal, leaving her for your father.

Deborah   Evil, you are. Like him.

Danielle #3   She thought she was special.

Deborah   I should have listened to that bastard doctor. I should have listened to him.

Danielle #3   She thought her piss was wine. Come on, let's go.

Danielle #2   I don't know.

Deborah   Don't go, Danielle.

Danielle #3   Your father going was one thing. But then you.

Deborah   Please. Don't go

Danielle #3   Come on, let's go. Move. You can't go backwards. Leave her. You can't go backwards. That's not the way it works. (*Pulling her*).

Leon *tells the audience what's for tea. Leads* **Danielle** *over to the microwave table.* **Deborah** *walks to breakfast table.*

Scene Nineteen: *East Glamorgan Hospital, Ward 5, 1996*

Deborah   Fucking grapes. I don't like grapes. It's their skin, mun. It irritates my throat. How many times have I got to tell him? Useless sod.

Danielle #3 *approaches, wearing a skirt.*

Deborah   Better.

Danielle #3 *sits down.*

Deborah   Too short though.

Danielle #3   I'm a tattooist now. I've got a studio in the precinct in Ponty. It's doing well, Mam.

Deborah   (*Stern*) I know what you are, gul. I've heard people talking about you in the market, haven't I? Complaining about

your monstrous tattoos and how ugly they look on everyone.
Snakes and bloody skulls. Why couldn't you have a normal job?
You know, work in a shop or something? On women as well.
You've got to have a screw loose to want to mark your body like
that, mun. If God wanted people to have tattoos they would have
been born with them, that's what my father always said.

Danielle #3   That's the whole point. You can't choose what
you're born with, can you? You've got your ears pierced, haven't
you?

Deborah   It's hardly the same thing. Earrings make you pretty.

Danielle #3   Earrings don't make you pretty. Just like tattoos
don't make you ugly. It's about identity, individuality. This woman
I had in today had been married for fifteen years to a loser from
up Glinc, violent, unfaithful. She got her divorce papers through
yesterday. She wanted the matter number tattooed under her
shoulder blade. Then in block capitals underneath, (*shapes her
hands around the words*) 'no more lies.'

Deborah   No shame, gul. Washing their dirty linen in public.
What'll people think when they see her in her cossie on Porthcawl
beach? 'Lesbos' they'll think. Butch old lesbos.

Danielle #3   Some people don't care what other people think.
That's the difference between you and me, Mam. If I did I'd
be in trouble. Talk of the town I was. 'There goes that alkie's
daughter, skinnier than a budgie's leg. She don't feed her properly,
see.' Because that's what they were really saying, wasn't it?
Everywhere I went I saw the pity in their eyes. You thought you
were the centre of attention, that people envied you. Pity! It was
pity. Where did it get you, Mam? All the vodka, all the lies?
Cirrhosis of the liver, that's where. Forty-four years old and laid
out on your death bed.

(*Noticing* **Deborah**'s *foot and pulling back, feeling guilty. Clicks
her tongue*) Look at your foot. Does it hurt?

Deborah   'Course it bloody hurts. Everything hurts. That's why
I'm here. Can't get a pair of shoes on now. What do I need shoes

for, anyway? I'm not going anywhere. Hey, you can have my shoes when I've gone. You always wanted them when you were little.

Danielle #1 *crosses the stage, taking her trainers off.*

Danielle #1   Stupid bloody things!

Deborah   Prettier than them. You might find yourself a nice boyfriend if you wore better shoes.

Danielle #3   I've got a boyfriend. You were always so obsessed with your shoes.

Deborah   (*Accusatory*) So were you!

Mr Morgan enters, following **Danielle #1**.

Danielle #1   Bore da Mr Morgan.

Mr Morgan   Interesting shoes, Danielle.

Danielle #1   Thanks Sir.

Mr Morgan   Not for school though. Take them off.

Danielle #1   (*Disappointed*) Oh, sir!

Mr Morgan   (*Mimicking her*) Oh, sir!

Scene Twenty: *Tattoo parlour, Pontypridd, 1996*

Danielle #3   (*Smiling*) There you are, then. If you can pay at the desk. Receptionist's got your details.

Tommy   There you are, lovely.

Danielle #3   Where else would I be?

Tommy   Well you haven't been to the hospital for a week.

Danielle #3   Oh, what's the point, Tom? She doesn't want me there. All she does is criticise me. I'm busy here. Fifteen sittings today alone. Tribal's the thing now. Thick, black. They take forever.

Tommy   It's worse, lovely. She's in and out of consciousness now. It could be any time. Could be tomorrow. Could be tonight.

Danielle #3   She told me the liver can repair itself.

Tommy   You've seen her, lovely. She's dying. The hospital have waived visiting hours. It could be anytime. I'm going home to change. She'll be alone for a couple of hours. It's your last chance, Dan.

Danielle #3   What's the point in anything if she's dead? Everything I've ever done, I did for her. Everything. I did it to impress her, to annoy her, to shock her. This. (*Gestures at the studio around her*) So that she'd notice me. So that she'd love me. So that she'd hate me. Anything. So now what?

Craig   Dan? Dan? Danielle? (*Going to her*)

Tommy   Alright, butt?

Scene Twenty One: *Kitchen, terraced house, Pontypridd, 1996*

Danielle #2 *is at the kitchen table with her homework, drawing and singing to herself.*

Danielle #2   How did you meet my mother, Dad?

Jerry   Well, now –

Danielle #2   In a pub?

Jerry   Outside a pub, actually. I was seeing this girl from the other valley, I was, and I took her out for a run in my new Sunbeam Tiger. Lovely car, that was. I don't know why we went through Pandy to be honest, but we did. Saturday afternoon. Sunny. I was driving past the Pandy Inn, and there in the corner of my eye: ta da. Your mother waiting at the bus stop. Yellow miniskirt, legs up to her flipping neck. I can remember it like it was yesterday, love. Out of this world, she was. Like a film star. She didn't look real. Well, I just lost control of my senses, didn't I? Lush, she was. Is that what you youngsters say these days? Lush?

Danielle #2   She *is* a lush, yeah.

Jerry   Well, I forgot about this poor girl in the car next to me. I slammed the brakes on and shouted out of the window: 'Where're you off to then, sexy? Waiting for a bus? Where're you off to?'

Deborah   Ponty ...

Jerry   Your mother says, sneering at me. See, it must have been strange for your mother because this girl was sitting next to me, but I'd forgotten all about her. After I saw your mother I don't think I ever looked properly at another woman again. I shouts at Debs: 'No you're not! You're coming on a date with me!' This other girl starts swearing, calling me all the F's and B's, slamming the car door, running off down towards the De Winton fields. You couldn't blame her really.

Danielle #2   Bet my mother loved that.

Jerry   Well, yeah, it seemed to work. Your mother got in the car and I took her to the pictures in Ponty. Closed down now. I didn't see a minute of that film. I spent the whole afternoon staring at your mother sat next to me; the prettiest thing I'd ever seen in my life. Would have walked over hot coals for your mother, I would.

Danielle #2   I miss her a bit, Dad. I didn't think I would, like. But I miss the way she called me 'sweetheart' when she wanted something. I know she couldn't cook but I miss the way she put too much milk in the tea so it was cold by the second sip. Margaret puts the milk in last 'cause she's a bit posh, isn't she?

Danielle #3   Fucking Margaret.

Deborah   Get me my lipstick sweetheart will you?

Jerry   I tried to teach your mother to cook. She wasn't interested. You know when we were first together, staying in your grancha's house? She got up one morning saying she was going to cook breakfast. Next thing, this terrible burning smell's drifting up the stairs. She was only trying to boil eggs in the electric kettle. She used to try to impress me in those days. That changed after the wedding. She was a hell of a girl, your mother. All layers. Like an onion.

Danielle #2   Yeah. Onions make you cry, don't they? (*Pause*)

Then there's the stuff I **don't** miss. Like when she had to go to the PTA meeting ...

Deborah   Do I look like the kind of woman who goes to parent teacher meetings? Do I? Tommy's gone to see a comedian up the Legion. I could have gone up there myself. Could have done with a pissin' laugh.

Mr Morgan *enters.*

Deborah   Well ding fucking dong.

Mr Morgan   Ah, hello, Mrs Davies. Sorry about the delay; just nipped to the loo. (*Looking around.*) Busy night.

Deborah   Call me Debs, darling. We're all friends here, aren't we? We're all here for Danielle.

Mr Morgan   So, er, Danielle? I'm Danielle's main tutor: her form teacher.

Deborah   Lucky Danielle.

Mr Morgan   We're very impressed with your daughter, Mrs Davies. (*Looking down at his notes*) She's advanced in her reading. In fact, she's a whole year advanced. She's recently started on the year eight reading list.

Deborah   Naturally. She's got my beans, see.

Mr Morgan   Beans?

Deborah   My beans. My NDA.

Mr Morgan   (*Not making eye contact*) And she's obviously blessed with a creative flair. I'm sure you've seen her drawings pinned up in the corridor. Some of them are highly original, I must say.

Deborah   Oh, you must. Hot in here, isn't it? Phew. I've got a mouth like an Arab's dap here. (*Goes in her bag for a bottle of vodka, swigs at it.*)

Mr Morgan   Our concern is that Danielle is often somewhat withdrawn, Mrs Davies. Quiet. Not always keen to participate in group activities, class discussions, that sort of thing.

Deborah   Are you sure about that, sweetheart? She's got a mouth on her in the house.

Mr Morgan *is embarrassed, searching frantically through his notes.*

Deborah   I'm joking, darling. I'm teasing you. Loosen up. (*Throws papers on the floor*) There you are. What were you saying?

Mr Morgan   Class discussions. We know she's bright. But she chooses not to engage –

Deborah   Well I always engage.

Mr Morgan   (**Deborah** *starts stroking his chest*) Confidence could be an issue here.

Deborah   Oh I don't think it will be love. (*Holding* **Mr Morgan***'s face*) Tell you what, handsome. Let's get out of this stuffy school hall, continue our little meeting somewhere more private?

Mr Morgan   We can't do this!

Jerry   Inappropriate.

Mr Morgan   No I really can't do this. Mrs Davies I'm going to have to ask you to leave. The door is that way, I'm going this way.

Jerry   Entirely inappropriate.

Deborah   What a boring bunch of bastards, you are. You wouldn't know what fun was if it turned up and shat in your laps. (*Notices a big rubber plant in the corner*) Now look at that. I've always wanted one of them. Must be my lucky day. (*Picks the plant up and dances with it, singing*) **The minute you walked in the joint, I could see you were a man of distinction, a real big spender. Good looking, so refined. Say, wouldn't you like to know what's going on in my mind. So let me get right to the**

point. (*About to exit*) **I don't pop my cork for every man I see.** (*Exits*) **Hey Big Spender!**

Jerry   Yeah. She was a hell of a girl, your mother. (*Gets up with a sigh and goes off to make his cup of tea.*)

Danielle #2   (*Mortified*) Oh my fucking God. I wish she'd listened that doctor. I wish the ground would have swallowed me, I swear.

Danielle #3   Don't worry about it. Believe me, you'll be able to laugh about in a few years' time. The funny thing is that after Dad went I used to dream she'd marry Mr Morgan. Someone stable. (*Pause*) So how's things? With loverboy?

Danielle #2   (*Looks at her, taking an interest*) Craig?

Danielle #3   Of course, Craig. (*Rolls eyes*) Who else?

Danielle #2   (*Looks despondent*) I don't think he's into the whole motorbike-boot-alcoholic's-daughter sort of thing.

Danielle #3   (*Laughs*) You've got to take the lead. Your legs are fab, babe. Wear the short skirt. To the party on Friday.

Danielle #2   They're bandy. *She* told me.

Danielle #3   (*Laughs bitterly. Scrapes* **Danielle #2**'s *hair out of her face. Look at her sadly*) They're perfect. Your legs are perfect. (*Pause*) And he's crazy about you, sweetheart. Don't you see? He gets a semi on every time he looks at you.

Danielle #2   Just a semi?

Jerry   Come on then, Dan, you'd better clear this up. Look, you've got charcoal here on Margaret's best table cloth. I hope that washes out. I've cleared you a space in the spare room for you to do your drawing. Margaret'll have a fit if she sees you by here.

Danielle #2   Of course it washes out. It's just charcoal, Dad.

Danielle #3   It's not permanent. It's not like tattoo ink or anything.

Jerry   (*Looks strangely at* **Danielle #3**, *almost acknowledging her, but not quite. Looks to* **Danielle #2**) This is her best filet lace, love. Come on, I tipped curry sauce on it once; she had my nutsack in a knot for a fortnight.

Scene Twenty Two: *Kitchen, terraced house, Tonypandy, 1992*

Danielle #2 *is sitting at the kitchen table surrounded by her art project.* **Deborah** *enters and goes to a mirror, fiddling with her hair and spraying hairspray.*

Danielle #2   (*Coughing*) Mam? Can I have some money? I'm running out of paper. I need to finish this project for school.

Deborah   Doesn't the school supply that these days?

Danielle #2   I need it now. It's homework. I've got to finish it before I go back on Monday.

Deborah   (*Takes the card out of an empty stocking packet and holds it up*) This any good?

Danielle #2   Don't be stupid. It's for school. It's important.

Deborah   Well you never minded before.

Danielle #2   I did mind, actually. All I wanted was real paper, like normal kids. How much is a pad anyway? It's cheaper than a pair of stockings. But you've got to have your stockings, haven't you. All I get is this. (*Rips the card in two*)

Deborah   You're so bloody ungrateful. Doesn't matter if I bought you all the paper in the world, you'd still be painting on everything in the house with my best nail polish. Normal kids don't go around painting on the furniture with their mother's best nail varnish, not at fifteen.

Danielle #2   No. 'Cause normal kids got paper. Normal kids got acrylic paints. Normal kids got normal mothers.

Deborah   Money doesn't grow on trees, girl.

Danielle #2   Money does grow on trees, Mam. It's paper, isn't it? (*Makes a face at her mother*). I'd get a paper round but you won't let me. Reckon I'll get molested. It's not that though, is it? You just want to have total control over me. You don't want me to have any money. It's only paper I want, mun. It's not like I'm asking for money for the school skiing trip, or my first new uniform in two years, or a bottle of vodka. Two flippin' pound. For a flippin' drawing pad. So I can actually pass my exam.

Deborah   Oh, I declare, Danielle. I really do.

Danielle #2   Yeah? I declare as well. (*Putting her things away in a pencil case*) I'm going down Nanna and Grancha's. They'll buy me paper.

Deborah   Don't you dare go down there, begging. Don't you ever go down there. Don't you dare! (*Quieter*) Don't you ever go down there.

Danielle #2   Well I need it for school. I'll get in trouble otherwise.

Deborah   Look, I'll buy you the bloody paper. Stop your mingeing, alright? I'll get some money off Tommy later, you can get it tomorrow.

Danielle #2   Mingeing? What the fuck? (*Staring at Debs*)

Deborah   Danielle! Stop your swearing. Give me some peace to get ready. You can have your pad tomorrow. Jesus wept.

Scene Twenty Three: *Living room, terraced house, Tonypandy, 1995*

Tommy   Debs? Deborah? (*Getting hold of her and trying to raise her onto the sofa*) Come on, love. Up we get.

Deborah   (*Shouting, barely coherent*) Danni? Danni?

Tommy   It's me, love. Come on.

Deborah   (*Trying to wrestle him off but she's too weak*) Get off me. Get off me. I'm OK.

Tommy   (*Looking around in desperation, still holding his nose*) You're not, love. You're ill. You're really ill and you've

– (*pointing at her to indicate she's soiled herself*) I'm phoning the doctor. I have to.

Deborah   I don't need no fucking doctor. Leave me alone.

Tommy   But you do, love. I'm sorry, love. You do. (*Going to the phone*)

Scene Twenty Four: *East Glamorgan Hospital, Ward 5, 1996*

Deborah   (*Struggling to speak*) Where've you been? I haven't seen you.

Danielle #3   I'm sorry, Mam. I've been busy. Work things.

Nurse   Not so good today. Can I get you anything from the trolley? A coffee?

Danielle #3   No. Thank you.

Danielle #3   You never told me you loved me. You never told me anything. Not one positive thing my entire life. What harm would it have done to encourage me? To tell me you were proud?

Deborah   (*Eyes closed and struggling*) You didn't need any encouragement.

Danielle #3   You rejected me. That made me love you more. I loved you so much I could have choked on it. No-one loved you more than me.

Deborah   You left.

Danielle #3   I would have strangled you.

Deborah   I made you strong.

Danielle #3   You made me hard.

Deborah   It's the same thing.

Danielle #3   No, it's not Mam. Admitting something doesn't make you weak. Telling your own child that you love them doesn't make you weak. Having feelings, being human, that doesn't make you weak. Say it. Tell me you love me.

Tommy   Dan? You OK, lovely? I'll take over now if you want.

Danielle #3   Yeah. Yeah, I have to go.

Deborah   Danni? You smell nice, sweetheart. New perfume?

Danielle #3   No.

Deborah   Oh, it smells nice. You smell nice, sweetheart. See you tomorrow, is it?

Danielle #3   (*Putting on a brave face*) Yep, see you tomorrow.

(*To Audience*) I saw her the next day. But she didn't see me. From the corner I watched her. Tommy was holding her hand. I thought she was too mean to die. And if she did die, I thought the world would end. That everything would explode.

Danielle #2   But there was no trouble.

Danielle #3   No bother.

Danielle #1   No Tonypandemonium.

Danielle #3   She slipped away, easy as a leaf falling from a tree. I looked around and everything was the same. (*They hold hands*)

The dinner lady was doing her rounds, whistling a tune.

Danielle #1   And when it happened the dinner lady didn't stop whistling.

Danielle #2   She just kept on going, whistling.

Danielle #3   And the clock kept chiming, like the world wasn't exploding, like the world would keep on going.

All Danielles   And the world just kept on going.

Danielle #1   Yep. We just kept on going.

The Radicalisation of Bradley Manning

Tim Price

The Radicalisation of Bradley Manning was commissioned and produced by National Theatre Wales. It was first performed on 12 April 2012 at Tasker Milward VC School, Haverfordwest, as part of National Theatre Wales's second year of work. The production then toured Wales and was re-mounted in 2013 at the Edinburgh Festival. The version featured in this anthology was prepared for the 2013 production. The play won the James Tait Black Prize for Drama 2013. The cast was as follows:

Matthew Aubrey
Harry Ferrier
Gwawr Loader
Kyle Rees
Naomi Everson
Michael Gilhooly

Director	John E McGrath
Designer	Chloe Lamford
Lighting Designer	Natasha Chivers
Sound Designer	Mike Beer
Multi-platform designer	Tom Beardshaw
Emerging Director	James Doyle-Roberts

'The story I tell happened in a time we cannot understand'
Jorge Luis Borges

'I will officially give up on the society we
have if nothing happens'
Bradass87

'Courage is contagious'
Billy Graham

Characters in order of appearance.

Marine 1 – *Guard in Quantico Brig.*

Bradley Manning – *(14–23) U.S. Soldier, accused of leaking the largest amount of classified material in history – to be played by every member of cast.*

Chorus – *See author's note.*

Mrs Stokes – *(50s) Inspirational history teacher.*

Mark Pritchard – *(14–17) Welsh teenager, class charmer.*

Gavin Hope – *(14–17) Welsh teenager, class thug.*

Lisa Williams – *(14–17) Welsh teenager, class beauty queen.*

Anthony Edwards – *(14–17) Welsh teenager, class whipping boy.*

Lady Gaga – *American popular music star.*

TFL worker – *(any age) Londoner.*

Commuter 1 – *(any age) London worker.*

Commuter 2 – *(any age) London worker.*

Commuter 3 – *(any age) London worker.*

Customer – *(any age).*

Tina – *Bradley's colleague in the U.S. service industry.*

Brian Manning – *(50s) Bradley's father.*

Waitress – *(any age).*

Drill Sergeant – *Instructor for U.S. Military basic training.*

Recruit 1 – *Fellow recruit of Bradley's to the U.S. Military.*

Recruit 2 – *Fellow recruit of Bradley's to the U.S. Military.*

Recruit 3 – *Fellow recruit of Bradley's to the U.S. Military.*

Reporter – *News reporter for Syracuse.com at Proposition 8 rally.*

Tyler Watkins – *(20) Gay student, Bradley's first love.*

Marine 2 – *Marine at Quantico Brig.*

Marine 3 – *Marine at Quantico Brig.*

Marine 4 – *Marine at Quantico Brig.*

David House – *(20) President of Builds, hackerspace at Boston University, one of the few people allowed to visit Bradley at Quantico.*

Kyle – *(20) Hacker.*

Alison – *(20) Hacktivist.*

Commander Browning – *Marine Commander in charge of Quantico Brig.*

Soldier 1 – *Soldier stationed at the Discharge Unit, awaiting dismissal from the army.*

Soldier 2 – *Soldier stationed at the Discharge Unit, awaiting dismissal from the army.*

Soldier 3 – *Soldier stationed at the Discharge Unit, awaiting release from the army.*

Private Miles – *Bradley's 'battle buddy'. Soldier assigned to Bradley at the discharge unit to help with the stress of transition from army to civilian life.*

Sergeant – *Sergeant at Discharge Unit tasked with recycling Bradley back into the army.*

Intel Officer 1 – *Fellow intelligence analyst of Bradley's at Forward Operating Base*

Hammer.

Intel Officer 2 – *Fellow intelligence analyst of Bradley's at Forward Operating Base*

Hammer.

IFP – *Iraqi Federal Police.*

Nidal – *Iraqi Federal Police.*

Major – *Major in charge of Bradley's Division.*

Deaf Counsellor – *U.S. Military Counsellor.*

Blind Counsellor – *U.S. Military Counsellor.*

Mute Counsellor – *U.S. Military Counsellor.*

Commander – *U.S. Military Commander in charge of Forward Operation Base*

Hammer, in Iraq.

/ – indicates when the next line should be spoken.

// – indicates the next following line should also interrupt.

- indicates an interruption by another thought or character.

*It is suggested lines in **bold** are to be delivered chorally. How that manifests itself is for the director to discover.*

Author's note

Throughout the play there are stage directions for the Chorus. These are just suggestions. All direction for the Chorus should be discovered by the director and cast in rehearsal. The Chorus should be on stage at all times, and should serve the story by creating the subtext of the scene, through physical language as well as bringing fluidity to the transitions between time and space. The cast should seek to blur the lines between characters and choral personalities, so that Chorus serves as a five-headed monster, holding the play together by pulling it apart.

Throughout the play there are directions when a new cast member should start playing Bradley and choral lines marked in bold. Again these are just suggestions and should be discovered by the director and cast.

Act One

Scene One – March 2011

Bradley on POI watch in Quantico

On Screen – Wales is a radical country. The Internet is a radical space. Both have a history of fighting corrupt concentrations of power. For Wales, the fight is over. For the Internet, it's only just begun ...

In this story Bradley Manning's school years have been imagined. Everything else is true.

Darkness.

Bradley lies in a smock on a bench.

Marine 1   *(off-stage)* Detainee 4335453 Are you okay?

Beat.

Bradley   What?

Marine 1   *(off-stage)* Answer affirmative or negative. Are you okay?

Beat.

Clanking sound of door opening ...

Scene Two – Present Day

Chorus 1   Bradley Manning is traitor.

Chorus 2   Bradley Manning is a hero.

Chorus 3   Bradley Manning is F***ing A-hole.

Chorus 4   Bradley Manning is a soldier.

Now Chorus speaks at the same time, over each other getting louder and louder trying to be heard.

Chorus 5   Bradley Manning is a sign of the times.

Chorus 6   Bradley Manning should fry!

Chorus 1   Bradley Manning is going to die in jail.

Chorus 2   Bradley Manning is not going to get a fair trial.

Chorus 3   Bradley Manning is a human rights issue.

Chorus 4   Bradley Manning is being held in inhumane conditions.

Chorus 5   Bradley Manning is an intelligence analyst.

Chorus 6   Bradley Manning should not have enlisted.

Chorus 1   Bradley Manning needs our help.

Chorus 2   Bradley Manning is only a boy.

Chorus 3   Bradley Manning caused the Arab Spring.

Chorus 4   Bradley Manning is gay!

Chorus 5   Bradley Manning was tortured.

Chorus 6   Bradley Manning was held in Kuwait.

Chorus 1   Bradley Manning's glasses were taken from him, which is a contravention of his human rights.

Chorus 2   Bradley Manning is a whistleblower.

Chorus 3   Bradley Manning is innocent.

Chorus 4   Bradley Manning is not a machine.

Chorus 5   Bradley Manning is a hot-headed loner.

Chorus 6   Bradley Manning is twenty-three.

Chorus 1   Bradley Manning is meh…

Chorus 2   Bradley Manning is in chains twenty-three hours a day.

Chorus 3   Bradley Manning is a communist.

Chorus 4   Bradley Manning should never have gone to Iraq, whose idea was that?

Chorus 5   Bradley Manning took an oath to serve his nation, and abide by the rules and regulations of the Armed Forces.

Chorus 6   Bradley Manning is a complex character deserving of our compassion.

Chorus 1   Bradley Manning was tired of being a victim.

Chorus 2   Bradley Manning's personal and sexual issues inform his decisions.

Chorus 3   Bradley Manning was let down by those above him, and if this is anyone's fault it's the army. And don't ask don't tell.

Chorus 4   Bradley Manning was witness to war crimes.

Chorus 5   Bradley Manning went too far.

Chorus 6   Bradley Manning is the WikiLeaks guy right?

Chorus 1   Bradley Manning was recycled.

Chorus 2   Bradley Manning is our Dan Ellsberg.

Chorus 3   Bradley Manning has security clearance.

Chorus 4   Bradley Manning was the kid who got all aggro on the X Factor right? Right?

Chorus 5   Bradley Manning sounds like a real cool guy, at least before they sent him crazy in detention.

Chorus 6   Bradley Manning knew when he leaked all of those records he had a pretty good idea he was going to pay for it down the road. He still did it. That's not cowardly.

Chorus 1   Bradley Manning is a fucking hero no matter how a trial plays out.

Chorus 2   Bradley Manning is just a dumb kid, and his actions really haven't changed anything.

Chorus 3   Bradley Manning worked at Starbucks.

Chorus 4   Bradley Manning didn't know what was in the cables he leaked.

Chorus 5 Bradley Manning's commentators have presumed he's guilty.

Chorus 6 Bradley Manning is guilty of nothing at this time.

Chorus 1 Bradley Manning saw what looked like a pattern of wrongdoing.

Chorus 2 Bradley Manning's case serves to illustrate how badly designed U.S. military networks are in terms of supporting information compartmentalisation and secrecy silos.

Chorus 3 Bradley Manning is a dickhead of colossal dimensions.

Chorus 4 Bradley Manning is rotting in the brig.

Chorus 5 Bradley Manning is too trusting.

Chorus 6 Bradley Manning is alleged to have released extensive U.S. military and government materials to WikiLeaks. These show how the U.S. and many other governments so often say one thing in public, another in private, and yet a third through their actions.

Chorus 1 Bradley Manning needs a bullet in the fucking head.

Chorus 2 Bradley Manning is no hero and neither is Julian Assange.

Chorus 3 Bradley Manning's actions are down to his frustrated sexuality and personal isolation.

Chorus 4 Bradley Manning is why we don't have gays in the military.

Chorus 5 Bradley Manning is still a soldier.

Chorus 6 Bradley Manning hadn't read hardly any of the stuff he leaked.

Chorus 1 Bradley Manning is a transvestite.

Chorus 2 Bradley Manning discovered his company was run by the mob.

Chorus 3   Bradley Manning is now left with the sinking feeling he doesn't have anything left.

Chorus 4   Bradley Manning is not allowed to hold a gun anymore.

Chorus 5   Bradley Manning is woken every twenty minutes.

Chorus 6   Bradley Manning's prison guards are being targeted by Anonymous.

Chorus 1   Bradley Manning likes Pi Day.

Chorus 2   Bradley Manning leaked footage of another botched job by your shitty and unprofessional military.

Chorus 3   Bradley Manning is a little squirt who betrayed his country and has risked the lives of all of us. This has been a lesson in what happens when you let homos in the army.

Chorus 4   Bradley Manning wants to work in the prison library.

Chorus 5   Bradley Manning is bi-polar.

Chorus 6   Bradley Manning heads our reader poll for who should win this year's Nobel Peace Prize.

Chorus 1   Bradley Manning worked at Abercrombie and Fitch.

Chorus 2   Bradley Manning is not a piece of equipment.

Chorus 3   Bradley Manning has an iphone.

Chorus moves into position so that **Mrs Stokes** *stands in front of a classroom of kids.*

Chorus 4   Bradley Manning is moving to a less harsh detention centre.

Chorus 5   Bradley Manning wants an air purifier.

Mrs Stokes   Bradley Manning is Welsh!

Scene Three

Tasker Milward School – October 2001

Mrs Stokes   So I don't want to hear any bullying or joking about his accent. He can play for Wales, so he has as much right to be here as any of you. Bradley?

The entire room looks at **Bradley** *who stands in the corner of the room holding a piece of paper – his timetable. Ad lib class muttering and talking.*

Bradley   Um … I don't know if I'm in the right period.

Class sniggers at his accent and 'period' – some imitate.

Mrs Stokes   Bradley, within this room you will find people you will love and people you will hate, I know I do. Mr Pritchard, / I assign Mr Manning, // it is your duty to get him to his next class and to make sure no-one sticks his head down the toilet until at least Thursday.

Mark   No no no no! Not me.

Gavin   Bummers!

Mrs Stokes   Bradley what do you know about the Norman invasion of Wales?

Bradley   Who's Norman? *Class erupts into hilarity. Lighting state change:*

Class continues to laugh in silence as **Mark** *walks* **Bradley** *around the room – An opportunity for* **Mark** *to pick out audience members as fellow pupils.*

Mark   Okay! Quickest way to Tesco's is through the lady's garden. Stick with us TASK boys avoid the ERM lot. Back here's the wasters. Don't lend him anything. She cries when she has her period. His Dad got caught with a rent boy. England supporter.

Beat.

(Gavin) Hard, *(Anthony)* wanker, *(Lisa)* psycho. Stokesy's alright, for a teacher. Keep hold of your bag and, don't take a shit in school.

Sequence over: class noise returns, normal lighting.

Mrs Stokes   Settle down! Bradley you'll get up to speed in no time. Having defeated King Harold in 1066, why did William the Conqueror build Chepstow castle in 1067, Mr Pritchard?

Mark   He wanted a palace.

Mrs Stokes   Mr Hope?

Gavin *shrugs. Class/Chorus is permanently harassing, giggling and talking to each other to grotesque degrees isolating* **Bradley**.

Mrs Stokes   Anyone? Ms Williams?

Lisa   Was it? Was it because; right, was it because he wanted to get away from where they'd just had a fight. Where was it?

Anthony   Has/tings.

Lisa   Hastings! I thought it was somewhere else then for a second. So, because he'd won there, did he want to like get far away from there so, they couldn't come back at him. I don't know where's Hastings?

Mrs Stokes   Mr Manning? Hazard a guess?

Silence.

Bradley   I, don't know.

Mrs Stokes   Why does it look like we're going to invade Afghanistan?

Bradley   The Taliban are / hiding Bin Laden.

Gavin   Ye-haw!

Mrs Stokes   Thank you Mr Hope. Throughout history the invaded countries have changed, but the reasons stay the same. *Strategy* drives America to invade Afghanistan, and *strategy* … drove William the Conqueror to build a fort at the edge of Wales.

A piece of paper hits the back of **Bradley**'s *head.*

Mrs Stokes   Through / military might and inter-marriage, // the Normans went on to take control of Wales.

Bradley   *(under)* What was that for?

Mark   *(under)* Don't.

More paper flies at **Bradley**, **Lisa** *throws paper.* **Anthony** *throws a piece of paper at Bradley.*

Bradley   What the fuck?

The frenzy of throwing stops as **Mrs Stokes** *turns.*

Mrs Stokes   What's going on? Bradley?

Silence.

She turns her back again.

The Mailed Fist as it was known, gripped Wales following the Norman Conquest.

More paper flies, **Anthony** *throws some paper and it hits* **Mark** *who takes umbrage at* **Anthony** *joining in.* **Mark** *stands up to throw paper at* **Anthony**, *but* **Mark** *becomes the target and gets totally plastered by the rest of the class.*

Mark *is overwhelmed until* **Bradley** *joins in, steps in front of* **Mark**, *and defends* **Mark**, *hurling paper back at Anthony.* **Mrs Stokes** *turns around, and the class immediately reverts to good behaviour. But* **Bradley** *is too slow. He is left standing alone pelting paper at* **Anthony**.

He realises he's alone.

Mrs Stokes   Bradley Manning. See me after class.

Bradley   It wasn't just me.

Mrs Stokes   You are the only one I saw.

Bradley   I'm not lying.

Mrs Stokes   You were the only one I saw.

Bradley   But that's / bullshit. I'm not lying.

Mrs Stokes   I won't ask you again.

Bradley   But-

Mrs Stokes   I won't tell you again.

Bradley   WHY WON'T YOU LISTEN?

Scene Four – August 2010

Quantico Brig

Marine 1   Contravenes regulations.

Beat.

No exercise.

Bradley   I'm / just.

Marine 1   No exercise.

Bradley *stops exercising.*

Bradley   I am still a soldier.

Marine 1   No exercise.

Bradley   Who's in charge here?

Scene Five – July 7 2005

King's Cross Station

Rolling screens say 'All trains cancelled'.

Bradley *is wearing a rucksack.*

TFL worker   I am, you have to leave.

Bradley   Can I use your phone?

TFL worker   It's not working mate you have to leave.

Bradley   Excuse me, can I use your phone? Is your phone working?

Commuter 1   I can't get through. / There's no dial tone.

Commuter 2   They take down the mobile networks when stuff like this happens.

Bradley   Stuff like what?

Commuter 2   Bombs. Bloke over there said it was two separate lines. Don't sound like gas. / You on your own mate?

Bradley   I'm trying to get the embassy. I've got a flight to the States tomorrow.

Commuter 2   Can't see any planes leaving London.

Commuter 1   Here have some water.

Bradley *and* **Commuter** *share water.*

My wife's in Paddington. I think there's an internet café over there / I'm gonna try and email her.

Bradley   I need a phone. Are there any phonebooths anywhere? I just need to make a call.

Commuter 3   There's no phones working.

Lady Gaga hands **Bradley** *a telephone.*

Bradley   Um, Dad? Have- have you seen the news? Turn on the news.

Beat.

What's it say? I'm at, I'm at King's Cross Station, I'm meant to be getting a new passport and then flying home tomorrow but there was this explosion and smoke and- what's the news saying?

Beat.

Oh my God. How many?

Beat.

Was there one on a bus? What's going- My phone doesn't work, everyone's being really kind- Oh My God, Oh my God. Have they said who it is? Is it Al Qaeda? I could've- what?

Beat.

I'm okay. I felt the explosion in my feet. I was that- It was underneath me I could have been on one of those subways Dad I could have- hang on. The boards are changing. It's changing. Everything's changing. Hangon I'll tell you what it says.

'I'm running away.'

Oh.

'I'm running away from Wales because, I'm a coward.'

Um. They're not saying. They're not saying. They don't have any new information.

'Like you.'

It's just … saying random things. Dad. Can you call Mom for me? She's- I don't want her worrying about me. She'll be worried about me. I don't want her worrying.

'Mom needed me, and I abandoned her. Just like you did.'

I'm in the middle of a fucking terrorist- Can you just call her? Please? Call her. Thank you.

'I have to show her I'm nothing like you.'

I'm fine! I've just- I was really close that's all.

'By making something of my life.'

I'm uh … I don't think my flight is uh, is … is going to be, running either so …

'I have to do something special.'

Yeah.

'For her.'

Yeah. Are you gonna call Mom?

Scene Six

Tasker Milward School – October 2001

Mrs Stokes   I won't be calling your mother this time Bradley but you do seem to have a problem with authority. Do you have a problem with authority?

Beat.

Why were you arguing with me?

Bradley   Because it's not fair.

Mrs Stokes   Who are you to say what's fair and what's not?

Bradley   Who are you to?

Pause.

Mrs Stokes   Think you've just answered my first question there Bradley.

Beat.

Listen. This is a new school. New teachers. New classmates.

Beat.

You're already at a huge disadvantage; you're American. You've joined late; you're not a big lad. You don't need to add a bad attitude to that mix.

Beat.

How's things at home.

Bradley shrugs.

Okay, next time you feel yourself filling up with anger, I want you to take a deep breath. Once you've taken that deep breath all your anger will go away and you'll have clarity. You'll know what you should do next, and I guarantee it will never be lash out.

Beat.

Will you try that for me?

Bradley *nods.*

Mrs Stokes   Who threw the first paper ball?

Bradley   Gavin Miss. Is that everything?

Scene Seven

Bradley in a McJob – April 2006

Customer: Yes just the soya latte.

Bradley   Flat white soya latte?

Tina hands the cup to **Bradley** *who hands it over to the* **Customer**. *Chorus performs service industry jobs, and ensures* **Bradley** *and* **Tina** *have right props.*

Customer: Thank you.

Bradley   Sorry for the- …

Customer *has left.*

Bradley *yawns.*

Tina   So where you living now?

Bradley   I was at my dad and step-mom's for a while didn't really belong there, so I got my own place in Midtown; landlord's kind of a crappy.

Tina   Okay.

Bradley   I'm just doing this till I get my own tech company up and running. Last place was a fucking joke. I'm not here long so, it's okay.

Bradley *and* **Tina** *start folding shirts.*

Tina   Everyone's just here for the summer.

Bradley   Yuh.

Tina   What's that supposed to mean?

Silence.

You think I want / to work here forever?

Bradley   No.

Beat.

I didn't mean that.

Beat.

I don't know what I meant.

Silence.

Tina *and* **Bradley** *stand at a counter with a factory line of burgers on it.* **Tina** *puts the lid of the bun on, and passes it to* **Bradley** *who closes the box.*

Beat.

I'm not being mean.

Tina   You are.

Bradley   Forget it. *Silence.*

Tina   My friend lives in Midtown, whereabouts?

Bradley   Uh, Brady Arts District, around there.

Beat.

I'm just saying, I've lived in the UK. I've built websites. I practically nursed my Mom on my own. I'm sorry if that's made me want to do something with my life.

Tina *squirts the surface with a cleaning product,* **Bradley** *mops the floor.*

These people don't. So I have nothing in common with them.

Beat.

If that makes me mean. Then fine. I'm mean.

Tina   You haven't tried talking to everyone.

Bradley   I have.

Tina   Really?

Bradley   Yes. Most of them.

Tina   Most of them.

Bradley   They don't wanna do anything with their lives. I can tell. There's no rush. I can't get out of here quick enough.

Tina   You look down on / people Bradley.

Pause.

Bradley   Maybe I do. They deserve to be looked down on, if they think this is all they're good for.

Tina *and* **Bradley** *put headsets on.*

Tina   Jason said he saw you sleeping in your car.

Beat.

Bradley   I was doing a double shift.

Tina   He's seen you a few times. *(To headset)* I'm just putting you through to our policy support team sir. Please hold! *(To* **Bradley***)* You sleep in your car.

Beat.

Bradley   I don't, sleep in my car.

Tina   You're always the last to leave and you have a toothbrush in your drawer.

Beat.

Bradley   I'm a hard worker.

Tina   Everyone's seen you brushing your teeth in the toilet.

Beat.

Bradley   That doesn't mean anything.

Tina   You look down on everyone and walk around telling everyone we're all stupid but you're the one who's homeless.

Beat.

Bradley   I share a place in Midtown.

Tina   I thought it was your *own* place? *(To headset)* Yes sir we're just waiting for one of my colleagues who's on another line. Sorry for the delay.

Beat.

I don't care if you sleep in a dumpster. Just don't act like you're smarter than everyone else. It'll bite you on the ass. You sleep in your car, and work a crappy job. You can't look down on *anyone*. You're just as trapped as the rest of us.

Scene Eight

Quantico Brig – Sept 2010

A clunking sound.

A plate of food is slid under door.

Bradley *approaches it. He looks at* **Tina**

He picks up his food, sits next to Tina and eats in silence.

Scene Nine

An American Diner – August 2007

Another **Bradley** *sits in a diner opposite* **Brian Manning**, *his father.* **Brian** *is played by the whole chorus.*

Nervously, **Bradley** *fiddles with a napkin.*

Bradley   Thanks for meeting me.

Brian   You eat yet? I think I'm going for pancakes. You think pancakes?

Bradley   I'm good.

Brian   You eat yet?

Bradley   I haven't got any / money so.

Brian   I can buy you breakfast Bradley.

Bradley   Pancakes are fine.

Brian   *(To waitress)* Two pancakes, both with maple syrup.

Brian   I ain't eat here before.

Bradley   It's good. It's / good.

Silence.

Brian   Stop that.

Silence, as **Bradley** *puts the napkin down.*

You not going to ask how your step-Mom is doing?

Bradley   How is she?

Brian   Doing just fine.

Beat.

Getting new carpet. House is a mess.

Silence, as **Bradley** *starts fiddling with the napkin again.* **Brian** *takes it off him.* **Bradley** *takes a deep calming breath.*

Bradley   I uh. I asked to see you today, Dad, because uh …

Brian   Where you living now?

Beat.

Bradley   I'm staying. I'm with friends. Around.

Chorus acts as Waitress to bring over two pancakes.

Bradley   Thank you.

Waitress becomes a **Brian**.

Bradley   I wanted to ask you. If uh, if you know, if you could help. If you had. If you could help, me pay my way to go to college.

Brian   *(Two Brians)* **You been looking at schools?**

Bradley   MIT, BU.

Silence.

I'll work. I'm working crappy jobs now, but I need to be going someplace else otherwise, all I am is someone who works crappy jobs. And living, you know, / with no-where.

Brian   Where are you working now?

Bradley   I was at Abercrombie and Fitch. Looking for something else. In-between.

Brian   You think the world owes you a career. Well it doesn't. / Your mother took you to Wales and you lost all sense of reality.

Bradley   This not because Mom took me to Wales when you walked out on us.

Silence.

Brian   *(Three Brians)* **You watch your mouth.**

Silence.

Eat your pancakes.

Beat.

You want to go to college.

Bradley   Yeah, major in computer sciences.

Silence.

Brian   You think that's going to fix everything?

Bradley   Ye/ah.

Brian   Well it's not.

Bradley   Are you going to help me or not?

A fourth **Brian** *counts out some money and puts it on the table.*

Take that money. Meet me here tomorrow with a resume, a clean shirt and tie. We head on down to the military / recruitment centre together.

Bradley   No Dad I'm not joining the army! I want to go to college!

Brian   When you were boy all you wanted to do was join the army.

Bradley   I want to go to college.

Brian   What's your problem with the military?

Bradley   I don't have a problem with the military Dad it's the Government / I have a problem with.

Brian   You get three square meals a day. A roof over your head.

Bradley   I don't know why I thought you'd help.

Brian   You can work with computers in intelligence. They've got the best hardware. You get three square meals, roof over your head and a skill base. And here's the thing. After four years' service, they pay for you to go to college.

Bradley   They pay you to go?

Brian   To any school you want. Ivy League. And they pay you wage. You have to wait but you're getting life experience and money in your pocket.

A fifth **Brian** *joins and physically leans on* **Bradley**.

Brian   Get your degree and get the hell out of there, with a degree and military credentials.

Silence.

Bradley   I could go to MiT?

Brian   You go where you want. For free.

Silence.

Bradley   I'm five two and I weigh a hundred / and five pounds.

Brian   You ain't going in for infantry. Basic will be tough.

Bradley   I'm gay. I'm not allowed to be open and in the military.

Beat.

Brian   Life's about compromises. D' you wanna to be a man, and join the army, or do you want to be gay and work in Starbucks?

Beat.

Brian *offers him the money.*

Bradley *takes the money.*

Bradley   Where do I go?

Scene Ten

Tasker Milward School – September 2002

Mrs Stokes   The front please Bradley, take the hot-seat. Today! We are learning about the Merthyr Rising of 1831!

Reluctantly, another **Bradley** *goes to the front of the class and sits down.*

A popular rising where the workers took control of the town. A time when revolutionary ideas threatened the status quo. The first time the red flag of revolution was raised, in the world.

Mrs Stokes *leans on* **Bradley**.

This twenty-three-year old man was executed for those ideas. Hanged to death outside the entrance to what is now Cardiff market.

Beat.

But he's come back from the grave for one afternoon to help you pass your GCSE's. So class, let's welcome;

(To **Bradley***)* Dic Penderyn. Who has a question for our hot-seated martyr. Lisa?

Lisa   Um … well, uh. Oh, um … I was gonna say … no. I. Whatyoucall? I had it then. No! Hang on. What's your, what's your real name?

Bradley   Richard Lewis.

Gavin   How old are you?

Bradley   Twenty-three.

Mark   Are you gay?

Class hilarity.

Offended, Bradley starts to get out of his seat and get up, Mrs Stokes indicates for him to take a breath. Bradley sits down and takes a deep calming breath.

Bradley   No. I'm not.

Mark   Have you ever kissed a boy?

Mrs Stokes   Thank you Mr Pritchard, I think this line of questioning has been exhausted.

Anthony   What was it like being hanged to death?

Bradley shrugs.

Mrs Stokes   Mr Penderyn?

Beat.

The class is silent.

Mrs Stokes   You have the class's attention Mr Penderyn.

Bradley   I didn't like, all the people watching and not doing anything. If I'd seen someone innocent getting punished for no reason I'd do something about it. All these people who I thought were my friends. Just let me die.

Silence.

Mrs Stokes   Just to clarify Mr Penderyn, there was a petition with over eleven thousand signatures, urging the Government to release you, but yes. That must have awful for you. What were your last words?

Bradley   I don't remember. I was too busy dying.

The class laughs. Bradley enjoys the moment.

Mrs Stokes   Your last words were 'Oh arglywdd, dyma gamwedd'? What do they mean? Test your Welsh.

Bradley   Arglywdd is God right?

Mrs Stokes   'Oh Lord, what an injustice' or 'Oh Lord, here is iniquity'. Why did you say that?

Bradley   Because I'm innocent. I didn't stab that soldier in the leg. I didn't stab anyone they got the wrong guy.

Gavin   What's it like being a martyr?

Bradley   I'm not a martyr/. That's the frustrating thing, I'm dead but I can't control what happens to my name.

Gavin   You are butt.

Bradley stands up.

Bradley   A martyr is someone who wants to die. I didn't want to die.

Mrs Stokes   That's not necessarily true.

Bradley   It is.

Mrs Stokes   A martyr is someone who died for a cause, not someone who killed themselves for a cause, there's a difference.

Bradley   Okay well I'm not a proper martyr.

Mark   What's someone, who's not a proper martyr?

Bradley   I'm not a martyr; I just got caught, and got blamed for something I didn't do. How does that make me a martyr?

Lisa   Because you got punished.

Bradley   Those guys that flew the planes into the World Trade Centre, they were martyrs. Suicide bombers in Afghanistan, they're martyrs. A martyr is someone who believes in something so much they'll kill themselves for it. Not someone like me who just got caught.

Mrs Stokes   Anyone agree with Mr Penderyn?

Pause.

Anyone want to disagree with him?

Lisa   It's not. It doesn't matter. What it is, is. Like you haven't got to. Just because you haven't done something, if the army or Government or whoever make you pay then … I don't know. I just. I don't know.

Mrs Stokes   Why were you protesting?

Bradley   Uh … poor working conditions. Debtors court. Um.

Mrs Stokes   Anyone else?

Mark   Truck shops.

Lisa   Low wages.

Mrs Stokes   You wanted reform? Yes?

Bradley   Yes.

Mrs Stokes   Mr Penderyn. Hanging you to death was a very severe punishment for maiming a soldier. Do you think the Government was threatened by your fighting skills or your ideas?

Pause.

You're not very good at fighting are you.

Bradley   I don't know.

Mrs Stokes   As a Government, you can't punish an idea, so you punish the man.

Beat.

And hope it acts as a deterrent. Is it Bradley's actions that threaten? Or the ideas he subscribes to?

Class   Ideas.

Mrs Stokes   What does that make you?

Bradley   A martyr.

Mrs Stokes   Very good Bradley. Excellent. Round of applause for Bradley.

Class claps.

Scene Eleven

Basic training at Fort Leonard Wood, Missouri – October 2007

Clapping becomes the sounds of military drums.

Through movement, **Bradley** *is ripped from his digital self.*
Bradley *is given a haircut, inoculations, and blood samples, given
a duffel bag, mouth guard, and fatigues.*

Chorus is given the same treatment, as **Bradley** *becomes part of a
unit.*

*Chorus becomes a platoon performing fitness training – squat
thrusts, burpies, callisthenics. Platoon marches to company area
led by* **Drill Sergeant**.

They perform the 'Bag Drill'.

Drill Sergeant   My name is Sergeant Adams! You may call me
Sergeant. You may not call me Sir; I work for my money. Why are
you blinking like that?

Recruit 1's *eye twitches.*

Recruit 1   It's a nervous / thing Sergeant.

Drill Sergeant   Stop blinking.

Beat.

STOP BLINKING.

Beat.

STOP BLINKING.

Beat.

I am your drill sergeant for BCT. The Patriot Phase of your
training. Most of you will quit. I want you to quit. I don't want
weak soldiers. I don't want soldiers I cannot trust. I don't want
soldiers who think for themselves. I want soldiers who think for
their platoon. WHY ARE YOU STILL BLINKING? STOP IT!

Beat.

Everyone empty your bags on the ground in one pile.

Recruits empty their bags into a pile on the floor.

Drill Sergeant *scoops up the stuff, messes it about, walks all over it, and then gets a clock watch out.*

Drill Sergeant   Thirty seconds reclaim your property.

Drill Sergeant *blows a whistle!*

Screen has a thirty-second count-down clock.

Recruits scramble for their stuff; immediately it's a nightmare of pushing, shoving, arguing, and **Bradley** *gets consumed in the melee. He vanishes.*

Another **Bradley** *is thrown out of the group –* **Bradley** *is isolated and can't get to his property.*

Thirty seconds is up: Whistle blows!

None of the recruits have their stuff.

Drill Sergeant   Fail! Empty your bags again.

Recruits reluctantly empty their stuff into a pile again.

Drill Sergeant *approaches* **Bradley**.

Drill Sergeant   Name!

Bradley   Bradley Manning Sergeant!

Drill Sergeant   Are you the runt of the platoon Bradley Manning?

Bradley   I don't think so Sergeant!

Drill Sergeant   I think you are. Are you going to prove me wrong Bradley Manning?

Bradley   Yes / Sergeant!

Drill Sergeant   Until then what are you?

Bradley   I don't understand Sergeant.

Drill Sergeant   I think you're the runt until you prove me wrong. So what are you?

Beat.

WHAT ARE YOU?

Beat.

WHAT ARE YOU?

Recruit 1   Say you're the runt.

Drill Sergeant   Am I talking to you recruit?

Recruit 1   No Sergeant.

Drill Sergeant   On the floor. Twenty.

Recruit starts press ups.

Drill Sergeant   What are you Manning?

Bradley   I'm … I'm the, the runt Sergeant.

Drill Sergeant   What?

Bradley   I'm the runt Sergeant.

Drill Sergeant   Louder.

Bradley   I am the runt Sergeant.

Drill Sergeant   I can't hear you.

Bradley   I AM THE RUNT SERGEANT.

Drill Sergeant *blows his whistle. Thirty-second countdown clock starts.*

Bradley *is slow off the mark, unnerved by the bullying.*

This time it's an even more ruthless scramble for property, **Bradley** *fights tooth and nail to get some stuff. Another* **Bradley** *pops out of the melee.*

Drill Sergeant *blows his whistle.*

There is still property on the floor.

Drill Sergeant *empties everyone's bag again, scoops it all up, messes it all up, walks all over it.*

Drill Sergeant   Thirty seconds! Starting from now.

Drill Sergeant *blows whistle. Thirty-second countdown clock.*

Bradley *is reluctant to try.*

Drill Sergeant   Manning! Are you defying an order?

Bradley   No Sergeant!

Bradley *tries to gather some of his things.*

Whistle blows!

Another **Bradley** *pops out of the scrum.* **Drill Sergeant** *starts emptying bag, platoon is disappointed.* **Drill Sergeant** *scoops them all up, walks over them throws them on the floor.*

Drill Sergeant   Thirty seconds.

Drill Sergeant *blows whistle.*

Platoon starts to work together and sort out their property, passing it to each other; **Bradley** *still struggles to get all of his stuff.*

Another **Bradley** *pops out of the melee. Everyone has a bag packed except* **Bradley** *who is on the floor scrambling for some final pieces.*

Whistle blows!

Drill Sergeant   Empty your bags!

Platoon groans.

Recruit 2   For fuck's sake Manning.

Drill Sergeant *scoops all the clothes up, and jumbles them up and walks over them.*

Recruit 3   Manning, get your shit together this time.

Recruit 1   Let's just help him.

Drill Sergeant   Looks like I'm not the only one who thinks you're the runt Manning! You fail and the whole platoon gives me fifty.

Whistle blows! Countdown clock starts again.

Recruits scramble. **Bradley** *is exasperated.*

Bradley   Why me?

Scene Twelve

A street protest against Proposition 8 – March 2008

Reporter   Because of the military reference on your sign. You're a soldier right?

Reporter puts a microphone in front of a surprised **Bradley**.

Tyler *watches from a distance.*

Bradley   Who are you with?

Reporter   Syracuse.com. What's your name?

Bradley   How about I just don't tell you my name? Best way to keep a secret is to never have it.

Reporter   That's fine.

Bradley   I'm here to protest against proposition eight. I'm currently serving in the military awaiting deployment to Iraq. I was kicked out of home and once lost my job because I'm gay. The world is not moving fast enough for us at home, work or the battlefield.

Reporter   Is Don't Ask Don't Tell the worst part about being in the military?

Bradley   Totally.

Standing in drag, **Tyler** *catches* **Bradley**'s *eye.*

My job, is about life and death, you'd think the army would value personal integrity. Instead they'd rather ten per cent of their employees to lie and mislead every single day about who they really are. Excuse me …

Bradley leans towards **Tyler** *and Chorus holds him back.*

Bradley   Hey?

Tyler *looks* **Bradley** *up and down.*

Tyler   Hello.

Bradley   I'm Brad.

Tyler   Tyler.

Bradley   Are you going to the rally?

Tyler   Probably, not.

Bradley   Oh.

Tyler   Speeches bore me.

Bradley   Me too yeah. *They start to walk together.*

Tyler   I'm guessing small town, something geeky, web developing, something with good health insurance.

Bradley   Soldier.

Tyler *laughs.*

I am.

Beat.

I'm with the Tenth Mountain Division.

Off **Tyler**'s *bemusement.*

I'm an intelligence analyst.

Tyler   Computers.

Bradley   Any kind of intelligence, cell, pamphlets.

Tyler   Computers / right?

Bradley   Basically computers yeah.

Tyler *and* **Bradley** *laugh, as they follow the march.*

Tyler   You like it?

Bradley   I do a really important job, if I do my job well, brief a brigade commander right, I save lives. I feel a great responsibility.

Tyler   Well, good luck with that.

Bradley   I'm not. I don't see myself, having a military career. I figure I can do a couple of years, get some kick-ass credentials. Get into politics. Pull ideas together.

Tyler   I don't even know what shoes to wear and you've got two careers mapped out.

Bradley   If you had my upbringing you'd work on your exit strategies. How about you?

Tyler   Brandeis. Neuroscience major.

Beat.

I'm also a classical musician and drag queen.

Bradley   That's. That's …

Tyler   Shall we go / find a bar?

Bradley   Yes. That's. Absolutely. Yes. I. Yes.

Tyler *walks off and* **Bradley** *follows,*

Scene Thirteen

Quantico Brig – January 2011

But the door slams in his face.

Chorus becomes a Free **Bradley** *Manning protest.*

Bradley *stands up. He listens hard. The chanting gets a little louder.*

Bradley *tries to press his ear as close to a wall as possible. The chanting becomes a little clearer. 'Free Bradley, Free Bradley Manning, Free Bradley Manning'.*

Bradley *is stunned. He stands stock still as he tries to digest what he's hearing.*

He is sure; he's hearing 'Free Bradley Manning'.

A sob escapes him, and he tries to compose himself.

He stands listening, with a huge smile on his face.

He stretches his arms out.

He starts to feel the adrenaline and he starts to fidget.

He hops up and down, and then tries to stand still.

He hops again and this time runs a little in his room. Punching the air. He jumps on his bed and jumps off it. He runs around the cell.

Marine 1   *(off-stage)* No exercise.

Bradley   *(delighted)* Okay!

Bradley *stands still. He can't help himself and he lets out a howl and punches the air, he runs around his cell.*

Clunking sound of a door opening.

Pumped up – four marines enter.

Marine One *applies handcuffs to* **Bradley**. **Marine Two** *applies leg-restraints to* **Bradley**.

Marine 1   Attention!

Bradley *stands at attention.*

The Marines pace around.

Marine 1   Detainee 4335453, at parade rest!

Bradley *stands with his feet shoulder width apart.*

Marine 2 *sticks his face in* **Bradley**'s *face.*

Bradley *tries to look ahead but can't help looking at* **Marine 2**.

Marine 2   Are you eyeballing me 4335453?

Bradley   No Sergeant!

Marine 1 Turn left!

Bradley *turns left.*

Marine 3 Don't turn left!

Bradley *corrects his direction.*

Marine 1 I said turn left!

Bradley Yes Corporal!

Marine 4 In the *Marines* we reply 'aye' not yes. Do you understand Private?

Bradley Yes Corporal.

Marine 3 YOU MEAN AYE!

Bradley Aye Corporal.

Marine 1 Turn right.

Marine 2 Don't turn right!

Bradley Ye- Aye Sergeant!

Marine 1 I said turn right!

Bradley Aye Corporal!

Marine 1 Stand still so we can remove your restraints.

Beat.

I SAID STAND STILL.

Marine 1 *eyeballs* **Bradley**, *who starts to shuffle in retreat.*

Marine 1 I told you to stand still!

Bradley Yes Corporal I am standing still.

Marine 4 *approaches* **Bradley** *menacingly.*

Marine 4 I thought we covered this you say 'aye' not 'yes' do you understand?

Bradley Aye / Corporal.

Marine 1   *(screamed)* STAND STILL!

Bradley   Yes Corporal I am standing still! I mean-

Marine 4   Are we going to have a problem? Do you have a problem with following orders?

Marine 2   Do you have an attitude problem 4335453?

Marine 4   Sergeant asked you question 4335453.

Bradley *starts to step backwards in fear.*

The Marines loom towards him.

Marine 2   SERGEANT ASKED YOU A QUESTION.

But **Bradley** *is too scared. He staggers and sits down.*

Bradley   I. I … I'm not; I'm not trying to do anything. I'm just trying to follow your orders.

Marine 4   DO YOU HAVE A PROBLEM WITH ORDERS?

Bradley   I'm. Please I'm just / trying to follow orders.

Marine 4   DO YOU HAVE A PROBLEM WITH ORDERS?

Silence.

Bradley   *(quietly)* No Corporal.

Marine 4 *holds his face in* **Bradley***'s face for an age.*

Bradley *looks at the floor.*

The four marines, stand at the corners of a square.

Marine 1   Commence your recreation 4335453.

Very long pause.

Marines stand stiff and straight, contrasting with **Bradley***'s slump.*

Slowly, **Bradley** *stands up.*

Keeping within the square the Marines have formed, **Bradley** *starts to walk.*

It becomes apparent **Bradley** *is walking figures of eight.*

Scene Fourteen

Tyler's student house – August 2008

He walks into **Tyler***'s arms and they kiss in a passionate drunken embrace.* **Tyler** *pulls at* **Bradley***'s clothes. Chorus pushes and pull them apart.*

Tyler   Been too long.

Bradley   I know.

Tyler   Get your shirt off, get your shirt off.

Tyler *pulls* **Bradley***'s shirt off.* **Bradley** *is covered in bruises.* **Tyler** *startles.*

Tyler   What the fuck is all that?

Bradley   It's okay.

He tries to re-engage **Tyler** *who resists.*

Don't worry about it.

Tyler *turns* **Bradley** *around to see all his bruising.*

Silence.

Bradley   You don't need to be worried / about this okay. It's my business.

Tyler   This is / your job. Normal people don't get beat up in an office.

Bradley   I fight back.

Beat.

Why are you looking at me like that?

Beat.

It's fine.

Tyler   Do you have people you can talk to?

Silence.

Bradley   Pete.

Tyler   What does / Pete have to say about all this?

Bradley   Yeah, he talks to me.

Beat.

If he hears me crying.

Bradley *stops putting his shirt on and stares at it.*

It won't be for much longer anyway.

Tyler   How come?

Silence.

Overwhelmed **Bradley** *puts his face in his shirt.*

Tyler   Hey.

For a few moments, **Bradley** *holds his face in his shirt.*

Tyler   Come on.

Bradley *recoils from* **Tyler**.

Silence as **Bradley** *gathers himself.*

Bradley   You go to class today?

Tyler   Uh yeah.

Beat.

Missed the first one, I slept in.

Bradley   Right.

Silence.

Tyler   You can sue them.

Bradley   You sound like such a fucking idiot; do you know how you sound sometimes?

Beat.

Like a fucking idiot.

Beat.

I'm outta here.

Bradley *gathers his things.*

Tyler   No.

Bradley   Out of my way.

Tyler   Please stay.

Bradley   GET OUT OF MY WAY.

Silence.

Tyler   I've seen guys like this you don't have to stand for it.

Bradley   What the fuck do you know about anything?

Beat.

I'm going through this every day, so I can be where you are, and you can't even get out of fucking bed for class.

Beat.

I'm beat up every day, I'm called faggot, and runt and chapter fifteen, people spit on me and- I do it to get where you are and you can't get out fucking bed?

Bradley *rips his shirt open.*

You wanna stay in bed with this?

Silence.

I only signed up so they'd pay for me to go college but I'm such a fuck-up I can't even pass basic training!

Beat.

They're kicking me out.

Beat.

So all this? It's for nothing anyway!

Tyler   Why are they kicking you out?

Bradley   Does it matter?

Scene Fifteen

Tasker Milward School 15 – January 2003

Anthony   Not, not to me.

Anthony *sits at a computer.*

I'm just saying.

Beat.

You're meant to have a hall pass to be in here.

Bradley *sits at a computer. The two work in silence.*

Bradley   What game you playing?

Anthony   I'm not playing a game.

Bradley   Jesus Anthony.

Beat.

I'm just asking.

Silence.

Anthony   I'm writing.

Beat.

A programme.

Bradley   Oh yeah?

Bradley *leans into* **Anthony**'s *screen.* **Anthony** *quickly hides it.*

What is it secret?

Anthony   It's not finished.

Bradley   I'm building a website.

Silence.

I could help. I'm pretty good with code.

Anthony   Thanks.

Bradley   Do you want help or not?

Beat.

Anthony?

Beat.

Bradley *goes over to* **Anthony**'*s screen; again* **Anthony** *shields it from him.*

Bradley   Let me see.

Beat.

I'm not going to steal anything; I've got enough of my own ideas.

Beat.

Come on.

Anthony *shakes his head.*

Why not?

Silence.

Anthony   It's fine. I don't mind if it's going to take ages.

Exasperated **Bradley** *returns to his computer. They both sit in silence as they work on their projects.*

Anthony   I don't like: going on the yard.

Silence.

Bradley *moves over to* **Anthony**'*s screen.* **Anthony** *doesn't hide it.*

Bradley   What are we doing here?

Scene Sixteen

Boston University hackerspace/Tasker Milward – November 2008 / 2003

Tyler   I want you to meet some of my computer geek buddies.
David!

A group of BU students sit around, checking out hardware.

David   Oh hey! Tyler.

Tyler   This is Bradley. This is more his kind of thing than mine.

David   Okay! Are you familiar with the open software, open
hardware movement? Builds is a space where students can
advocate for that movement as well as a space for student-led DIY
learning to take place.

Beat.

So! Hang around, check things out, if you've got the knowhow,
share it. We've got the Open Organisation of Lock Pickers coming
along to do a demonstration later and Free Software Foundation
dropping by to talk to us too.

David *leaves.*

Bradley   I want to go home.

Tyler   We're here for *you*, this is *your* thing. You need to meet
other geeks and I don't know. / Make some new friends.

Bradley   They're *all* students.

Tyler   You're smarter than all these people put together.

Kyle   Hey?

Tyler   Hey.

Kyle   Kyle.

Tyler   Tyler, Bradley.

Kyle   What happened to your face man?

Pause.

Tyler   He's a soldier.

Kyle   You're a *soldier*?

Bradley   Intel.

Kyle   Wow! Check out this red robot mouse I built.

Kyle *produces a remote control and drives a robot mouse into their personal space.*

Bradley, **Tyler** *and* **Kyle** *look at the floor, as* **Kyle** *reverses the mouse, turns the mouse around in circles, sends it back and forth.*

Silence.

Tyler   That's great.

Bradley   Yeah great; work.

Tyler *and* **Bradley** *drift away from* **Kyle**.

Bradley   Can we go home?

Tyler   Seriously?

Bradley   I'm about to lose my job, and my one chance of going to college, and you bring me to a place full of people getting computer science majors and all they're doing is building fucking *robot mice.*

David *overhears this.*

David   So! Bradley, how about you come meet Alison?

Bradley   Um, I don't know.

Tyler *indicates for him to go.* **David** *brings* **Bradley** *over to* **Alison**'s *group.*

Tyler *drifts away from* **Bradley** *and joins another group of people who are sitting around debating and drinking from red plastic cups.*

Alison   Levy outlines six hacker ethics, 'access to a computer and anything else that might teach you how the world works, should be unlimited'. 'All information should be free'. 'Mistrust authority – promote decentralisation.' Um how many have I said? Oh – 'Hackers should be judged on their hacking not on anything like education, race, sexuality'. This is my favourite, 'you can create beauty on a computer'.

David   Six?

Alison   Fuck, man.

David   'Computers can change your life for the better.'

Kyle*'s mouse darts past the group, followed by* **Kyle** *running after it. Everyone watches* **Kyle** *exit, chasing red robotic mouse.*

Silence.

Alison   I said the thing about not judging anyone right?

David   Yeah.

Alison   Where we are now. This is the Mesopotamia of hacking. MiT, BU sort of.

Everyone laughs.

Hacking, cyber activism / this is the where it all started.

David   Is she doing her enlightenment / schtick again?

Alison   Yes I am!

David   She always / does this.

Alison   I'm sharing information!

Everyone laughs at the in-joke.

Okay. When Gutenberg built the printing press it took thirty years for the first porn publication and a *hundred* years for the first scientific journal. We've had our cyber-porn goldrush. Now it's time for our global enlightenment. The printing presses tore down the self-interest of the church in Europe. Web 2.0 will tear down the self-interest of the corporate state. How do we do that?

Beat.

I'm asking how do we do that?

Bradley   Oh I'm sorry, I thought you knew.

Alison   No I'm I'd like to know how we do that.

David   I think it's something do with reverse engineering. Have you seen the lock-pickers over there?

Bradley   Yeah what's that about?

David   It's symbolic.

Alison   Like a metaphor for hacking.

David *picks up a lock and brings it over to them and hands it to* **Bradley***, he gives him a pin.*

David   When you pick a lock for the first time, you learn that the only barriers in the world are psychological. You hold the key to your life, not corporations, parents or University administrators.

Alison   And so, the more people who think like that …

David   The bigger things we can reverse engineer.

Bradley   Like what?

Alison   We can do anything I guess?

Bradley *pops his lock open – everyone is pleased.*

Tyler   You want to head off before they start chanting?

Bradley   *(to* **Alison***)* How could we, reverse engineer a Government?

Mrs Stokes *picks up a bin.*

Mrs Stokes   By throwing conventional wisdom into this bin.

Mrs Stokes *drops a book into a bin.*

Come on, books in the bin.

Class scrambles towards the front of the class to throw their history books into the bin.

Mrs Stokes   Today we're looking at the Rebecca Riots of 1839. All of you find a costume.

This action takes place as **Mrs Stokes** *talks.*

Mrs Stokes *lifts another bin up, the class scramble to it and pull out traditional Welsh clothes and start to dress up as traditional Welsh women.* **Antony** *gets there first but gets robbed of everything he gets his hand on, so his outfit is the least complete.*

The class individually giggle and communicate to each other their delight.

We're going to help you remember some facts about the riots. And we're going to do it, by having a riot of our own.

Confusion as **Mrs Stokes** *jumps up onto a table and starts stamping on the table!*

Mrs Stokes   Who's with me?

Silence.

I said who's with me?

Gavin   What? We're rioting?

Lisa   In class like? In class.

Mrs Stokes   Yes!

She bangs on the desk!

I said who's with me!

Class   *(ad lib)* I am! Yeah! Fucking come on! Let's do it!

Mrs Stokes   I'm not taking / any more of this! Are you with me?

Class   *(ad lib)* Yeah! Let's go nuts! Come on! Go on Stokesy! Let's go down town!

Class get up on the chairs and desks and push chairs around a bit.

Mrs Stokes   Gavin! Why are you here today?

Gavin   I don't know / I'm. It's!

Mrs Stokes   Who knows why we've come here, dressed as women, in the cold?

Mark   For a meeting!

Mrs Stokes   What am I standing on?

Gavin   Desk!

Anthony   A toll-gate!

Mrs Stokes   A toll-gate yes! And what are we going to do?

Bradley   Tear it down!

Mrs Stokes   Why?

Bradley   Because we're sick of having to pay every time we go to market!

Class cheers.

Lisa   And we're sick of paying tithes to the church!

Class cheers.

Mark   I hate the vicar!

Class cheers.

Gavin   Vicar's a prick.

Class cheers.

Anthony   Wet harvest.

Class cheers.

Gavin   *(under)* You can't riot about the weather, or we'll be out every night.

Bradley   English landlords!

Gavin   Sidebars!

Lisa   Poor rates!

Anthony   Taxes!

Lisa   Why are all the landlords English?

Bradley *gets up on the desk.*

Bradley   We're the ones who know how to farm.

Cheer.

Know how to raise cattle and harvest corn! What the fuck does council do except collect money?

Cheers!

What does the church do? Except collect money?

Cheer

What do the landlords do except collect money?

Cheers

And what do the fucking turnpikes do for us? Collect money!

Class   NOTHING!

The class tips over the final tables and wrecks the 'toll-gate'

In the background **Anthony** *picks up a chair and throws it.*

Anthony   I'm not a fucking pushover!

Silence.

Everyone stares at a panting **Anthony**.

Mrs Stokes   Anthony, step out of the room.

Silence.

Step outside.

Gavin   Why are you / such a knob Anthony?

Lisa   You spoil everything.

Mrs Stokes   Step outside Anthony.

Anthony   But ...

Anthony *leaves the room,* **Bradley** *feels terrible for* **Anthony**.

Mrs Stokes   Right ... tell me now. Why did the riots keep happening? What did trashing the classroom feel like?

Mark   It was good. I didn't know I knew all that stuff.

Lisa I've never you know. What it is, I've never done nothing like that before in a classroom. Not with a whatyoucall there. Teacher.

Mrs Stokes You felt free of normal school rules? Just as these people felt free of the normal rules of society?

Lisa Yeah.

Gavin That was awesome.

Mrs Stokes What do you think Bradley?

Bradley I don't know.

Mrs Stokes If you feel stupid just take a look round at your classmates.

Bradley *looks at his classmates dressed as women.*

The class giggles.

Bradley I don't know. I guess, for a moment; I didn't feel like.

Mrs Stokes What?

Bradley I didn't feel like the new kid.

Beat.

People were listening.

Mrs Stokes Can you see why the riots kept happening?

Lisa It was fun.

Gavin Can we do it in Maths?

Mrs Stokes I wouldn't recommend it. Anyone else got any thoughts.

Mark Sort of. Like if. By showing no respect to the tollgate, we sort of got …

Bradley Self-respect.

Mark Yeah.

Bradley *takes his bonnet off.*

Mrs Stokes   Why is dressing up as women, important?

Lisa   That's fun too.

Mrs Stokes   Absolutely. Gives a sense of occasion. There's something else.

Beat.

What did dressing up give them?

Bradley   Anonymity.

Mrs Stokes   And what does that give you?

Bradley   Freedom.

Mrs Stokes   Yes. If society casts you as powerless. Why follow society's rules? Put a hoodie on and move freely. Act without compromise. Right, tidy up the class while I talk to Anthony.

Bradley   Miss I don't think you should punish Anthony.

Mrs Stokes   Take a deep breath Bradley.

Scene Seventeen

Quantico Brig – January 2011

Bradley *takes a deep breath and stands to attention.*

Commander Browning enters.

Commander Browning   At ease.

Bradley *stands at parade rest.*

Commander Browning   What happened today at recreation call?

Bradley   I was trying to follow orders sir, but the Marines seemed intent on causing me distress by giving conflicting orders sir, and demanding I respond as a Marine even though I am not.

Beat.

I'd like to make a complaint sir, I'd like you to investigate / those Marines.

Commander Browning   I am the commander and no one tells me what to do.

Silence.

There a problem detainee?

Bradley   I'm making a complaint sir.

Commander Browning   I am the commander here that means, for practical purposes, I am God.

Silence.

Bradley   Everyone has a boss who they have to answer to.

Commander Browning   Did I hear that right?

Bradley   You still have to follow brig procedures sir, whatever. It's not my fault if there's a protest outside.

Commander Browning   Marines!

The Marines enter the cell.

Place Detainee 4335453 under Suicide Risk Status and POI.

Bradley   What? No! Why are you doing this? I HAVE DONE NOTHING WRONG.

Commander Browning   Strip Detainee 4335453 of his clothes.

With no ceremony Two Guards strip **Bradley** *of his clothes.*
Bradley *starts crying.*

Bradley   Why are you doing this to me! What have I done? Please no? Please! I'm begging you.

Beat.

Tell me what you want me to do and I'll do it?

Beat.

Just tell me! I don't understand! What have I done?

Commander Browning *leaves followed by The Marines.*

Bradley *stands naked in the cell crying.*

Scene Eighteen

*Tasker Milward's Computer room / U.S Army Discharge Unit
– November*

2003/April 2009

Another **Bradley** *and* **Anthony** *sit in the computer room.*

Anthony   It's okay. Let me see.

Anthony *fixes something on* **Bradley***'s screen.*

Bradley   Mrs Stokes can be a dick.

Anthony   Everyone thinks she's tidy, but …

Beat.

Only if you do exactly what she wants.

The rest of the class enters.

Mark   Bradders!

Lisa   Bradley!

Gavin   Here he is!

Gavin *jumps up on a desk.*

Gavin   We will fight them on the beaches, we will fight them in
Wetherspoons, we will fight them in Pwll! We will fight them in
Llanidloes!

Mark   Come on Bradley / give us another speech.

Bradley   I'm in the middle of something guys.

Gavin   We / will fight them in our underwear! We fight them in
their underwear, we will fight them without underwear!

Class   Speee-eeech! Speee-eeech! Speeee-eeech!

The gang lift **Bradley** *up in the air, and* **Bradley** *is laughing, everyone is laughing and joking and throwing him up in the air like a hero.* **Anthony** *is isolated.*

Bradley   *(laughing)* No guys put me down! Put me down! Come on guys please.

Suddenly the actions turn less playful and **Bradley** *is in pain.*

He screams.

We are now in the Fort Leonard Wood, Missouri – the Discharge Unit. **Bradley** *is held by a group of American soldiers who are inflicting pain on him.*

Soldier 1   Say I am chapter fifteen!

Bradley   Fuck you!

Soldier 1   Say I'm chapter fifteen!

Bradley   Let me go!

Soldier 1   Say it!

Bradley   Let me go! Get the fuck off me you fucking assholes GETOFFME!!

Soldier 1   Say it Manning! Fucking say it! You like to suck dick and you're a chapter fifteen!

Bradley   AAA/HHHHHHFUUUUUUCCCKK YOU!

Soldier 1   SAY IT!

Bradley   GEEETTTTOFFFFMEEEE!!!

With a huge effort **Bradley** *kicks himself free. Soldier and his gang burst out laughing;* **Bradley** *grabs a chair and holds it over his head.*

Bradley   Stay the / fuck away from me!

Soldier 1   What you gonna do / Chapter fifteen? Fuck the chair? Come on pretty boy, let's see you drop your pants and fuck the chair.

Bradley   STAY THE FUCK AWAY.

Soldier 2   Drop your pants.

Silence.

You're on your own Manning.

Bradley   Stay the fuck away from me, I'm warning you, I'll fucking, I'll fucking kill you.

Soldier 2   What you gonna do? Cry on me?

*Soldiers laugh at **Bradley**.*

Soldier 2   My nephew's tougher than you he's eight.

Bradley   I'll fucking kill your nephew.

Soldier 2 *startles towards* **Bradley**, **Soldier 3** *holds him back.*

Soldier 3   You know how hard it is to sleep with you crying all the time?

Beat.

Crying and fucking screaming like a bitch.

Beat.

Like some kind of freak.

Beat.

Crying like a baby.

Beat.

Soldier 1   Got anything to say chapter fifteen?

Beat.

*The Soldier goes for **Bradley**, **Bradley** swings a chair.*

*The Soldier goes for him again. **Bradley** swings a chair.*

Bradley *wets himself.*

Soldier 2 *leans into* **Soldier 1** *and points at* **Bradley**'*s trousers.*

Soldier 2   Hell Manning you just pissed your pants!

Private Miles *enters.*

Everyone tries to act normally.

Private Miles   What the hell is going on here?

Beat.

Specialist Manning put that chair down.

Pause.

Specialist Manning!

Bradley   NO / SIR!

Private Miles   Put the chair down!

Bradley   NO! I'm fucking…

Private Miles   Specialist Manning this may be a discharge unit but you are not a civilian yet. Put that chair down, that's an order.

Pause.

Bradley *throws the chair to guffaws and cat-calling from the other Soldiers.*

Private Miles   Pick up the chair Manning.

Soldier 2   **Yeah pick up the chair Manning.** *Bradley catches his breath.*

Private Miles   Specialist Manning pick up the chair.

Beat.

I SAID PICK UP THE CHAIR.

Bradley   I'M NOT A FUCKING PUSHOVER!

Private Miles *grabs* **Bradley** *and drags him towards the door.*

No! No! Get off!

Chorus whoops with delight and laughs at **Bradley**'s *humiliation.*

Let go!

Beat!

Let me go! FUCK YOU! I'LL FUCKING KILL YOU!

Bradley *is dragged kicking and screaming out of the door and the Chorus cheers and laughs at him.*

Scene Nineteen

Tasker Milward School – December 2003

Mrs Stokes   Silence!

She looks at her table.

Mrs Stokes   Vandalising school property is serious.

Beat.

I want a name.

Beat.

NOW!

Beat.

Who has done this?

She points to the desk.

If I don't get a name, you will all be punished. If you're happy to protect a vandal then you shall be punished like vandals. Mark? Do you know who has carved this disgusting image on my desk.

Mark   No miss.

Mrs Stokes   Lisa?

Lisa   Didn't see anyone Miss.

Mrs Stokes   Anthony?

Anthony *shrugs.*

Mrs Stokes   Bradley?

Bradley   Didn't see anything Miss.

Mrs Stokes   Gavin?

Gavin   Didn't see nothing Miss.

Mrs Stokes   Fine. I'll see what Mr Roberts has to say about this. All of you will see me after school for detention and I will be speaking to Mr Roberts about getting ALL of your parents involved in this.

Class groans.

Bradley   That's not fair.

Mrs Stokes   You have something to say Bradley.

Bradley   You haven't got to get my Mom involved for something I didn't do.

Mrs Stokes   Give me a name and I won't.

Bradley   It's your fault! / You can't say riot in one lesson and then …

Mrs Stokes   Shut up Bradley.

Bradley   What have I don't wrong?

Scene Twenty

U.S Army Discharge Unit – October 2009

Sergeant   At ease Specialist.

Bradley stands at parade rest, but is ill-disciplined with his posture – he is defeated. Bradley has a black eye. Sergeant goes through some paperwork.

Sergeant   Who's supporting you through your discharge process here?

Beat.

Who's your battle buddy?

Bradley   They keep changing Sergeant.

Sergeant   Who's it today?

Bradley   Miles.

Sergeant   Miles!

In comes a much bigger, strapping soldier – **Private Miles**, *who salutes.*

Sergeant   At ease.

Private Miles *stands at parade rest.* **Bradley** *can barely stand straight.* **Sergeant** *can't look at* **Bradley**.

Sergeant   Specialist, do you know what the term 'recycled' means.

Private Miles *double takes. Chorus gasps and is in shock?*

Bradley   No sir.

Sergeant   It's a term we use. Private Miles will be familiar, where the army halts a discharge process. Do you follow Specialist?

Bradley   I / guess.

Private Miles   Permission to speak sir?

Sergeant   Granted.

Pause.

Private Miles   Sir.

Beat.

Are we?

Beat.

Are you saying; Specialist Manning is uh, to be. Is to be recycled sir?

Sergeant   Yes Private.

Beat.

There a problem?

Pause.

Private Miles   No sir.

Sergeant   So, to be clear Specialist, the major has taken a look at the assessments you failed and decided to give you a second chance.

Beat.

We're at war and the army needs you.

Beat.

You will be attached to the 10th Mountain Division as Intel Specialist, you will be …

Chorus plays Miles' disbelief.

Private Miles.

Private Miles *tries to straighten himself.*

Private Miles   Sir.

Sergeant   You will be deployed to Eastern Baghdad at Forward … at Forward Operating.

Beat.

Base.

Sergeant *clears his throat.*

Operating Base.

Staring at the sheet, **Sergeant** *tries to focus.* **Bradley** *sways.*

Hammer.

Sergeant *discards the paperwork and takes a moment.*

Sergeant   How'd you feel about … about serving your country Bradley?

Bradley *sways.*

Bradley   I'd be proud sir.

Beat.

I thought I was getting kicked out.

Private Miles *looks to the heavens.*

Sergeant   Good. (*Clears throat*) Good man.

Private Miles   Permission to speak sir.

Sergeant   Granted.

Private Miles   Sir should I take Specialist Manning to speak with the Judge Advocate Group sir?

Chorus thinks this is a great idea and is about to bundle **Bradley** *away when ...*

Sergeant   I have their paperwork here, they've signed off for recycling. It's all. It's signed off.

Chorus checks the paperwork and is in shock.

Sergeant   Your skills, are highly valuable to us Specialist. / Highly valuable.

Bradley   Yes sir.

Sergeant   We need every, every Intel Specialist we have to be on top of their game, because your Brigade commander will be relying on your briefings before sending his men into theatre.

Beat.

I hope you realise what an important job you have Specialist, and what a privilege it is to serve in the U.S. Army.

Bradley   Yes sir, / I won't let you down sir.

Sergeant   Before ... Before deployment, you will be stationed in Fort Drum. Good luck Manning, you're dismissed.

Bradley *straightens himself and gives a proud salute and starts to march to the door.* **Private Miles** *and* **Sergeant**, *share a look before* **Private Miles** *follows* **Bradley**.

Private Miles   Sir.

Sergeant   Specialist Manning. Do you have; do you have anyone, who can support you through deployment?

Bradley   I have met someone sir.

Sergeant   You have a *girlfriend* Manning?

Bradley   Yes sir, I do.

Scene Twenty One

Forward Operating Base Hammer – Eastern Baghdad – 2009

Tableau sequence.

Computers, paperwork, TV screens are on every wall with live feeds from the war as the US engages the enemy.

Post-it notes are on every computer.

Another **Bradley** *stands watching the screens as his fellow Intel Officers throw stress toys around, mess about, and show each other things on screen that makes each other laugh.*

They are oblivious to **Bradley**, *and they are oblivious to the horrors of war footage being broadcast on the screens.*

Bradley *is drawn to the screens. He can't escape the screens, as everyone else goes about their work.*

Intel Officer, steals a piece of paper from **Bradley**.

Intel Officer 1: What have you got there Manning? Oooh! Manning's got his first commendation. Specialist Manning's dedication led to the detainment of Malik Fadil al-Ugayli, a Tier two level target.

Intel Officer 2: Make sure you tell your Mom Manning.

Intel Officer 1: While you're there ask her why you're such a faggot Manning.

Waves of digital, information, code, intelligence, crash over **Bradley**.

Bradley's head is spun as he turns from screen to screen, standing fixed in one spot; unable to tear himself away from the images he is seeing.

All the time his colleagues do not look at the footage.

Tableau sequence over.

Intel Officer   Hey anyone else read this CIED Sigact from the Diyala province?

General 'no's.

Intel Officer   Roadside IED, targeting a convoy heading South East on Miami, carload of civilians manoeuvre off-road to allow convoy passage, activating a road-side IED. Four civilians injured and one dead at the scene, all personnel present and accounted for. HOO-HAAA!

Intel Officers: HOO-HAAA!

Intel Officers high-five and draw **Bradley** *into an unwanted high-five.*

Bradley   Yeah.

Intel Officer   HOO-HAA!

Scene Twenty Two

Tasker Milward School – April 2004

Class erupts as **Mrs Stokes** *is absent.*

Mark *picks up* **Anthony's** *bag.*

Anthony   Fuck off Mark.

Mark   You fuck off.

Mark   Your bag smells of ham. Does anyone need a protractor?

Anthony   Why don't you / fucking pick on someone else Mark; stop being such a prick to me all the time.

Mark   Is there anything anyone needs? Lisa? Protractor, roller-ruler? This pen's got a compass in it, look at that? That's cool I'm having that. Bradders you haven't got a protractor have you?

Anthony   Bradley?

Bradley   Give his stuff back.

Mark   Why? It's Anthony.

Bradley   Mark come on.

Mark   No way, he's a wanker.

Mark *continues to look in the bag and disregard* **Anthony***'s feelings.*

Unable to take it anymore, **Bradley** *grabs the bag from and hands it to* **Anthony**. **Mark** *retaliates by grabbing it from* **Anthony**. **Bradley** *grabs it from* **Mark***, there's a tussle and* **Bradley** *finally gets the bag.*

Mark *chases* **Bradley** *around the room, while the class jeers. The chase ends with* **Bradley** *standing on* **Mrs Stokes***' desk.*

The class falls silent as **Mrs Stokes** *enters.*

Mrs Stokes   What the hell is going on here?

Mark   He stole my bag miss.

Mrs Stokes   Get down.

Beat.

NOW!

Bradley *gets down off the table.*

Mrs Stokes   I leave the room for two minutes.

Bradley   Miss.

Mrs Stokes   I don't want your excuses Bradley. Who wants to go and get Mr Roberts?

Whole class put their hands up except **Bradley**.

Scene Twenty Three

Iraqi Police Jail / Forward Operating Base Hammer – February 2010

Chorus are Iraqi Federal Police and detainees in Iraqi jail. Movement sequence as Iraqi Federal Police mistreat detainees.

Bradley *and* **Nidal** *are in FOB Hammer looking over some Sig Acts.*

Bradley   Major Browning asked me to assess your fifteen detainees arrested November ten.

Nidal: Insurgents.

Bradley *shuffles paper.*

Bradley   They weren't armed on arrest.

Nidal: They distribute Al Qaeda literature.

Beat.

They are insurgents.

Bradley   Right.

An Iraqi Federal police beats detainees.

Bradley   Where were they / detained?

Nidal: Out. In street.

Bradley   Okay. They were handing out / insurgency literature, in the street.

Nidal: In the street, yes.

IFP beats detainees – **Bradley** *is unnerved.*

Bradley   *(urgent)* Do you have any of their papers? / Where's their papers?

Nidal: Nothing.

Another beating – increasing pressure on **Bradley**.

Bradley   I need more information, what does the literature say?

Nidal: America must die. They are / insurgents.

Iraqi Federal Police beats another detainee.

Bradley   Stop! Listen We need to find out who these people are, what group they're associated with, why they're just handing stuff out in the street.

Beat.

I need to know who they are; can we, can we work together, on this?

Beat.

Nidal.

Nidal: Yes.

Bradley   I need to know who / they're working with. I have to write this up.

Nidal: Yes.

Bradley   When you identify these people you're going to liaise with me.

Nidal: Yes.

Bradley   I have to write a report on this. The Major wants a report on this. / I have to identify them, you understand what I'm saying?

Nidal: Yes.

Bradley   This doesn't make sense.

Nidal: Yes.

Bradley *is dragged into the beating. He stops it.*

Bradley   They don't look like fighters.

Beat.

Give me what they were handing out.

Nidal hands over the literature.

Bradley *takes it and walks to the Major's desk and stands at attention.*

Major   Specialist.

Bradley   Sir. I investigated the fifteen people arrested by the IFP on Nov ten. The IFP claimed they were insurgents distributing anti-American literature and were part of a wider organisation.

Major   And?

Bradley   Sir, they're not insurgents.

Beat.

They're just. They're just protestors.

Major   I don't understand.

Bradley   This is the literature the IFP retrieved, I had it translated. It's not anti-American sir. It's not even anti Sunni. It's. You can read it for yourself; they're accusing the Iraqi Government of corruption. They're accusing the Iraqi Government of stealing aid.

Beat.

Major   Who authorised this translation?

Bradley   We're wasting our time on them sir. They're not insurgents.

Major   *(louder)* who authorised the translation?

Pause.

Bradley   I did sir.

Silence.

I was using my initiative sir.

Silence.

I had. I thought. I had suspicions that these weren't. They didn't look like insurgents sir. I think. By doing this. I've, I've saved us resources so we don't spend time gathering intel on these fifteen / when, when they're just, regular.

Major   *(loud)* your role is to support our brigades on the ground by identifying and tracking insurgents.

Bradley   Yes sir.

Major   How the hell does this support our brigades?

Major *holds Iraqi translation literature.*

Silence.

Bradley   I've stopped us wasting time gathering intel / on people who aren't the enemy.

Major   How does *this*, help support our brigade?

Silence.

Bradley   I've saved resources sir.

Major   Do you have an attitude problem Specialist?

Bradley   Sir no sir.

Major   Do you know have a problem following orders Specialist?

Bradley   Sir no sir.

Major   If the IFP says that's an insurgent, that's insurgent, you do not spend time proving their innocence you spend time finding more! Do you understand Specialist? You want to show some initiative, come in here in two days' time, and say you've doubled the IFP haul, do I make myself clear?

Beat.

I want more / insurgents not less!

Scene Twenty Four

Tyler's Student house April 2010

Sound of mortar fire and Chorus hits the floor. It could be a post-student house party. It could be dead Iraqi civilians. Some are dead, some are nearly dead.

Bradley   That's a fucking joke.

Bradley *sits at a laptop,* **Tyler** *stands behind him.*

Beat.

You forget your pass you just knock on the door and someone lets you in. Passwords to every computer are on sticky notes pressed onto monitors. Why has no one leaked anything?

Beat.

Tyler   Sounds, crazy.

Bradley   Did you read the 9/11 pagers released on WikiLeaks?

Tyler   Uh, no.

Bradley   That definitely came from someone in the NSA because I've read those on the inside.

Beat.

Tyler.

Tyler   What?

Bradley   They can't crack the encryption. Somebody leaked but the FBI can't figure out who. They've got no one. If WikiLeaks don't know who uploaded it, how can the FBI?

Tyler   Bradley.

Bradley   Do you know they brought gravel and pebbles from Turkey so that the KBR contractors don't get their feet too dirty when it rains?

Beat.

Man I'm so glad to be out of that room, I thought I was going insane. Fourteen hours a day I'm looking at a screen, or sweeping the floor in the same room. Six days a week, I'm bombarded with all this information that no one's allowed to see, and I can see it, as long as I act like I don't care.

Beat.

I can read about plots to assassinate heads of state, but I can't tell anyone about *you*.

Tyler   Bradley *listen*, the reason / why I said you needed to come over this weekend.

Bradley   Sorry, I haven't finished, when I was a kid I used to hack into programmes, because that was the only time I felt free. Now I don't even need to hack, this stuff is just there. When I was kid, it was ... exciting to find stuff. Now. I wish I hadn't seen half of it.

Bradley looks at the dead bodies.

Yeah.

Beat.

Now I can't get it out of my mind.

Beat.

So. I'm thinking of leaking something myself.

Silence.

I've worked out how I can do it. It's simple I just take in a re-writable CD with something like Lady Gaga written on. Stick it in a machine, and the re-write with all the classified info and lip-synch while I drag and drop the shit out of those servers.

He laughs nervously.

Tyler   Okay, just stop, / for a minute.

Bradley   There's a video. I just found it in a zip file.

Beat.

It's an Apache helicopter shooting civilians on the street with a thirty millimetre cannon.

Beat.

And.

Beat.

I *can't* stop watching it.

Beat.

They circle them for a while.

Beat.

You'd think they'd all be looking up at the helicopter, but they can't see or hear it because the Apache's nearly a mile away. They fire and these people don't know where they're being shot at from. Some hide behind a wall, but because they can't see the helicopter, they don't realise the helicopter can see them.

Beat.

One guy sort of just ... explodes.

Beat.

And, I can't, stop, watching it. Nobody asks any questions if you're watching stuff like that because, everyone's watching videos like that.

Beat.

We're supposed to make sense of it.

Silence

All I can think ... every time I watch it, I think ...

Beat.

Maybe *this* time they'll get away.

Beat.

Tyler   Don't look at me. I don't know what you expect me to do with all this.

Beat.

Bradley   I can't be myself, because if I try to be myself, I have to do something. The longer I'm there, the more I feel like I don't have a choice.

Beat.

I'm sorry I'm just … I need a drink or something.

Tyler *looks around the room – can he see the bodies that haunt* **Bradley***? Does a body reach out to* **Tyler** *for help?*

Tyler   I don't want, you using all your leave to come see me.

Bradley   *(flirty)* Shut up.

Tyler   I don't want you using all your leave on me.

Bradley   I *want* to come see you.

Tyler   I know.

Tyler *backs away from the bodies.*

I just think you should use your- maybe some other folks would like to see you; I don't want to hog / you from your family.

Bradley   Who am I going to go and see? My Dad?

Tyler   You know what / I'm saying.

Bradley   Being stupid Tyler.

Tyler   I'm thinking of you.

Bradley   And I think of you every single second I'm in that box. I count down the hours till I can see you again.

Bradley *kisses* **Tyler***,* **Tyler** *is non-committal.*

Tyler   I know.

Bradley *senses* **Tyler***'s distancing.*

Bradley   What?

Tyler   It's nothing.

Bradley   You're such a headfuck.

Tyler   I'm sorry.

Tyler *backs away from the bodies.*

It's just. I've got, finals coming up. You're a *soldier.*

Silence.

I'm just a student.

Beat.

We're just.

Beat.

I've got, finals coming up.

Scene Twenty Five

Tasker Milward School May 2004

Mrs Stokes   You've *all* got finals coming up. So today we're going to concentrate on Chartism and The Newport Rising. Lisa. Stop talking.

Beat.

In 1839, the last armed rebellion against the Government on mainland Britain, descended on Newport. Who's John Frost Gavin?

Gavin   Chartist Miss.

Mrs Stokes   Chartist leader Gavin. He'd made more public speeches, written more pamphlets than anyone else. But now the rising was happening, he wasn't sure it was the right thing to do and he tried to persuade the workers to go back home but they refused. Mark. Stop talking.

Beat.

So did John Frost, turn his back on history and go back to writing and thinking about change. Or did he take action? Lisa?

Lisa   Um …

Mrs Stokes   What did John Frost do?

Lisa   Um … he like. Was he. / No hang on. I know.

Mrs Stokes   Bradley stand by the board and write the names of anyone who tries to talk while I'm talking. The last person on the board at the end of the class gets detention. You keep an eye on the class, in case I miss anyone.

Bradley *gets up picks up a piece of chalk.*

Mrs Stokes   *(to Bradley)* Lisa.

Bradley writes Lisa on the board.

He took action, and led the uprising. He was arrested and sent to Australia for his part.

(To **Bradley***)* Gavin.

This time **Bradley** *takes his time writing* **Gavin***.*

John Frost is one name, in a long list of Welsh radicals. I want you to show wider reading in your exams so you have a task. Go home and research on the internet the following people, Gwynfor Evans, James Keir Hardie, Tyrone O'Sullivan, The Women For Life On Earth, Aneurin Bevan. All these people, found themselves at pivotal moments in history and had no choice but to act – such was the power of their convictions. Mark are you chewing gum?

Mark   No Miss.

Mrs Stokes   Then you're talking. Bradley.

Bradley *doesn't respond.*

Mrs Stokes   Bradley put Mark's name down.

Bradley *doesn't. He puts the chalk down and heads to his desk.*

Mrs Stokes   What are you doing Bradley?

Bradley   I'm not putting anyone else's name on the board.

Mrs Stokes   Why not?

Bradley   I'm just not.

Beat.

Mrs Stokes   Fine I'll get someone / else to do it.

Bradley   I don't think anyone else should either.

Mrs Stokes   What do you mean by that?

Bradley   I don't think any of us should. We don't have to help you punish us.

Bradley *sits down.*

Mrs Stokes   Lisa. Go to the front please, pick up some chalk. As I was saying, these figures in history-

Lisa *doesn't move.*

Lisa.

Beat.

Go to the front.

Beat.

Gavin. Front of the class please. Pick up a piece of chalk.

Gavin   No I'm alright here Miss, I want to get all this down.

Mrs Stokes   Mark? Front of the class.

Beat.

Mark   I've done it before Miss.

Mrs Stokes   I don't want to have to put you in detention. What's the matter with you?

Scene Twenty Six

Forward Operating Base Hammer – May 2010

One ensemble member plays **Counsellor** – *Rest of ensemble play* **Bradley** *as he increasingly 'fractures' into two, then, three, then four, then five, further and further apart – ensemble are to elaborate on choral delivery.*

Bradley   If I knew I wouldn't be here.

Counsellor   How is work? And your relationship? What do you want to talk about

Bradley?

Bradley   **You have no idea, what it's like trying to talk to you.**

Deaf Counsellor   I'm a trained army therapist. I know acute stress when I see it. What's the first thing that comes to mind?

Bradley   **Command; asked me to look into … why, these two groups were meeting in Basra.**

Beat.

Recommended a sourcing mission.

Beat.

Did not recommend; engagement.

Counsellor   But they were engaged. What did the log say, was it enemy or friendly action?

Bradley   **Log said enemy.**

Silence.

Why would, the CCIR warn against negative publicity?

Beat.

Why say that, if they were enemy kills?

Beat.

Counsellor   You have to trust the OIC.

Bradley   **I do.**

Beat.

I don't know, what, they're dealing with.

Counsellor   Why is this troubling you? *Silence.*

**Bradley   I read; on my girlfriend's and Facebook status …
She now considers herself …**

Beat.

Single.

Counsellor   Your relationship is over?

Bradley   Not for, for me, seems that way for hi-her.

Counsellor   How were things when you last saw her?

Very long silence.

Bradley   She's in Brandeis so.

Beat.

Everyone.

Beat.

That's her status. Only it's patently not.

Beat.

**There's someone half-way, half-way round the world, in a
warzone. Crying. I'm crying every night because I, because
she, she won't reply to any messages.**

Beat.

**What he … What she's put. I want. I. Her relationship status
is not true. It's not true. It might be what; she wants, but it's
not that's not … how it is.**

Beat.

I've.

Beat.

She's got all the …

Mute **Counsellor** *nods in understanding.*

I can see how, someone … can try to just; wipe someone from existence. How can? How can someone just deny a year-long relationship ever existed: with a sentence?

Pause.

And … it's got me thinking, you know. About the logs.

Bradley looks at the bodies.

Why would we *ever* record a mistake?

Silence.

Counsellor   Because we're the professionals.

Bradley   That gives us *every* reason not to record mistakes.

I. Some guy … left his house today, and four hundred klicks away I couldn't decide what his politics were from his fucking cell use, so he got shot in the head.

Beat.

You know, it's, it's just one. It's just one letter … on a, on a keypad. Add an E to the KIA and no-one asks any questions. Enemy killed in action.

Beat.

The world can't be like this, or I can't be in it.

Scene Twenty Seven

Quantico Brig – February 2011

Bradley *makes sounds to re-acquaint himself with his voice.*

Bradley   I'M KINDA BUSY K-K-K KINDA BUSY.

Beat.

K-K-K-K-K-K-K-KINDA BUSY.

I.I.I.I.I.I.I'M KINDA CHAPTER FIFTEEN.

CH-CH-CH-CHAPTER FIFTEEN.

CHA-CHA-CHA!

He makes more sounds re-acquainting himself with his voice.

I.I.I.I.I.I.I.I.I.I.I.I.I.I.I.I.I.

Beat.

I missss.

MMMMMMMmmmmmiiiiiissssssssssssssss

I miss.

Beat.

I missssssssssssss

Beat.

My mother.

Bradley *makes sounds. Beat.*

Gay.

Beat.

Chapter fifteen.

Beat.

Gay.

Beat.

G-uuhh

Beat.

G-uuuuuuhhhh.

Beat.

G-uuuuuuaaaaaayyyyy. Gay. Gay. Gay. Gay.

Maximum!

Beat.

Maximum.

Beat.

Maxi-mum.

Maxi-mum. Maxinum. Mnaxinum. Aximum. Maxinum.
Manaximum. Manningaximum. Manaxing. Man. Man.
Mannnnnnning. Mannnnning. Manning

Beat.

Manning. Mmm. *Beat.* MMMMmmmmmmmmmmmm.

He makes sounds as if he's warming up his voice.

A meal slides out from under the door into the middle of the room.

FOOD! F-F-F-F-FOOOOOOOD. DUH. DUH. DUH. Beans!

Thanks!

Beat.

Thank you!

Beat.

Thank you for my food! Foood!

Silence.

*Confronted with the silence, **Bradley** turns to his food. He tries to eat but can't. He stares at the plate.*

Beat.

He screams with frustration and hurls the plate and food against a wall.

As the plate hits the wall, a Female Chorus hits the floor.

Scene Twenty Eight

Forward Operating Base Hammer – May 2010

Commander   Specialist Manning you have been reported for striking a superior officer!

Holding his gun **Bradley** *stands before a* **Commander**. *Chorus bodies sprawl around.*

Do you have anything to say on the matter?

Bradley   No sir!

Commander   I am issuing you with Company Grade Article Fifteen; you will be reduced in rank to Private.

Beat.

Hand me your weapon.

Bradley   My weapon sir?

Commander *takes* **Bradley**'s *gun from him.* **Commander** *stares at* **Bradley**. **Bradley** *looks straight ahead.*

Commander   Behavioural Health sent me your psych files.

He turns pages.

Anything you want to say Private?

Long pause.

Bradley   No sir.

Silence.

I thought; my medical files were, confidential sir.

Commander *thumbs through the files.*

Commander   Anything else you want to say Private?

Silence.

Commander *turns a page.*

Silence

Commander *turns a page.*

Silence.

Commander *turns a page.*

Silence.

Commander *turns a page.*

Silence.

Commander *turns a page.*

Bradley   Sir. Can I ask why you took my weapon sir?

Commander *turns a page.*

Commander   Because I have to ensure the safety of everyone on this base. Including yourself Manning.

Bradley   I'm not a risk to myself or anyone else sir.

Commander   I have a female sergeant with a bust lip that might disagree with you Manning.

Silence.

Commander *turns another page.*

Silence.

Commander   The behavioural unit has put your actions down to 'adjustment disorder'.

Beat.

Your time at FOB Hammer is over. In three days' time you will be back in Fort Leavenworth where the Discharge Unit will start to process you and end your military service.

Beat.

I want you take the last few days of your security clearance to finish any unwritten reports, liaise with Specialist Marino so we have continuity with briefings, then you will be assigned to the supply office while you wait for redeployment to the states. Your discharge cannot jeopardise any ongoing operations. The war is over / for you Manning.

Bradley   Sir, I lost my temper, but I still have a lot to offer the Brigade.

Commander   *(reading)* 'The persona I'm forced to take on, is killing the fuck out of me.'

Bradley   *(rising)* Sir I understood my counselling to be confidential.

Commander   *(rising)* 'I don't know, I think I'm weird I guess. I can't separate myself from others. I feel connected to everybody, like they were a distant family.'

Bradley   *(rising)* Sir, that's…

Commander   'Specialist Manning recalled dressing as a woman while on leave.'

Bradley   *(rising)* THAT IS NOT YOUR BUS/INESS.

Commander   IT IS MY BUSINESS BECAUSE I DON'T TRUST / YOU.

Bradley   AND I DON'T TRUST YOU! I'M NOT A FUCKING PIECE OF EQUIPMENT!

Commander   YOUR CAREER IS OVER MANNING. AND SO IS YOUR WAR. DISMISSED.

Bradley *turns.*

Commander   Salute your superior.

With zero respect, **Bradley** *salutes.*

Scene Twenty Nine

Bradley and the Lady Gaga huge download – May 2010

Intel Officer   Hey Manning, I've sent you the video of the hellfire taking a guy's head off.

Bradley *stands in the INTEL room.*

Intel officers sit around, as usual chewing gum, watching videos, listening to music and throwing stress balls around.

Bradley   Great.

Intel Officer   Boom!

Bradley *sits at a computer console.*

The rest of the department go about their business. Passing files around, logging reports. Answering phones, working on computers.

Trying to hide his fears, **Bradley** *looks around the room.*

Bradley *takes a deep, long breath.*

Pause.

Professionally, **Bradley** *goes to his bag and gets a CD out. He puts headphones on.*

He puts a CD into a computer and starts to mine the data and transfer it to his CD.

Quietly, **Bradley** *starts mouthing the words to Lady Gaga 'Born This Way'.*

Bradley *finally finds himself using his anonymity for good.*

Tableau sequence.

Spotlight on **Bradley** *at his computer, spotlight on Lady Gaga singing 'Born This Way'.*

Lady Gaga intercepts Intel Officers as they try to engage **Bradley** *with work; she acts as an intermediary, passing papers, cables, passes, coffee, around to protect* **Bradley**.

Secret embassy cables, and war logs from the Afghan and Iraq Wars fall on the audience.

At some point in the sequence, all Intel Officers hit the floor and form the dead bodies that have haunted **Bradley**. *One by one, they come alive to become:*

Another **Bradley** *at the Prop 8 March.*

Another **Bradley** *dressed as a soldier cries, surrounded by his property.*

Another **Bradley** *lies in cell.*

Another **Bradley** *serves coffee.*

Another **Bradley** *stands on a desk in a Welsh costume.*

Scene Thirty

Bradley in Quantico – March 2011

Bradley *breaks down as he is tortured with repetitive questioning.*

Marine   Detainee 4335453 are you okay?

Bradley   Yes.

Marine   Detainee 4335453 are you okay?

Bradley   Yes.

Marine   Detainee 4335453 are you okay?

Bradley   Yes.

Marine   Detainee 4335453 are you okay?

Bradley   Yes. I'm fine.

Marine   Detainee 4335453 are you okay?

Bradley   Yes.

Marine   Detainee 4335453 are you okay?

Bradley   Yes.

Marine   Detainee 4335453 are you okay?

Bradley   Yes.

Marine   Detainee 4335453 are you okay?

Bradley   Yes. We don't have to do this every five minutes.

Marine   Detainee 4335453 are you okay?

Bradley   Yes.

Marine   Detainee 4335453 are you okay?

Bradley   Yes.

Marine   Detainee 4335453 are you okay?

Bradley   Yes.

Marine   Detainee 4335453 are you okay?

Bradley   Yes.

Marine   Detainee 4335453 are you okay?

Bradley   Yes.

Marine   Detainee 4335453 are you okay?

Bradley   Yes.

Marine   Detainee 4335453 are you okay?

Bradley   Yes.

Marine   Detainee 4335453 are you okay?

Bradley   Yes.

Marine   Detainee 4335453 are you okay?

Bradley   Yes.

Marine   Detainee 4335453 are you okay?

Bradley   Yes.

Marine   Detainee 4335453 are you okay?

Bradley   Yes.

Marine   Detainee 4335453 are you okay?

Bradley   Yes.

Marine   Detainee 4335453 are you okay?

Bradley   Yes.

Marine   Detainee 4335453 are you okay?

Bradley   Yes.

Marine   Detainee 4335453 are you okay?

Bradley   Yes. I'm not a risk to myself.

Marine   Detainee 4335453 are you okay?

Bradley   Yes.

Marine   Detainee 4335453 are you okay?

Bradley   Yes.

Marine   Detainee 4335453 are you okay?

Bradley   Yes.

Marine   Detainee 4335453 are you okay?

Bradley   Yes.

Marine   Detainee 4335453 are you okay?

Bradley   Yes.

Marine   Detainee 4335453 are you okay?

Bradley   Yes.

Marine   Detainee 4335453 are you okay?

Bradley   Yes.

Marine   Detainee 4335453 are you okay?

Bradley   Yes.

Marine   Detainee 4335453 are you okay?

Bradley   Yes.

Marine   Detainee 4335453 are you okay?

Bradley   Yes.

Marine   Detainee 4335453 are you okay?

Bradley   Yes.

Marine   Detainee 4335453 are you okay?

Bradley   Yes.

Marine   Detainee 4335453 are you okay?

Bradley   Yes.

Marine   Detainee 4335453 are you okay?

Bradley   Yes.

Marine   Detainee 4335453 are you okay?

Bradley   Yes.

Marine   Detainee 4335453 are you okay?

Bradley   Yes.

Marine   Detainee 4335453 are you okay?

Bradley   Yes.

Marine   Detainee 4335453 are you okay?

Bradley   Yes.

Marine   Detainee 4335453 are you okay?

Bradley   Yes.

Marine   Detainee 4335453 are you okay?

Bradley   Yes.

Marine   Detainee 4335453 are you okay?

Bradley   Yes.

Marine   Detainee 4335453 are you okay?

Bradley *gathers himself.*

Bradley   Yes.

Marine   Detainee 4335453 are you okay? **Bradley** *stands up and stands to attention.*

Bradley   Yes.

Marine   Detainee 4335453 are you okay?

Bradley   Yes.

Marine   Detainee 4335453 are you okay?

Bradley   Yes.

Black.

On Screen –

February 28th 2013, the U.S. Government finally brought Bradley to court. Bradley had been in jail for 1025 days.

The legal limit without trial is 120 days.

Bradley took full responsibility for the leaking of information to Wikileaks, pleading guilty to ten of twenty-two charges.

Amnesty International has called on the U.S. Government to drop the charge of 'aiding the enemy', which carries the death penalty.

Judge Colonel Denise Lind ruled that any sentence Bradley receives will be reduced by 112 days, due to his torture at the Quantico Brig.

The twenty-five-year-old has been nominated for the Nobel Peace Prize 3 years running.

President Obama has imprisoned more whistleblowers than every other President in the history of the United States of America, combined.

Bradley's Court Martial continues.

Scene Thirty One

Tasker Milward School – May 2004

Mrs Stokes   Detention over!

Class bursts out of its chairs.

Mrs Stokes   Except you Bradley.

He sits back down. They are alone.

Mrs Stokes   Do you like it here?

He shrugs.

Mrs Stokes   Think you might stay here?

Bradley   I don't know.

Silence.

Mrs Stokes   I thought you were going to try and take a deep breath for me before opening your mouth and getting into trouble.

Bradley   I kept my promise.

Mrs Stokes   So why did I just have a whole class revolting against me?

Bradley   I did what you / said.

Mrs Stokes   No you didn't, you got into an argument like you always do.

Bradley   No, I did what you said.

Beat.

Mrs Stokes   And?

Bradley   It worked. I got clarity.

Silence.

Mrs Stokes   I don't know how your Mam copes with you.

Bradley *shrugs.*

Bradley   I'm sort of. Taking care of her.

Beat.

Me and Anthony we've built this website, it's sort of like a news aggregator, and social network for the county. People can come and post local news and stuff. Hoping that'll take off.

Beat.

We need the money.

Mrs Stokes   Is that what you'd like to do? Run something like Apple.

Silence.

Bradley   I don't know.

Beat.

I'm smart I can do stuff. But I want to use it to help people. I see all these people walking around and. None of them know how much I can help them.

Mrs Stokes   That's very noble. I don't hear many boys your age, talk about a desire to serve their community.

Beat.

Bradley   I guess that's why I think I'll probably join the U.S. Army.

Mrs Stokes   Why's that?

Bradley   We have to protect our country. I love America.

Beat.

Mrs Stokes   Don't you love Wales?

Bradley   Yeah. But.

Beat.

If I want to make help people, make the world a better place I can't think of anywhere better than the U.S. Army.

Mrs Stokes   I don't want you to join the army.

Beat.

Bradley   I don't have a choice Miss.

Lights down.

End.

Gardening: For the Unfulfilled and Alienated

Brad Birch

Gardening: For the Unfulfilled and Alienated received its first production on 1 August 2013 in the Pleasance Courtyard at the Edinburgh Festival Fringe where it received a Scotsman Fringe First award, in a production by Undeb Theatre Company and with the following cast:

Owain   Richard Corgan

Director   Hannah Banister
Designer   Madeleine Girling
Producer   Francesca Moody

Characters

Owain

Owain *is sat in his shed.*

Owain   There's some stuff you don't talk about.
Some things you keep to yourself.
You know?

We're all entitled to some part of our lives
that we shouldn't have to defend.
Some things that just *are*.

That's how it should be.
I don't believe in much but I believe in that.

Some people don't get it.
They don't understand it.
They think you must have got something to hide.
Something to … yeah.

Pause.

Ann calls me ignorant.
I'm not ignorant.
I just don't go poking around
in other people's business.

Got to seem polite.
How are you doing?
How are the kids?

I don't expect you to care.
Not really.
You see because I don't really care about yours.
There's only so much room in my head.
Energy, effort.
You're fine and I'm fine and that's it.
That's as far as it needs to go.

I'm just a man in my garden.
Leave me alone.

Pause.

Everyone needs to have a hole.

Somewhere they can bury themselves.
Thoughts, worries, ideas.
You need to lose yourself.
Need to be able to lose yourself.

Got to make sure you know the way back.
That's the thing.
Got to make sure you know how to get back.

Course there's some folk who want to get
their nose in that too.
In your head.
What are you thinking about?
I'm not.
What's wrong?
Nothing.

Some things you don't let on.
Some things you can't.
There's some things you'd never share
because people will never understand.
And all you'd be doing is spreading worry.
All you'd be doing is smearing it
across people who never need to know.

Pause.

I used to think I'd fallen out of love with my house.
We got married and bought it.
Help from her parents.
Had our two kids here.
Memories.
But then again it's just a building.
I can't get past that now.
Just space filled in.

Ann didn't need to know.
Didn't need to worry about it.
Course she'd only see it as me blaming her.
Blaming the kids.

I don't blame anyone.
Maybe myself.
I became bored of life.
And it's not one thing or another
I just lost it.
Dropped whatever it is that keeps you going.
Keeps you bothered.
I wasn't bothered.
I didn't mind.

Pause.

Space is important.
Room to be yourself.
No, not even that.
Room to be *nothing*.

I've got the garden.
Ann doesn't get it.
Doesn't understand what it's doing for me.
What are you up to in there?
What are you up to in that fucking shed?

I tell her I don't know what she thinks I'm doing.
It's a shed, not the Albert Hall.
I just sit here.

I think she thinks I come in here
to have a wank.

Pause.

I struggle.
I glide through my days with a mild panic.
I'll be sat at my desk and things will land
into my inbox
things I will never understand
and then an hour later I'll get another email
saying thanks for sorting it.

The garden grows at my pace.

My dad had a den, see.
A place of his own.
None of us were ever allowed in.
I've got to share my den with the lawnmower
but I'll take what I can get.

It was the only place in the house he could smoke.
Every evening and after Grandstand on Sundays.
In his den, smoking.
That's where he was a man.
That's where he was content.

He died of throat cancer, mind.
The cigarettes ravaged him in the end.
So maybe it wasn't the healthiest thing.
But it was the happiest thing.
I want that.
Not cancer – happiness.

Pause.

I panicked.
That's how it started.
It began with a panic like everything does.
Nothing changes when we're happy.
Change comes about by distress.

It all started when Matthew in the office
won a competition.
Won a lifetime supply of cereal.
He gets a box a month delivered for two hundred
and seventy five months.
But that only gives him about twenty years.
That's a life, is it?
That's what you get.
Twenty years.

　　And I thought is this it?
I was waking up in the morning yawning.
But yawning not out of tiredness
but boredom.

   And I panicked because I didn't know
what I could do.
I was spending my days swallowing the thoughts
I didn't want others to know
and keeping as still as I possibly could at work.
That's no life.

The world in which you live is soiled
because you are compelled to share it with others.
And the little patch you're donated
you're expected to fill with other people.
Family, friends.
Neighbours.
And before you know it
even that patch isn't yours any more.
It's mortgaged and it's a debt.
The world is not your oyster.
It's your fucking lobster and it's being boiled alive.

And I just thought …
I mean don't you ever
just get to that point in your life
where you think fuck it.
Fuck it and fuck this.
I don't want to do it anymore.

Pause.

It wasn't like I was reaching out for anything.
Maybe I was.
Can you reach out for something without realising?

I found the book one day in the canteen at lunch.
I say that.
I don't know who found who, really.

I was sat there with my beige sandwich.
I don't know what it is about sandwiches.
But the moment you wrap them up
and take them to work
they always end up going beige.

I normally read the magazines that are left there.
There to distract you and waste your breaks.
Well Mike from accounts came in
returning from the toilet
clutching a whole bundle of the magazines
and that didn't leave me with much enthusiasm
to leaf through them while eating my lunch.

I tried to find an alternative.
But there was nothing in the canteen cupboards
other than a few manuals on
how to use and repair the toaster
how to unblock the sink
and what to do if a fire rampages through the building and traps
you by the coffee machine.

There was nothing to read
and I began to resign myself to the prospect
of breathing in molecules of Mike from accounts
as I flick through the magazines still warm
that he brought back from the toilet.

But in one drawer.
The last drawer.
Underneath the kitchen roll and cloths
I pulled out a book.
A thick book.
Hardback with its cover battered
and squashed by stores of cloth and roll
stuffed and kept over time.
But despite the weathering
in bright colours it read
Gardening: for the Unfulfilled and Alienated.

Worry not
it said
if you are one of life's almost men.
For you too can have some beauty in your life.

Bit grand, I thought.

I didn't take to it straight away.
I've never been that fucked about gardening.
Never appealed to me.
Old people, kids and pets.
That's what gardens are for.
It's just the bit of your house
that there's no house on.
Nothing more than that.

Never been one for nature.
The wild.
Why on earth would you want to be somewhere
called *wild*?
How can that be good?

But then see I read a bit of the book
and that's rule one already broken.
I've put myself up a barrier.
Gardens shouldn't have barriers.
Barriers like mental states.

A happy garden is a happy home.
It's the soul of your house
because it is the only part of your house
which is alive.

What the book tells you is that with a garden
you are shaping life.
The garden is a canvas
on which we can express ourselves.
Making art through living things.

You know plants are older than we are?
And they'll be here long after we've gone
I tell you.
There's food for thought.
Who's cultivating who?

    The book didn't change me.
Not straight away.
But it asked me a few questions that lingered.

That touched close.
A bit too close.

Go confidently into your garden.
Live the life you imagine and grow yourself.
Because it's not what you see that matters
it's what you plant.
Go into your garden
and live deliberately if you want to live at all.
The essential facts of life.
The birth of life.
And you will learn what cannot be taught
and what you discover cannot be forgotten.

It asked me
Are you a man devoid of expression or beauty?
And I said no I'm not.
Or at least I don't have to be.

I was late back from lunch that day.

Pause.

I took the book home.
Snuck it out.
Yeah I know.
It might seem like a daft thing
for me to be interested in.
There's hardly precedence
for administrators
in the map categorisation department
to get into flowers.
But then again there's hardly precedence
for administrators in the map
categorisation department
to do anything with their lives.

The wife didn't understand it.
Where did you get that book from?
The kids didn't even notice.

Well I didn't care.
I wasn't doing it for them.
The book said
make a garden for yourself first
and for the world second.
And eventually you'll find
you have made a world out of your garden.

I didn't have a fucking clue what I was doing.
Before I got into flowers
this garden was just cat shit and crisp packets.
We don't eat crisps.
And we don't even have a cat.
How does that work?

All I wanted was something for myself.
Something that was good.
You need something to cling onto.
And I had a grasp of something special.
I'm not letting that go.

You know there's a real power behind
the beauty of a flower.
It makes you run home.
It makes you stop wasting time.

Ah you might find it stupid.
You know I don't expect you
to find such existential significance
in a chapter on chrysanthemums.
But then again you're not me.

You get your kicks the way you do
and I get mine out here.
You don't work in the department
of map categorisation
and you don't suffer from an unutterable
sadness about how bland and stifling your life
has become.
Well maybe you do.

But if you do all I can say to you, friend
is have you ever thought about
making yourself a trellis?

I cleared the place up
ripped out all the weeds
and flattened the mole hills.
But it did nothing to inspire the place.
Just ended up looking like a bomb site.
Desolate.
Dark.
But that's okay
because it was just my canvas, see.
My starting point.

But the problem was
I mean
that's all it ever was.
Nothing grew.

The book didn't tell me what to do.
It went straight from seeds to flowers
to happiness.
It just skipped past the bit
I was having trouble with.

Well I just wrote it off.
Wrote it off that nothing with any symbolic
or literal beauty will ever sprout and bud
again in my life.
I had my flourish.
I had my blossom.
Now it was just cat shit.
A mysterious cat leaving unmysterious shits
in my Basra of a fucking garden.

And that's when Trevor started to take notice.
Poking his smug face over the fence.
Good luck with that mate.

Course his garden was beautiful.
A bit of a water feature.

I'd look at his and I'd look at mine
and I could never understand it.
He wasn't an enlightened man.
And course with flowers comes an artistry.
A way around the materials.
I'm no connoisseur.
But I didn't think he was either.
Some people are just lucky like that.

I didn't get that he was bluffing.
He was bluffing with shrubbery.
Smoke and mirrors.
But that was chapter eight, you know?
I didn't know at the time.
I was impressed.
The bastard.

It's not that I hate him.
It's nothing personal.

Pause.

Yes it is.
It's very personal.
It's the person part of him that I hate.

Pause.

It started with a pigeon.
My garden.
Things began to happen because of one of those
fat little pigeons.

He started coming to the house.
I don't know.
Maybe he thought I'd cleared him a landing strip.
The kids might have been feeding it.
They love animals.

Grown up with it.
Attenborough on the telly.

Well the little shit kept coming.
The kids thought it was hilarious.
Started seeing it as a pet.
They laughed when I'd struggle
trying to get it out of the house.
I had to get a blanket and kind of throw it
over the little thing.
Catch him then chuck him out.

Course with their sense of humour
this was fantastic fun.
Watching me trying to catch
a little fucking bird.
They called it Peter.
Peter the pigeon.
Peter the pigeon taking the piss out of dad.

He was a favourite but Peter peaked too soon.
He never had a chance.
Performance cut short.
He died, see.

Woke one day
and the bird was there dead in the garden.
We figured he'd been ill for a while
and had just been trying to get in the house
for safety.

Bit like your dad
I said to Ann.
Course she didn't find that funny.
They'd laugh at a pigeon flapping about
but I thought that was quite quick.

The kids were upset.
I told Ann it was a good lesson for them.
Death, mortality.
I tried to explain it was a beautiful thing.

She said I had to bury it in the garden.
Here endeth the lesson.
Things die and you hide it.

What would you rather do with it
throw it in the fucking bin?

She was on one.
I don't know what I'd have rather done with it.
Maybe not establish such
an anthropomorphised relationship with it
in the first place.
Peter the fucking pigeon.

Well whatever.
I buried it.

And that was it.
I don't know what happened.
I don't know what it meant
but a few days later I get home from work
and there where I'd buried the pigeon
was a little sprout of something.

That tuft turned out to be nasturtiums.
Hadn't tried nasturtiums for months.

And not only did they grow
they grew at twice the speed
and double the volume.
Now I don't believe in any hokum
but that was fantastic.

I went back to the book, see.
I went back to it to see what could cause a ...
what could cause that kind of thing.
I didn't look for pigeons, exactly.
But you know.

Turned out it said nothing.
I mean the book spoke of breathing life

into the garden.
But not a pigeon's life.

Ann didn't care
The kids didn't.
They could barely remember the pigeon.
Crying all morning one day about it.
What pigeon, the next.
That's the YouTube generation for you.
But to me it was something.

Must be something in the water.
That's what I thought.
Something that got into the pigeon.
Chemistry.
Some chemicals that the pigeon digested.

I tried to forget it.
A tuft of hope in an otherwise desolate world.
I kept an eye on the garden.
See if it triggered anything.
See if it ignited a bit of ...
But no.
Just that freak bunch of flowers.

But that was until one day
when I was out there stood watching
the nasturtiums heave out of the ground
when I turned and trod on a snail.
Crack.
Dead.

Now I'm not a ridiculous man.
I'm not a man that pursues fancy.
As the book says
I'm a *man who searches for the logic
and blooms only the sunlight of reason.*
Now there was no reason or logic in this
but where the snail was crushed

two days later
were the first sprouts of a lavender bush.

The book didn't say a thing about death.
In fact it went so far as to imply
death didn't really happen
and was just a state of mind.

Because one cannot die
in an environment of constant regrowth.
Like a sage scrub.

And I didn't know what it meant.
But it seemed simple.
Where things were dead in my garden
in their place something grew.

I tried to get in touch with the author of the book.
To see if he could give me any advice.
I googled him.
He was dead.
Died years ago.

On his Wikipedia page
it had a picture of his gravesite.
And on top of where he was buried
a great big mound of plantlife grew.
A million fucking colours.
And it said that they have to cut it back
every single day
because the plants there grew so thick
and so dense.

Meanwhile Ann just mentions casually
over breakfast one morning
how I seem to be starting to get
some success in the garden.
And that's what it was.
Success.
And that sat with me.
I was so worried and so concerned

about how it was happening
that I didn't for a moment just sit down
and appreciate it for what it was.
A nice fucking garden.

I had figured that death meant something.
That it was something about these dead animals
that gave the garden life.
How death gave breath.
I couldn't understand it.
And when Ann turned to me and said
oh that garden's looking a bit better.
All I could say was *yeah.*

I suppose that's all that needed to be said.

Pause.

And soon I started killing whatever I could.
Course I don't mean anything proper.
Snails, spiders, worms.
Things that generally don't have faces.
And the garden just drank it in.
Out came this cacophony of colour and light
and freshness.

And I felt like I was feeding off it some days.
Some days it felt as though it's my garden
that was giving life to *me.*
Silly that.
I know it's stupid.
I still felt it though.

It was almost worth it alone for Trevor's face.
And not only did we look like a house on the street
that finally belonged
we looked like a family that people admired.
No one's ever admired me in my life.

Do you believe in God?

Pause.

I went back to the book.
I wanted to go to the next level.
Yes my garden was good
and yes I was getting somewhere
But I really wanted to know
when the happiness would kick in.

But there was nothing.
It just petered out.
Just some bits on repotting
and how to rescue a waterlogged conifer.

I was confused.
Let down.
I knew the book was about gardening
but was that all it was meant to give you?
A better garden?
I mean a garden's just a fucking …

I had channelled so much into it.
I had given so much.

Now that's not to say I stopped.
That's not to say I could stop.
And not only did I carry on burying the things
I'd killed in the back
I also found myself looking out the front.

Now I'm not a murderer.
But a garden like mine is hard to maintain.

And I'd be lying if I said
I didn't go for something a little bigger.
A little …

My first cat was a traumatic one.
I didn't kill it though.
I found it.
I was driving and spied this dead cat in the kerb.
Its head was cracked like an egg
and something had burst its stomach.

Couldn't face picking it up.
I'd have had to kind of shovel it in my hands.

A dog had been at it or something.
I presume a dog.
Couldn't imagine Mrs Hinge having a gnaw at it
on the way to the bank.

I thought what's the worst that could happen?
We'd have a random cat's bones in the garden?
Be seen shovelling roadkill into the back of my car?
Well maybe that's pretty weird.
But fuck it because I did it.
And I took it home and snuck it out the back.

And that was it.
And I saw it in Ann's eyes.
The way she'd look at the orchestra of colour
that beamed out of the ground
where I'd buried the dead cat.

And that's the most important thing.
I wasn't thinking about
nicking dead cats off the street or pigeons
or whatever else was down there
buried among the shit and crisp packets.
There was a moment of magic
and there was a moment of pride.

It wasn't weird.
Creepy.
It was art.
First time in our lives
I actually did something right.

Course I couldn't tell Ann what I was doing.
How could I ever explain?
Whisper into her ear that it's the bodies
of dead animals making this happen?
That the blood on my hands

cold or not
is feeding the life on our land?

Pause.

Like all innovations there are challenges.
Persecution.
Trevor's on to me.
In one way or another.
He knows it's more than just seeds and watering.
He buys the same seeds
he uses the same water.
He knows there's something more.
He's sharp, see.

But what with him
and this insatiable demand to keep stuff growing.
Mrs Hinge has some really promising petunias
and my kids have just started to notice me again.

Do you know how long I spend
coasting round these estates
for knocked over cats?
Do you know how tempting it is
to knock them over yourself?

I sometimes pass a fresh one and think
did I knock that down last night
and blank it out?
Blank it out so that in the morning
I can pick it up
and still live with myself?

Course I've never had a thing against them.
Cats or whatever.

What is the cost of a beautiful garden?
And what is the price that's acceptable to pay?

If anything I'm giving them an extra life.
Do you get what I mean?
This is what they'd have wanted.

No, that's not true.
They'd have rather not died.
But fucking hell.
I'd have rathered not spend my life
clinging onto whatever passes me
and spending my evenings
hiding in my shed with bin bags of dead animals.

There's the pressure to keep going.
The pressure to ...
Ever since his dog went missing
Trevor's been at it at that window.
Just staring.
And I can't meet his eye.
I can't tell him that he's now a patch of bluebells.

I see old women and I don't see them as they are
but as their potential.
Cats and dogs and pigeons are good enough.
But can you imagine a person?
Can you imagine how magnificent it would be?

I know there's no way this could end well.
But then nothing does, really.
Does it?

End

Llwyth

Dafydd James

Llwyth was first commissioned and produced by Sherman Cymru and was performed in Wales and London, with its first performance taking place on 15 April 2010 at Chapter Arts Centre, Cardiff. It was subsequently revised for the Edinburgh Festival Fringe in 2011, co-produced by Sherman Cymru and Theatr Genedlaethol Cymru. The final version, in its present form, was performed on its last tour which was to the Taipei Arts Festival and Wales in August/September 2012. The original cast featured:

Aneurin/Duncan	Simon Watts
Dada/Terry/Mam	Danny Grehan
Gareth/Darren	Michael Humphreys
Gavin	Siôn Young
Rhys/Clare	Paul Morgans
Director	Arwel Gruffydd
Musical director, composer and arranger	Dafydd James
Designer	Tom Rogers
Lighting designer	Johanna Town
Sound production and additional arrangements	James Clarke
Dramaturgy	Arwel Gruffydd and Siân Summers

Introduction to *Llwyth*

I first encountered Dafydd James when I read an English-language play ['After the Storm'] that he had sent to me when I was literary manager of the then national new writing theatre company for Wales, *Sgript Cymru*. I was immediately struck by the dramatic and emotional intelligence that this then unknown young writer was able to apply in the expression and manipulation of passionate, erotic, philosophical and psychologically complex material. Hitherto, in his work as a writer and performer, it appeared that Dafydd sought only to express those aspects of his identity, imagination and creativity that only his second language (English) could allow. By his own admission, he seemed to fear unhindered freedom of expression in his mother tongue and that a Welsh-language play, even Welsh-language culture in general, was maybe unable to contain or convey the ambition, vivacity and naughtiness of his creative mind. This was perhaps not surprising; a Welsh language culture and tradition in a population of just over 560,000 – constantly grappling to assert itself in the constant presence of a dominant, global, avaricious, *colonial* language culture – is perhaps quite understandably conservative, protective and defensive by nature. It is a fact that any language under siege seeks to protect itself from outside influences – the need to fight off linguistic influences that threaten its very existence: the creeping Anglicisation and the diminution of grammatical standards. However, such anxieties may scare off artists, writers and potential speakers of the language alike. This fear may be characterised by a sense of 'I dare not express a thought in Welsh for fear of getting it wrong – grammatically – being criticised or judged for that'. Although there are many who thrive on working in their mother tongue, for others, life through the medium of a lesser used language culture can feel from within, backward, small-minded and limiting.

Nonetheless, I challenged Dafydd to pitch an idea to us for a Welsh-language play, which eventually became *Llwyth* ['Tribe']. Sexual promiscuity among the gay community seems an unlikely narrative base camp (pun intended!) for a Welsh-language play, given the conservative instinct of a lesser-used language – and yet it proved to be the most effective and fruitful ground for an exploration of identity. Was an unsuspecting Welsh-language audience ready for such an irreverent play? Yes, as it transpired – they were gagging for it! *Llwyth* took Wales by storm. The story of *Llwyth*, as a play and theatre production, somehow encapsulates the complex notions of belonging and not belonging often experienced by Welsh-speakers, the frustrations, doubts and anxieties around language and cultural identity, and an ambition to explore the world and talk to it about 'otherness'. Welsh speakers are continually confronted with issues of identity but seeing Welsh-language identity through a gay prism was not only bold and at times shocking but more immediately it was refreshing, fun and unexpectedly revealing. At the heart of this vision of Welshness is an assertion that being a Welsh speaker is like being gay; there is an innate queerness about lesser-used language identity. There is a moment in the play when young Gavin grapples with these issues and the seeming incongruity of Welshness and gayness. He questions, "Mae Cymraeg yn *queer*?" [Welsh is queer?], and Dada affirms, "Yn gallu bod" [Can be]. The play's vivacity was partly due to its very contemporary use of language – the free flow of English-language words and cadences throughout the play. This was a beautiful moment of utter emancipation for the minority within a minority – that is, the Welsh-speaking gays: a coming of age for a language, when it absolutely embraced gay culture and celebrated Welsh camp. In so doing, it unexpectedly acknowledged that any self-respecting and viable language culture needs to be progressive and to celebrate its own minorities within. During the first Welsh tour, part of the strategy of bridging between 'traditional' and contemporary Welsh-language culture was the involvement and recruitment of local choirs for each performance. The 'mash-ups' they performed during the performance – fusing popular Welsh music with gay anthems – also enacted a conscious synthesis of what had previously appeared, perhaps, as two conflicting 'tribes'.

I had the honour of working with Dafydd on the development of this play before subsequently directing its production. Not only did *Llwyth* take Wales by storm, playing to packed houses and rapturous audiences up and down the land, it also had a sell-out run in London and was a huge success at the Edinburgh Fringe. It also delighted audiences at the Taipei Arts Festival. There was something beautifully resonant about hearing a Taiwanese choir singing in Welsh. It reminded us that the experiences of Welsh-language culture could resonate globally. Due to the often-fraught relationship between Taiwan and China and the issues of identity around the island's many languages – including Taiwanese, the dominant Mandarin and its many minority languages (including the Hokkien language) – the audiences in Taipei enthusiastically embraced *Llwyth*'s negotiation of difference.

Twice revived – unheard of before for a Welsh-language theatre production – *Llwyth* became something of a phenomenon, approaching almost cult status. It seemed, in many ways that this was the play Welsh-language audiences had been waiting for. In a nation that has undergone a revolution in terms of gay rights in recent years, *Llwyth* was a moment in Welsh-language history when not only was it OK to be both a Welsh-speaker and gay, but when Welsh-speaking gays stormed the building, stole the limelight, and went international!

Arwel Gruffydd
Artistic Director, Theatr Genedlaethol Cymru

Golygfa Un

Bore Sadwrn, ddiwedd Mawrth.
Mae Rhys yn canu iddo'i hun ychydig linellau o Ysbryd y Nos.
Yna mae Rhys yn ymarfer gyda chôr mewn festri capel yng
Nghaerdydd. Mae'r gerddoriaeth yn gyfuniad o Y Cwm *a*
Chwarae'n Troi'n Chwerw.
Mae'r gerddoriaeth yn oedi.
Mae Aneurin yn gwibio lawr Burghley Road, Llundain.

Aneurin:
Haul braf
A'i nwyd yn cydio.
Vest-tops cynta'r gwanwyn,
Bechgyn yn prancio a
Dynion.
Llwyth o ddynion,
Llwyth o gyhyrau;
Cnawd ar gerdded,
Tra bo fi ar feic ar frys
yn chwys diferol.
Ond ma' 'na flas ar y chwys;
Blas braf,
Blas chwant.
A Llundain, fel fi,
Yn hyfryd yn yr haul.
O! Dwi'n dwli ar y ddinas fawr ddrwg.
Ymgolli drwyddi draw.
Colli fy hun,
Ffeindio fy hun.
Mor hawdd perthyn i'r amhersonol.

Heb enw, heb enwad,
Getting lost; letting go …
Ond wrth gwrs,
Dwi'n gwbod yn iawn le odw i nawr.
Lawr Burghley Road,
Troi i'r dde,
Ac ar y gorwel mae'r llyn fel petai'n chwerthin.

Dwi bron yn gallu clywed y llyn yn chwerthin.

    – Fuck you!

  – Sorry. Didn't see you there!

Crotchety fat breeder â wyneb fel hwrdd,
Tri o blant yn sgrechen fel moch.
Ei buggy fel tanc yn mynnu tiriogaeth.
A hithau'r jeli blonegog chwyslyd
Yn rhegi ei hawl i'r pafin.

Oblegid Duw a ddwedodd:
Agor dy goesau, beichioga'n ddiarwybod.
A thi a geir freintiau a budd-daliadau
Yn wobr am ddod â'r bastards bach i'r byd.

Dwi bron yna.
Mae'r glesni ar y gorwel,
A'r bobol fel llygod yn heidio at

  – Cheese

  – Shit! Sorry!

O wel,
Fydd honna'n werth arian rhyw ddiwrnod:

Mae'r côr yn cael egwyl o'r ymarfer. Mae Rhys yn mynd ati i alw Aneurin.

The black blur is indeed Aneurin Wyn Roberts,
Winner of last year's Booker Prize
For his fantastic first novel,
Racing past the tennis court
To get some well-deserved ...

Mae ffôn yn dirgrynu ym mhoced Aneurin.

Blydi hell.
Not now, Dad, not now.
This is my time, my time.

Mae Aneurin yn estyn ei ffôn o'i boced i weld yn union pwy sy'n galw.

Oh!
My favourite gay!

Aneurin   Beth ti moyn?

Rhys   Ble wyt ti?

Aneurin   Ble ti'n feddwl?

Rhys   Ar fore Sadwrn?

Aneurin   Last chance, lovely.

Rhys   Slag.

Aneurin   Rhys Thomas, I take offence at that! Ti'n canu ar fore Sadwrn, that's equally anifeilaidd.

Rhys   Ni off w'thnos i heddi, nagyn ni? Taipei, here I come …

Aneurin   Rho hanner awr i fi and I'll be coming too.

Rhys   Twat.

Aneurin   Knob.

Rhys   Make notes. Fydd Gareth moyn gwbod popeth …

Aneurin   I'll report back with all the gory details! It's my gwobr. Am fy narganfyddiad ysgytwol am Iolo Morganwg …

Rhys   Really?

Aneurin   'Weda'i heno.

Rhys   Megabus?

Aneurin   Yep. Kingsway, quarter past five. See you then.

Rhys   Fydd hi'n bedlam. Mae'r match prynhawn 'ma.

Aneurin   Fydd hi'n bedlam achos fydda i nôl. Love you.

Rhys   Whatever.

Aneurin   Who's your favourite Aneurin?

Rhys   Aneurin Bevan.

Aneurin   Ta-ra twat.

Rhys   Ta-ra!

Mae Rhys yn mynd i ail-ymuno gyda'r côr. Mae'r ymarfer yn ail-ddechrau.

Aneurin:
Sdim llonydd i ga'l.
Ond 'mla'n â fi.
Gan osgoi mamau a phlant and a …
Blydi hell!
A skunk on a lead.
On a lead!
Only in London.

Mae'r côr yn canu cytgan olaf **Chwarae'n Troi'n Chwerw.**

A dwi'n hedfan
Lawr y tyle
A ma' pawb yn edrych:
Look at him go!
Isn't he sexy!
Isn't he clever!
Isn't he wonderful!
Yes, thank you very much everybody,
Yes I am!
And my audience awaits.

Rownd y gornel, rownd y llwyn,
The berth gives birth to
(Thank fuck it's the weekend!)
An ocean of Orthodox Jews and
Glorious, glorious gays.
Helo Hampstead Heath!
Ma' Aneurin Wyn Roberts wedi dyfod o'r diwedd.

Golygfa Dau

Fflat Dada, Celestia, Bae Caerdydd.
Mae Dada'n ymlacio gyda gwydr mawr o win coch.
Rhys ac Aneurin yn cyrraedd.

Dada   Co hi!

Rhys   The wanderer returns!

Dada   Y'ch chi'n iawn?

Aneurin   Bloody marvellous. Pour me a wine, Dada.

Dada   Coch?

Aneurin   Gwyn, plîs. Make it a big one.

Dada   I wouldn't have it any other way.

Rhys   Ble ma' fe?

Dada   Toilet.

Rhys   Odi e'n pissed?

Dada   Gad e fod, mae'n dathlu.

Aneurin   Dathlu be'?

Dada   Promotion.

Rhys   Manager.

Aneurin   Y gym?

Rhys   Na, Lady Gaga!

Aneurin   Ond mae'n rhy ifanc, nagyw e?

Dada   Obviously not.

Aneurin   Manager?

Rhys   Ydi. Gareth yn frenin ar holl fuscles y fro. The smell of sweat. 'Mor wlyb, mor chwaethus o wlyb' ...

Aneurin   That's hot, Rhys.

Rhys   Wy'n gwbod. Odi e'n pissed?

Dada   Tipsy.

Aneurin   Excellent.

Dada   Nawr 'te ti, 'rosa gytre' am 'chydig bach. Dada missed you.

Aneurin   Do fe?

Dada   Do. S'o fe r'un peth hebddo ti.

Rhys   Odi e 'di bihafio, though?

Dada   Fel angel.

Rhys   O'dd Lucifer yn angel.

Dada   Co ti, darling. Ti nôl am sbel tro hyn?

Curiad.

Dada   Shwt ma' dy Dad?

Rhys   Ie, sut ma' ddi?

Aneurin   S'o Dad 'di ca'l sex change.

Rhys   Dy fam, you idiot.

Aneurin   Bloody fine. Siarad dwli am vol-au-vents. Right as rain.

Rhys   Vol-au-vents?

Aneurin   Chicken and mushroom. Mmm, ma' hwn yn neis iawn, Dada.

Rhys   'Na'i ddod 'da ti i weld hi rhywbryd wythnos 'ma.

Aneurin   I wouldn't bother, tro diwetha o'dd hi'n meddwl mai Margaret Williams o't ti.

Dada   Easy mistake.

Rhys   Thank you, Dada!

Dada   Www, beth am i ni ga'l bach o Margaret, i leddfu'r ysbryd.

Mae Dada yn mynd i nôl albwm ohoni.

Aneurin   S'dim byd yn bod 'da'n ysbryd i, thank you very much.

Dada   O, dewch 'mla'n (*gan anwesu llun y clawr*), mae mor biwtiffwl.

Aneurin/
Rhys   Na!

Daw Gareth i mewn.

Gareth   Evening all!

Dada   Co hi!

Rhys   Ti *yn* pissed.

Aneurin   How's my clever boy then?

Gareth   Mr Roberts. Yey!

Mae'n cydio yn Aneurin.

Gareth   Any rudies?

Aneurin   Loads.

Rhys   Gareth!

Gareth   What?

Rhys   Newydd ddod miwn ma' fe!

Gareth   So? I want to know. Faint?

Dada   Faint o'r gloch yw hi?

Aneurin   Faint?

Gareth/
Dada   Ie.

Rhys/
Aneurin   Six-thirty / Five plus.

Dada   Pryd ma' *Strictly*?

Aneurin   S'o ti'n watcho *Strictly*.

Dada   Plîs? *Comic relief* special.

Aneurin   Ges *i* comic relief unwaith – clown o Borthmadog.

Dada   Esgidiau mawr?

Aneurin   Gigantic.

Gareth   What does five *plus* mean?

Aneurin   You what?

Gareth   Five *plus*, rudies with five plus.

Aneurin   Well, rudies three involved several, so I'm not really sure.

Gareth   Why?

Aneurin   It was pitch black.

Dada   Ych a fi!

Rhys   Siarada Gymraeg 'da fe, Aneurin, ma' isie i fe ymarfer.

Aneurin   Bysen i yn 'sen i'n gwbod beth oedd y gair Cymraeg am orgy.

Dada   Mwy o win?

Aneurin   Beth am y Bollinger?

Dada   S'o ni'n agor y Bollinger.

Aneurin   Oh, go on!

Dada   Special occasion.

Aneurin   Mae *yn* special occasion. 'Wi gytre'.

Dada   O't ti gytre' tair wythnos nôl.

Aneurin   So? Golles di fi?

Dada   Llefen bob nos.

Gareth   A fi.

Rhys   Bob nos.

Gareth   Except for ddoe.

Aneurin   Beth ddigwyddodd ddo'?

Rhys   Be' ti'n feddwl?

Aneurin   Rudies?

Gareth   Ie!

Rhys   O'dd e'n fachgen da ddo'. Dath e rownd
B and Q 'da fi.

Gareth   And Homebase.

Rhys   A Homebase.

Dada   Iyffach. 'Wi'n mynd rownd Homebase drwy'r amser and
no such luck.

Aneurin   You should try Asda.

Dada   S'o Dada'n mynd i Asda. Ma' Asda'n common.

Aneurin   Ie, ond yr holl scallies!

Dada   So?

Aneurin   Ar rollerblades withe 'fyd.

Dada   Well definitely not, 'te. Ti'n gwbod shwt 'wi'n teimlo
ymbyti rollerblades.

Rhys   A gan fod e 'di eistedd drwy gyngerdd y côr wythnos
diwetha', ga'th e'r full works.

Dada   Pwp-dwll?

Rhys   Pwp-dwll.

Aneurin   'Sen i'n gorfod iste trwy *Hafan Gobaith*, I'd want pwp-dwll *a* civil partnership.

Rhys   Well ... (*Yn canu*) 'maybe next time, he'll be lucky, maybe next time' ...

Gareth   I enjoyed *Hafan Gobaith*!

Dada   Wnes i 'fyd. Very rousing.

Gareth   And that one you had a solo in, what was that?

Dada   *Ysbryd y nos*.

Gareth   It's lush, that is.

Aneurin   Smo chi'n canu hwnna'n Taiwan, ych chi?

Rhys   Odyn; clasuron Cymraeg – *Chwarae Troi'n Chwerw* ...

Gareth   *Y Cwm* ...

Rhys   *Y Cwm*! Brownie points, Gareth Lloyd ...

Aneurin   Pam ddiawl bydde 'da'r Chinese ddiddordeb yn ...

Gareth   They're not Chinese, they're Taiwanese!

Aneurin   ... y Taiwanese ddiddordeb yn Caryl Parry Jones a Huw Chiswell?

Dada   Pam lai? Dangosodd un ohonyn nhw ddiddordeb ynot ti yn *Mardi Gras* llynedd, os wi'n cofio'n iawn, a smo ti hanner mor dalentog.

Aneurin   That's not what he said.

Gareth   Oh yeah! Guan ... Guan ...

Rhys   Ting.

Gareth   That's right. Guan-Ting.

Dada   Wan-King? Enw addas!

Rhys   Apparently so. Os wela'i e, I'll send your love.

Aneurin   Bollinger?

Dada   Na. 'Wi 'di dweud, special occasion.

Aneurin   Mae'n International day; co ti special occasion.

Dada   S'o hwnna'n golygu dim byd i ti!

Gareth   And we lost.

Aneurin   I know. Brilliant, fydd isie bach o faldod ar y rugby boys.

Gareth   They're off to X tonight too.

Rhys   S'o ni'n mynd mas.

Aneurin   Rubgy boys on E; I can feel the love already. 'Na chi rheswm i ddathlu. Come on, Dada!

Dada   Na, na, na. Ma' hwnna i fi a neb arall.

Aneurin   Pryd ddiawl ti'n mynd i agor hi, 'te?

Curiad.

Dada   That's for me to know and you to find out.

Rhys   Www, ti jyst fel Mrs Madrigal.

Gareth   Mrs who?

Rhys   Never mind.

Aneurin   Beth am pan fenna i'n llyfr?

Dada   Chance would be a fine thing.

Aneurin   Actually Mrs Madrigal, 'wi ar y bennod olaf.

Gareth   O ie! How's the God-squad?

Aneurin   God*oddin*. Gododdin.

Gareth   Gododdin. Alright?

Aneurin   Good. About to reach its climax.

Dada   I do hope it's messy.

Aneurin   Gloriously so.

Gareth   What was that line again?

Aneurin   'A queer transhistorial love story' ...

Aneurin/
Rhys   ... 'for the *Dr Who* generation'.

Aneurin   Very good, Rhys.

Dada   Beautiful.

Gareth   Trans-what?

Aneurin   Transhistorical.

Dada   Danny la Rue. Now there's a trans-historical. God rest her soul.

Aneurin   Not the same thing.

Gareth   Beth yw transhistorical?

Aneurin   Drwy hanes. I've told you this before ...

Gareth   Remind me.

Aneurin   It's about time travel. Am foi sy'n teithio drwy'r space-time continuum yn cael loads o one night stands, cyn bod ...

Dada   O le mae'r boi yn dod?

Aneurin   Pwy?

Dada   Y boi. Y time traveller. Thingamajig ...

Aneurin   Owain. Owain Marro.

Dada   As in Owain fab Marro?

Aneurin   Ie ond yn yn fersiwn i mae'n half-italian ac yn byw uwchben Merola's yn Grangetown ...

Dada   Fabulous.

Aneurin   ... sydd wedi ei adeiladu ar rift yn y space-time continuum a dyna sut mae'n teithio nôl i'r hen ogledd i yfed medd ac ymladd 'da'r Gododdin ...

Gareth   Who were … ?

Aneurin   Gay.

Gareth   You what?

Aneurin   An ancient Welsh troop made up of pairs of gay lovers.

Gareth   Hot!

Curiad.

Dada   Woah funud fach. o'dd y Gododdin ddim yn gay!

Aneurin   Shwt ti'n gwybod?

Dada   Achos sai'n cofio 'Gwŷr a grysiasant am goc' yn y traddodiad barddol.

Aneurin   Dramatic licence.

Dada   Very dramatic.

Aneurin   Wel os o'dd e'n wir am y sacred Band of Thebes, it could have been wir am y Gododdin. They fought for their lovers in Ancient Greece, I reckon Aneurin was dicking Owain fab Marro yn yr hen Ogledd:

'Greddf gŵr, oed gwas
Gwryd am ddias;
Meirch mwth, myngfras –
O dan forddwyd mygrwas
Ysgwydd ysgafn, llydan
Ar bedrain meinfuan
Cleddyfawr glas, glân
Eddi aur affan'
TOTAL homo.

Gareth   That wasn't Welsh, that was a minor stroke.

Dada   Jyst achos na'th dy rieni di alw'n ti'n Aneurin, s'o hwnna'n rhoi'r hawl i ti fastardeiddio'r Gododdin.

Aneurin   It's just my take. I reckon they were all at it.

Rhys   No wonder nethon nhw gyd farw, o'n nhw 'di blino cyn cychwyn, poor dabs.

Gareth   Is your novel a porno?

Aneurin   No! It's romantic. It's about love.

Rhys   A Iolo Morganwg?

Aneurin   A-ha!

Dada   *Strictly*!

Rhys   Na, 'wi isie gwbod am Iolo Morganwg.

Gareth   What, one of your London shags?

Dada   Ma' fe 'di marw, bach.

Gareth   Marw? You slept with a dead man?

Aneurin   Naddo!

Rhys   Wouldn't put it past you.

Gareth   Who's Iolo Morganwg?

Dada   Ti'n gwbod. Y boi nath greu'r orsedd.

Gareth   What? Mr Urdd?

Rhys   Gareth, shut up!

Gareth   What?

Rhys   Ti'n bod yn stupid.

Gareth   But I don't get it.

Dada   Na'th e farw yn y nineteenth century, darling. Bardd. Poet.

Gareth   Well why didn't you say so?!

Rhys   'Wi 'di dweud 'na wrthot ti. 'Wi 'di dweud ymbiti Iolo Morganwg. Sawl tro.

Gareth   I'm not thick, Rhys.

Rhys   'Wedes i 'na?

Gareth   Might as well have.

Aneurin   I reckon he's a gay.

Gareth   Of course I'm a gay.

Rhys   Not you, stupid!

Gareth   I'm not stupid. Oh for fuck's sake.

Dada   Tynnu dy go's di ma' fe.

Gareth   I'm having a line. Who wants a line?

Mae Gareth yn paratoi llinellau o cocaine.

Dada   Www, naughty! S'o Dada 'di dablo ers *Eurovision*.

Gareth   Want to dabble, Dada?

Dada   Go on then, ni *yn* dathlu.

Rhys   O'n i'n meddwl bod ti moyn watcho *Strictly*?

Dada   Well I'll be dancing myself now in a minute.

Aneurin   'Wi newydd 'weud fod Iolo Morganwg yn gay. It's revolutionary.

Dada   Paid â bod yn soft, anyone who puts hundreds of men in frocks has to be a poof.

Mae Dada'n cymryd llinell.

Dada   Mmm, neis.

Curiad.

Ooh, it feels sacrilegious with Elaine Page watching. She never approved.

Gareth   What about Liza Minnelli?

Mae Dada'n codi ei aeliau'n awgrymog.

Dada   O's 'da ti dystiolaeth fod e'n boof?

Aneurin   O's 'da ti dystiolaeth fod e'n syth?

Gan weld Gareth yn cymryd llinell.

Aneurin   Oi, oi! Sai'n ca'l cynnig?

Gareth   Wrth gwrs, Mr Roberts. Thought you'd never ask.

Mae ffôn Aneurin yn dirgrynu.

Rhys   Come on! O's rhaid?

Dada   Jyst dychmyga mai medd yw e.

Rhys   They all died!

Dada   S'o ti'n mynd i ateb hwnna?

Aneurin   Ignore it. It's my sister.

Mae Aneurin yn cymryd llinell.

Gareth   Come on, Rhys.

Rhys   Na.

Aneurin   Mmm, that hit the spot.

Rhys   Dada, ddylet ti w'bod yn well.

Aneurin   Come on, Rhys. Dwi newydd sgwennu pennod chwyldroadol.

Rhys   Chwyldroadol?

Aneurin   Ie.

Rhys   Paid dweud. Owain a Iolo?

Aneurin   Jacpot!

Rhys   Mae'n siŵr o roi (*ffug-barchus*) ysgytwad i'r academi Gymreig heteronormative!

Aneurin   Very good, Rhys!

Gareth   'Heteronormative'?!

Dada   O'dd Iolo Morganwg yn briod.

Aneurin   O'dd Ron Davies yn briod.

Dada   Touché. Line, Rhys?

Gareth   'Heteronormative'?!

Aneurin   Two point four kids, picket fence …

Dada   Line?

Aneurin   Cats and dogs, my holier than thou, self-righteous, whinging sister …

Rhys   Ma' dy wâr di'n lovely, Aneurin.

Aneurin   Mae'n wâr i'n berffaith.

Dada   Rhys?

Rhys   Oh fuck. Go on 'te. Ni'n mynd mas nawr, yndyn ni?

Dada   It's a full moon tonight!

Maent i gyd yn udo.

Dada   Oh, it never gets tired. A cyn i ni fynd mas beth am bach o *Strictly*?

Pawb   Na!

Dada   Plîs?

Aneurin   O blydi hell. Rho fe 'mla'n, Rhys. Unrhyw beth am bach o dawelwch.

Dada   Diolch i ti, bach. Sdim byd fel watcho Bruce Forsyth when you're whizzing off your tits.

Aneurin:
Cymundeb,
Cymuned.
Un teulu fel atalnod
Yn nodi man ein oedi.
Dada'n swnian am

Dada   Sparkles, let there be sparkles!

A Gareth a Rhys yn wenau i gyd.
Ond dwi,

Dwi'n ysu,
Ysu am fwy.
Mae'r dudalen heno'n lân:
Fi yw awdur fy nhynged!
Dim oedi,
Dim meddwl,
Achos
Pan ddaw yfory
Rhaid dweud ffarwel
A rhoi pob dim ...

Rhys　Yn ôl y papurau, dyma'r peth caleta mae 'di neud.

Dada　I don't care. Deborah Meaden should never have attempted the cha-cha.

Aneurin　A co ni'n mynd ...

Golygfa Tri

Mermaid Quay, Bae Caerdydd. Mae'r pedwar yn cerdded i lawr y stryd.

Aneurin:
Un uned ar garlam,
Ar ras wyllt i'r goleuni.
Dada'n dawnsio disco'n ...

Dada　Fabulous!

Aneurin:
Heibio Tesco a'r Eli Jenkins.
Rhys a Gareth mewn.

Rhys/
Gareth　His and her's matching tops.

Rhys　His is a Ralph Lauren ...

Gareth　And his is from Asda, George selection.

Rhys　No one will ever know.

Aneurin:
Mae'r ddinas i gyd ar garlam heno.
A ninnau fel bleiddiaid yn glafoerio.
Gwaed yn ein gyrru ar gyfeiliorn,
Gwaed ar garlam drwy'n gwythiennau
A chamau'n traed yn …

Dada   Un fach cloi?

Rhys   Beth am y taxi?

Gareth   Fuck the taxi.

Aneurin:
Wrth i ni herio samba'r nos
Gyda rhythm ein gwrthbwynt dieflig.

Terra Nova, Bae Caerdydd.

Aneurin   Bitter and three lagers please!

Gareth   Wow!

Rhys   Gareth, rho dy dafod yn dy geg.

Gareth   Three o'clock!

Aneurin   Beth?

Gareth yn tynnu llun cylch yn yr awyr.

Aneurin   Dish?

Gareth   Total.

Aneurin   Ble?

Gareth   Eight o'clock now. Quick or he'll turn into a pumpkin.

Dada   Www, neis.

Rhys   Aneurin, slow down!

Gareth   Another one?

Rhys   Na, quick one o'dd hwn i fod.

Gareth   It was! Really quick.

Rhys   Usually is, darling.

Gareth   Piss off.

Aneurin:

Ac at y bar â ni cyn i chware droi'n …

Gareth   Bitter, please, and a …

Dada   Alla'i ga'l gin, darling? Ma' Dada'n dechre teimlo'n bloated.

Rhys   Lager i fi …

Aneurin   And a Vodka Red Bull, please. Come on, boys!

Rhys   Christ, Aneurin – ti ar mission heno.

Aneurin   No rest for the …

Darren yn ymddangos yn sydyn.

Darren   (*acen Trelai*) Wicked bra! Where've you been 'iding mate!

Aneurin   Fuck.

Rhys   Welai di'n y taxi rank.

Aneurin:
Darren Boner Hughes.
So called
As he …

Darren   Was up … ?!

Aneurin:
In school
All the time.
Oversexed.

Darren   Ain't seen you since school. 'Eard you've been doing alright, though. Making a film, right?

Aneurin   Writing a book.

Darren   Yer, that's it. Writin' a book. You were always fucking smart, you cunt. What's it about?

Aneurin   The Gododdin.

Darren   The what?

Aneurin   Have you heard of the Sacred Band of Thebes?

Darren   Rock band, innit?

Aneurin   Something like that.

Darren   Wicked!

Aneurin:
And on we go.
Ymlaen, ymlaen, ymlaen.

Gareth   Taxi!

Aneurin   Ddim hwnna.

Gareth   Pam?

Aneurin   I've 'ad im.

Gareth   Fair enough. Have you 'ad *him*?

Aneurin   No.

Curiad.

But I will.

A'r tasci'n ein tywys
Yn dywysogion y nos.

Alright, drive?
Busy tonight?
Been out long?
Finishing late?

Yackity-yackity-yackity-yack.
Teiar ar darmac,
Olwyn ac olew,
Yn iro'n llwybr i uffern.

Pob cwestiwn
Yn ail-ddarllediad:
Adlais parhaol
Ystrydeb y stryd.
A ni,
Yr ystrydebau llon,
Yn dadlwytho'n dwt i'r dref.

Heol y Santes Fair.

Gareth nawr
Fel ci bach ffyddlon
Yn ceisio rhoi clamp o dafod yng nghlust ei berchennog
Cyn bowndio nôl
Ar hyd St Mary Street fel …

Rhys   Bloody twat!

Aneurin:
A bwrw mewn i ryw ferch o'r enw

Mae Gavin yn ymddangos yn sydyn.

Gavin   Watch where you're fucking going … oh, hia Mr
Thomas!

Aneurin:
Sori, *bachgen* o'r enw …

Rhys   Gavin. Shwt wyt ti?

Gavin   Fi'n grêt, Mr Thomas. Fi'n cael amser gwych. Fi wedi
bod i Reflex gyda … Oi, Chanise – wait a sec. Sori, Mr Thomas.
Mae'n bursting. Bet you didn't recognise me. Mae'n fancy-dress
yn Pulse heno. Fi yw Thelma, she's Louise.

Rhys   Deg mas o ddeg am ymdrech, Gavin.

Gavin   Ydych chi'n gay, Mr Thomas?

Rhys   Pa fath o gwestiwn yw hwnna i ofyn i dy athro?

Gavin   Wel s'o ti'n dysgu fi rhagor, wyt ti? So mae'n OK. *Fi'n*
gay.

Rhys   Wyt ti nawr?

Gavin   Ie. Ond mae'n cool. Mam fi wedi dod gyda fi i'r Golden a popeth. A mae wedi gadael i fi gwisgo make-up hi.

Rhys   Hyfryd iawn, Gavin.

Gavin   Ie. Mae yn. Mae Mam fi'n lysh. Fi'n caru hi loads. Mae'n bos fi! Serious, yn Greggs. Boring, like, ond mae'n golygu fi'n gallu mynd allan, and it's not forever. Fi'n mynd i gwneud performing arts blwyddyn nesa. Ti'n mynd i gweld name fi in lights.

Rhys   'Na'i ddisgwyl 'mlaen i hynny, Gavin.

Gavin   Sori o'n i mor crap yn neud maths. O'n i'n hoffi ti.

Rhys   Diolch, Gavin.

Gavin   Oes boyfriend gyda ti?

Rhys   Gavin!

Gavin   Worth a try. Ti'n hot.

Aneurin:
Ac mae Gavin yn diflannu
Tu ôl i fôr o grysau burberry
Sy'n symud yn amwys araf
Tuag at Liquid Bar.

Gareth   You're cute.

Rhys   Beth ti'n feddwl?

Gareth   That was cute. You're cute.

Aneurin:
Mae'n garnifal yr anifeiliaid heno:
Teigrod yn ysgyrnygu am gnawd,
Saith buwch mewn boob-tube a …

Dada   Beth yw hwnna?

Aneurin:
A …

Gareth   Oh my God!

Aneurin:
A …

Mae pawb yn syllu i'r un cyfeiriad.

Dada   Morlo marw ar y ffordd.

Gareth   Fuck me, that's Clare. Clare? Clare? Clare, darling, you alright?

Clare   I fuckin' loves you. It's my ex, girls. It's my ex!

Dada   Pwy ddiawl yw hi?

Gareth   You've 'ad one too many, love.

Clare   We lost! Gar! We lost.

Gareth   I know, darling. Oh, not on the shirt, not on the shirt!

Aneurin:
Ac mae'n troi ei phen yr eiliad ola
I …

Mae Clare yn chwydu.

Clare   I fuckin' loves you.

Dada   Ych a fi!

Gareth   Will somebody call an ambulance? Boys?!

Dada   Fydd hi'n iawn. Gâd hi i'r seven dwarfs.

Aneurin:
Ac ymlaen â ni.

Dada   O't ti'n arfer mynd mas 'da honna?!

Gareth   We all have our pasts?

Dada   Yes, but your past has a vagina.

Gareth   And yours has Elaine Page.

Curiad.

Aneurin   Elaine Page has a vagina.

Dada/
Gareth   Shut up, Aneurin.

Curiad.

Rhys   'Mla'n â ni, ife?

Curiad.

Aneurin:
Paramedics fel paratroopers
Yn stormio diffeithwch ein celfyddyd.
Chwydfa o bolystyrene a bagiau siop chips
Yn leinio stumog y stryd.
A ninnau'n cerdded,
Cerdded ymlaen,
Cerdded drwy hŵd a thân,
Cerdded â ffydd yn ein cân,
Ymlaen,
Ymlaen,
Ymlaen!

Gareth   Fancy a quick one?

Dada   Thought you'd never ask.

Aneurin:
A mewn â ni
I gysgod y dafarn ddieflig
Lle mae Satan yn wên o glust i glust
A Kylie ar y juke box.

Golygfa Pedwar

Kings Cross

Aneurin:
Pedwar Aftershock yn ddiweddarach …

Gareth   Rhif un?

Aneurin   Vicar, CP, Covent Garden.

Gareth   Beth yw CP?

Aneurin   Corporal punishment.

Gareth   You what?

Rhys   Spanking, Gareth.

Gareth   Cool.

Rhys   Vicar? Mae hwnna bach yn …

Aneurin   Oedipal?

Rhys   Wel … ie, a dweud y lleia.

Aneurin   My father's a gweinidog not a vicar.

Gareth   Did he look like your father?

Rhys   Gareth!

Dada   CP, CP! S'o Dada'n lico meddwl am vicars brwnt yn cael eu dwylo bach blewog arnat ti.

Aneurin   O'dd hwn ddim yn flewog, o'dd e'n wacso.

Dada   Wacso? A waxing vicar? Whatever next?

Aneurin   A hairy biker.

Dada   Www, 'sen i ddim yn gallu neud 'ny. Smo fi'n lico poen.

Aneurin   Be', y wacso neu'r CP?

Dada   Y wacso. I enjoy a spanking.

Aneurin   He had lovely eyes and a very firm hand.

Dada   Bravo. Lle ffindes di fe, 'te?

Aneurin   Grindr. But get this, right, o'dd rhif dau yn well. Muscleman with a fetish for lycra. Co fe'n dod rownd i'r fflat 'da'r bag massive 'ma and there's me thinking, 'fuck I've gone and copped off with Fred West'. Ond ddiflannodd e mewn i'r bathroom, a dod mas five minutes later wedi gwisgo fel …

Pawb   Ie?

Aneurin   Superman.

Rhys   Superman?

Aneurin   Serious. Boots and all. Figure-hugging lycra.

Gareth   A muscleman dressed as superman?

Aneurin   Yep. Se *ti* 'di dwli arno fe. Huge, I mean, HUGE biceps. Dychmyga …

Dada   Sori, ma' hwnna just yn weird. Hyd yn oed i ti.

Rhys   Not as weird as custard-pie man.

Dada   O na, ti'n iawn. O'dd hwnna'n disgusting.

Gareth   So what happened?

Aneurin   Dim byd really. O'n i ddim hyd yn oed yn ca'l tynnu'r lycra off. O'dd e just moyn gorwedd ar ei gefn ar y llawr 'da fi yn gorwedd ar ei ben e yn … wel …

Dada   Beth? Syrffo?

Aneurin   Na … it was kind of like … body worship.

Rhys   Be' 'nes di, canu emyn?

Aneurin   A little bit of kissing, nibbling, stroking. 'Na ni really.

Dada   Ddylet ti 'di canu *Craig yr Oesoedd*.

Gareth   Awesome!

Rhys   Boring.

Dada   Wel, 'sen i 'di o leiaf mynnu ei fod e'n yn rhoi i mewn ffrog a 'ngalw i'n Lois (*sef Lois Lane*).

Rhys   Be', nethoch chi ddim hyd yn oed … ?

Aneurin   Certainly not. Jyst minnau fel pererin … 'mewn anial dir, yn crwydro yma a thraw' …

Rhys   Ti'n gweld … beth o'dd ei enw e?

Aneurin   Dunno. Superman?

Rhys   Ti'n gweld Superman 'to?

Aneurin   Fydd rhaid i fi. He left his left boot.

Dada   Jiw, jiw. Shwt a'th e gytre' heb ei esgid?

Aneurin   Hedfan.

Gareth   Shall we go?

Rhys   Gareth!

Gareth   But I want to go.

Aneurin   Fair enough.

Gareth   Let's go to X. I want to dance.

Rhys   Mae'n rhy gynnar. Fydd neb 'na.

Gareth   Oh come on, I'm bored here.

Rhys   Ti wastad yn bored.

Gareth   Well, things are often boring.

Curiad.

Dada   Www, pwy yw'r hunky-spunky wrth y fruit machine?

Rhys   O blydi hell, co nhw fan hyn nawr.

Gareth   Who?

Rhys   Terry Williams.

Gareth   Fuck off! Where?

Aneurin   Fyna, drws nesa i'r trannie.

Gareth   And he is.

Rhys   A blydi Duncan Colefield … God, ma' nhw gyd 'ma.

Aneurin   Pwy?

Rhys   Rhiwbeina firsts. 'Ffrindiau' Gareth.

Gareth   Don't be sarky. They're fine.

Rhys   They're apes …

Dada   Who cares … this is better than porn!

Rhys   This isn't porn, it's *Gorillas in the Mist.*

Mae Terry'n ymuno â nhw.

Gareth   Alright, Terr?

Terry   Alright, boys? Gar?

Gareth   Good thanks. Gutted though.

Terry   Fucking shit, I tell you. But there you go, we should be proud, at least we're consistent …

Gareth   Aye.

Terry   Brilliant losers. That's what we are. No one can take that away from us. If there's one thing to be said about the Welsh, it's that we're fucking brilliant at losing!

Gareth   Too right! Yn gollwyr gwych.

Terry   Very nice, Gareth Lloyd.

Gareth   Thank you, I've been practising. Treiglads and everything. Yn gollwyr gwych.

Terry   Yn gollwyr gwych, aye!

Gareth   Aye.

Terry   Buddugoliaethus o wych!

Gareth   Aye.

Terry   What do you reckon, boys?

Pawb   Aye.

Terry   So I don't know about you but I'm going to celebrate that. The one thing we do bloody well as a nation. Dwi'n cynnig llwncdestun i ni, y Cymry! As losers, we stand as one. Iechyd da, boys!

Pawb   Iechyd da!

Mae Terry'n gadael.

Rhys   Twat.

Gareth   Hypocrite.

Rhys   Be' ti'n feddwl, hypocrite?

Gareth   You were the one wishing him good health.

Rhys   Ie, ond dan yn anadl i, I was wishing him AIDS.

Aneurin   Neu diabetes. Apparently it's worse.

Rhys   Serious?

Dada   Ma' fe'n iawn: Dad had his leg chopped off, but Sissy, from the sauna, *she*'s having the best sex she's ever had, medde hi.

Gareth   Boys!

Aneurin   Be'?

Gareth   What the hell's wrong with you? You're talking about a human being.

Rhys   Really? A 'na le o'n i'n meddwl bod ni'n siarad am King Kong.

Gareth   You're such a bigot, Rhys.

Rhys   Os ti'n lico fe gyment pam 'nes di stopo ware 'da nhw 'te?

Gareth   You know why, I wanted to play for the lions.

Aneurin   Ti'n ware i'r lions?

Gareth   I haven't actually played for them yet. Just joined.

Aneurin   The gay rugby team?

Gareth   Ie.

Rhys   Ie. A *pam* ti'n ware i'r lions?

Gareth   'Cause I have more fun in the showers.

Curiad.

Gareth   God, I'm joking, mun!

Rhys   A dwi ddim yn bigot. Na'th y boi 'na sellotapo fi i'r ffenest yn yr ail flwyddyn a hwpo permanent marker coch lan yn nostril i.

Gareth   In the *ail* flwyddyn, Rhys! That was like …

Aneurin   Sixteen.

Gareth   Sixteen years ago. Get over it.

Rhys   Ma' nhw dal yn galw fi'n Rudolph! Pam ddylen i?

Gareth   'Cause you're gorgeous, you've got a good job, good friends and an alright boyfriend who loves you very much so it doesn't really matter in the grand scheme of things, so why should you care?

Rhys   Because I do, and therefore the 'alright' boyfriend who loves me very much should do too, but he doesn't, and therefore in the grand scheme of things I've got even more to be pissed off about.

Curiad.

Aneurin   O's rhywun moyn clywed am yr orgy ges i?

Gareth/
Rhys   Na.

Saib.

Gareth   I'm going for a fag.

Mae Gareth yn gadael.

Saib.

Aneurin   Rhys …

Rhys   Paid.

Aneurin   O'dd hwnna bach yn uncalled for.

Rhys   Fel dy gyngor di, so kindly shut up.

Aneurin   Beth sy'n bod, bach?

Rhys   Dim.

Curiad.

Rhys   Fi'n mynd i'r toilet.

Mae'n gadael.

Dada   Lovers' tiff?

Aneurin   As always.

Dada   Chi o'n i'n olygu.

Aneurin   I don't think so.

Dada   Dwed di.

Aneurin   Beth?

Dada   Dim.

Curiad.

Dada   Tell me about the orgy.

Aneurin   Na, sa'i moyn.

Dada   Paid â pwdu.

Aneurin   Sa'i moyn.

Dada   Faint?

Aneurin   No idea.

Dada   Amcangyfrif?

Curiad.

Aneurin   Pymtheg?

Dada   Pymtheg? My God, pwy o'n nhw? Y Rhiwbeina firsts?

Aneurin   Dunno who they were. O'dd hi'n dywyll.

Dada   Ble o't ti?

Aneurin   Vault 147, *boots only* night.

Dada   Boots only?

Aneurin   Ie. Boots *only.*

Dada   O!

Aneurin   Chi'n gadel eich dillad wrth y drws. Ma' nhw'n rhoi plastig bag i chi gadw'ch arian.

Dada   A co fi'n meddwl bydde 'na ddigon o slots i hwpo'r newid.

Aneurin   Dada! Y'ch chi'n ddrwg!

Dada   Yndyf i! So beth ddigwyddodd?

Aneurin   All sorts. Ar un pryd o'dd 'da fi goc yn bob llaw, a'n un i mewn ceg. O'n i'n shiglo gyment, I could have been an epileptic.

Dada   Aneurin! Fucking hell!

Aneurin   Na, fucking heaven!

Rhys yn dychwelyd.

Rhys   Ma' fe 'di mynd.

Dada   Pwy? Gareth?

Rhys   Ie.

Aneurin   Gytre'?

Rhys   Na, X.

Curiad.

Rhys   With the fucking Rhiwbina firsts.

Curiad.

Dada   Could be worse.

Rhys   Shwt 'ny?

Dada   He could have gone with the seconds.

Curiad.

Aneurin   Beth ti moyn neud, cariad?

Rhys   Wel, sai'n mynd i redeg ar ôl e. Falle bo fi
'di bod bach yn fyrbwyll ond sa'i mynd i ymddiheuro. Sa'i mynd
i adel i fe ga'l y boddhad. Geith e neud fel mae e moyn, a fi 'fyd –
we're not tied at the hip, you know.

We can do as we please.

Curiad.

Aneurin   Ti moyn mynd i X, yn dwyt ti?

Rhys   Odw.

Dada   Oh shame. Mae'r cabaret ar fin dechre.

Aneurin   If you want to see bad make-up and miming, tro'r
volume lawr ar 'Dechrau Canu, Dechrau Canmol'.

Aneurin:
A thrwy'r drws â ni,
A'r drag queen
Yn rhochian ar ein holau

'Exit left the Three Muskequeers ...
Come on boys –
Let's 'ave a go on your swords!'

Cyn llabuddio

Dada   (*Yn canu*) 'I am what I am!'

Curiad.

Aneurin:
But now it's time to forget who we are ...

Mae Aneurin yn cymryd Ecstasy.
Mae curiadau Techno'n cynyddu.

Golygfa Pump

Club X, Charles Street.

Aneurin:
Lawr y grisie
I dywyllwch.
Mae'n dywyll yma.
Cancr ein rhywioldeb:
The ghost of lovers past.
Salwch meddwl lle bu saliva;
Wellwn ni fyth o'r feirws.
Munudau gwag,
Oriau o euogrwydd,
A diafoliaid y duwch yn dawnsio.
Pob cornel yn adrodd stori:
Of bankers, and sportsmen, and benefit thieves.
In here
Sex, not death,
Is the great leveller.
We are all but wankers,
This is the democracy of dicking around:
This is our 'poetics of promiscuity'.
Gofod gwag
Where the dark room used to be.
Gofod gwag a'r gwacter yn tyfu.
Goleuade llachar
Yn wincian Morse code:
SAVE OUR SOULS!
Ha, ha,
You stupid fuckers,
We've SOLD OUR SOULS:
Punt y peint ac
Enaid am E.
Mae pob Alice 'di byta'i chacen
And the house is about to explode.

Gareth   I love you, Rhys! I love you, Rhys!

Aneurin:
Spaniel cariadus
Yn rhuthro i gynnig ei foliant.

Gareth   I love you, I love you, I love you!

Aneurin:
Yn gi o dafod
Yn llyfu am faddeuant.
The lolloping, loveable …

Rhys   Gareth, ti'n hanging!

Aneurin:
A channwyll ei lygaid yn wenfflam:
Ffowc o goelcerth,
Dwy seren o serotonin.

Gareth   I love you! I love you! I love you!

Rhys   Wrth gwrs dy fod di. You're high as a kite. Nawr cer nôl i gyrato ar y podium. The BelAmi boy looks like he's missing you.

Gareth   Fi'n lyfo ti, Rhys!

Rhys   Gwed 'na wrthai pan ti'n sobor.

Gareth   Fi yn.

Rhys   Cer.

Gareth   Rhys!

Rhys   You're sweating all over me. Cer.

Aneurin:
Ac mae Gareth
Yn dychwelyd i'r dance floor
I ddawnsio ei ofid yn chwys.

Curiad.

Rhys   Paid â dweud dim byd.

Aneurin   Wedes i ddim.

Rhys   Ti moyn, though.

Aneurin   Odw i?

Rhys   Wyt.

Aneurin   Be' ti'n feddwl 'wi moyn dweud?

Rhys   Bo' fi'n anheg, yn afresymol ac yn hen fitch bossy.

Aneurin   Now, why would I want to go and say a thing like that?

Curiad.

Aneurin   It's 'cause you're turning thirty.

Rhys   Beth ma' hwnna i neud 'da fe.

Aneurin   Ti'n paranoid.

Rhys   Na. Fi'n realist.

Mae ffôn Aneurin yn dirgrynu.

Aneurin   Oh for fuck's sake.

Mae'n ei dynnu o'i boced i weld yn union pwy sy'n galw. Yna mae'n ei roi yn ôl heb ei ateb.

Rhys   Pwy yw hwnna?

Aneurin   Gad hi …

Curiad.

Rhys   Beth sy'n mynd 'mlaen?

Aneurin   It's fine. Ga'd hi.

Curiad.

Aneurin   Because 'out there', Rhys Thomas, 'out there, it's their time; in here, in here it's our time'.

Rhys   Have you just quoted *The Goonies*?

Aneurin   Totally.

Dada'n ymddangos.

Dada   Co fi!

Aneurin   Ti'n OK?

Dada   Odw! 'Wi newydd ga'l pi-pi drws nesa i un o'r gorillas. Y capten.

Rhys   King Kong?

Dada   Na, King Dong!

Rhys   Pam s'o nhw'n aros ar batchyn eu hunen?

Aneurin   Wedes di helo?

Dada   Na … jyst shiglo llaw. Cyn i fe ca'l cyfle i olchi'i ddwylo!

Aneurin   Dada!

Rhys   Chi moyn dawnso?

Aneurin   Odw. I'm coming up. Dada?

Dada   Be'?

Aneurin   Dance floor?

Dada   Ie.

Mae curiadau Techno'n cynyddu.

Aneurin:
'Ie' fach ac mae'r frwydr yn cychwyn.
'Ie' fach ac ymlaen â ni i'r gâd.
Un sgwâr fach o dir gwastad:
Tirwedd ein mebyd,
Haen o Smirnoff Ice
Yn sugno ein sodlau,
Wrth i ryfel y ddawns gydio.
Because sometimes, damn it, it is.
It's war.
Survival of the fucking fittest.
Between the Straights and the Gays,
the Jocks and the Geeks,
the Bears, the Cubs and the Chasers,

the BelAmi Twinks and the Triga Chavs,
the Butch Dykes and the Lipstick Femmes,
the Spice Girls and the Spice Boys,
the Emos and Goths and
the Queens, the Welshies a fi.

Fi.
Achos heno,
Heno, hen blant bach,
Fi yw'r fucking fittest!

It's in my blood.
It's in my genes.
What's in your genes?
What's in your jeans?

Pennau i lawr a …
Cloi!
Breichiau'n …
Cloi!
Scrum yn granc o gnawd
Yn symud yn
Igam-ogam,
O gam, i gam,
O gam, igam-ogam.
Beat.
Curo?
Curiad.
Curiad ein cariad,
Un cranc mawreddog o gariad.
Nid brwydr yw hon mwyach
Ond cymundeb ein brawdoliaeth.

A co fe'n dod:
The final push,
Yes, yes …
YES!

Mae'r curiadau Techno'n cyrraedd uchafbwynt.

And we're off,

We're going for it,
The multiple beats of our maswedd:
Mwy, mwy, mwy,
Ymlaen, ymlaen, ymlaen.
Dwylo'n ymestyn i'r awyr yn crafangu am atebion –
Ein gweddïau seciwlar anweledig.
Tonight we are Gods!
Pob un ohonom,
Pob un wan jac.
Pob un wanker.

Yn un anadl,
We take a breather.
Mae'r miwsig yn suo ein seibiant.

Mae yna elfen o ffantasi i'r cyfnewid yma.

Gavin   Helô.

Dada   Fi?

Gavin   Ie. Ti!

Dada   Helô.

Gavin   Ti yw ffrind Mr Thomas, nag ife?

Dada   Ie. A chi yw Thelma. Lle mae Louise?

Gavin   A'th hi off gyda Brad Pitt. Dwi'n hoffi feather boa ti.

Dada   Wel diolch.

Aneurin:
Hanner amser.
Ond gêm o ddwy hanner fydd hon.

Mae'r golau'n newid.

Dada   A 'na le o'n i 'da Lorraine Kelly ar un fraich a Barbara Windsor ar y llall yn canu *Brown Girl in the Ring* i Floella Benjamin. Jiw, gethon ni sbort. Ydych chi'n lico musicals?

Gavin   Caru nhw. *Moulin Rouge* yw favourite movie fi.

Dada   Jiw, jiw – a fi. Nid sioe gerdd draddodiadol wrth gwrs ond eithafol yn yr un modd. (*Yn canu*) 'Come what may! Come what may!' Wyddoch chi mai dyna yw hoff gân karaoke Mr Thomas? Mae wedi ennill sawl tro gyda honno.

Gavin   Mae Mr Thomas yn canu?

Dada   O, odi. Just fel Barbara Streisand, heb y trwyn.

Gavin   'Sen i'n lyfo gweld hwnna: Mr Thomas yn canu'r best song o *Moulin Rouge*.

Dada   Falle bod nhw'n sporty ond ma' Australians hefyd yn gw'bod shwt ma' bod yn camp. *Muriel's Wedding* – 'na chi glasur!

Gavin   A Kylie Minogue!

Dada   A Kylie Minogue, yn union. A ma' 'da hi waed Cymraeg.

Gavin   Ie ond s'o Cymru mor dda am neud camp.

Dada   Good God, odi: Jenny Ogwen, Heulwen Hâf … mae'n siŵr ma'r Cymry a'th â camp i wlad yr Aborigini 'da'r convicts.

Gavin   Jenny who?

Dada   Dim ots.

Gavin   Fi'n hoffi camp.

Dada   Alla'i weld 'ny.

Gavin   A fi'n hoffi musicals. (*Yn canu*) 'I will love you until my dying day'!

Dada   'Na lais pert sy' 'da chi! Musicals o'n i'n arfer neud. 'Nes i rannu llwyfan 'da Elaine Page.

Gavin   Serious?

Dada   Do, *Cats*. Am flwyddyn gyfan 'nes i fewian yn bwsi bach yn gyfeiliant i'w Grizabella.

Gavin   O't ti yn *Cats*? Ma' hwnna'n amazing. Fi'n caru *Cats*. Pan fi'n marw fi moyn Elaine Page yn canu *Memory* pan fi'n cael fy cremato. Bydd e'n really touching fi'n meddwl.

Curiad.

Gavin   Beth ti moyn pan ti'n cael dy cremato?

Dada   *Wonderwoman.*

Saib.

Dada   Neu *O'r Fan Acw*, Margaret Williams. Always gets me.

Curiad.

Gavin   Beth arall ti wedi bod yn?

Dada   Wel bues i yn *Starlight Express* am wythnos ond ges i hernia. Sa'i 'di bod ar rollerskates ers 'ny. Dwi'n ei chael hi'n anodd gwylio *Dancing on Ice* ... flashbacks. Ond y peth gore o'dd *West Side Story*. Fues i'n Jet wyddoch chi.

Gavin   You're joking! Pan o'n i'n fach o'n i'n like totally ffansïo pawb o' nhw, Jets a Sharks, a methu penderfynu pwy oedd favourite fi.

Dada   Cariad, what do you think press night is for? Try them all!

Mae Gavin yn chwerthin.

Gavin   Ti'n funny.

Dada   Chi'n annwyl. Ewch chi'n bell.

Gavin   Pam ti'n galw fi'n 'chi'?

Dada   Dwi'n eich parchu chi.

Gavin   Ond chi'n much older na fi.

Dada   Dim ond mewn oedran, darling boy. Dwi'n ifanc fy ysbryd.

Gavin   Ti eisiau cael sex gyda fi?

Dada   Good God, nagw. Dwi'n ddigon hen i fod yn dad i chi.

Gavin   Fi'n lico chi'n galw fi'n 'chi'! Fi'n teimlo'n posh. The other day, es i mewn i Burger King a wedodd y fenyw 'What can I get you, sir?' Sir! Yn Burger King! As if I were the friggin' king!

I've never been called 'sir' before. Neu 'chi'. Fi'n lico fe. Mae fel bod ni'n byw yn y 1920s neu rhywbeth.

Dada   Hoffech chi ddiod, syr?

Gavin   Ie plîs … Hoff … af?

Dada   Wel fe gewch â chroeso? Lager?

Gavin   WKD blue?

Dada   Na Gavin, ry'ch chi'n rhy ddiwylliedig i fwynhau diod sy'n staenio'ch dannedd yn las.

Gavin   Ydw i?

Dada   Ydych.

Gavin   Ok, um … martini? Neu gin a … thonic?

Dada   Www, da, Gavin. Treiglad llaes penigamp.

Gavin   Mae Cymraeg yn weird, nagyw e? Much as I like the 'ti's and 'chi's and all that, mae jyst yn neud pethau'n complicated. It just gets in the way. Nagwyt ti'n meddwl?

Dada   Mae parch yn bwysig.

Gavin   Ie ond mae'n like bod e'n rhoi airs and graces i pobol who *don't* deserve it, fel. Like half the teachers in my school are wankers. Why should they be 'chi'? Not Mr Thomas, wrth gwrs, mae fe'n brilliant, he's a total 'chi', but there's other ones sy' ddim, a fi'n pissed off bod fi'n gorfod rhoi respect i nhw, specially pan mae nhw'n fforso ti i neud. So then I don't want to play by their rules. If pawb was 'ti' falle bydd mwy o pobol yn siarad e.

Dada   Chi'n hen gommunist bach, yn dy'chi?

Gavin   Ond mae'n piso fi off, fel. Like pam mae'n rhaid i pob gair bod yn benywaidd neu gwrywaidd? Mae'n sexist.

Dada   Ma' rhai yn gallu bod yn fenywaidd ac yn wrywaidd, Gavin.

Gavin   Really?

Dada   Really.

Gavin   Mae Cymraeg yn queer?

Dada   Yn gallu bod.

Gavin   Wicked.

Curiad.

Ond beth am y gair 'gay' yn Cymraeg … gwrw … gwrw-thingy?

Dada   … gydiwr. Gwrwgydiwr.

Gavin   Ie, that's it. Gwrwgydiwr! Man-gripper. What's that about? Makes me sound like a JCB.

Dada   Beth am hoyw?

Gavin   That's equally shit.

Dada   Pam?

Curiad.

Gavin   Mae'n soundo'n gay.

Curiad.

Gavin   Beth yw'r gair Cymraeg am camp?

Curiad.

Dada   Derek Brockway?

Gavin   No wonder fi'n confused.

Aneurin:
Ac o bell,
Dwi'n arolygu'r olygfa.
Dacw Dada,
Lawr ar y soffa,
Yn ymofyn am noddfa anaddas
Yr ieuainc wrth yr hen.

Mae Dada'n dychwelyd at Gavin â dau gin a thonic.

Dada   Co chi.

Gavin   Diolch. Ooh, umbrella and everything.

Dada   Wrth gwrs.

Gavin   (*Yn canu*) 'I'm singin' in the rain, just singin' in the rain'!

Gavin/   (*Yn canu gyda'i gilydd*)
Dada   'What a glorious feeling, I'm happy again' …

Gavin   Ok. Gene Kelly neu … Fred Astaire?

Dada   Gene Kelly, bob tro.

Gavin   Pam?

Dada   Dannedd gwell. Ac ma' unrhyw un sy'n gallu dawnsio fel 'na pan fo'r ffliw arnyn nhw yn haeddu moliant i'r eithaf. Pan wi'n ca'l y ffliw mae'n struggle i fi ddeialu 'This Morning'.

Curiad.

Gavin   Pam ma' nhw'n galw ti'n Dada?

Dada   Achos dwi'n hen.

Gavin   Na ti ddim. Pwy mor hen wyt ti?

Dada   Pa fath o gwestiwn yw hwnna i ofyn i lady?

Gavin   Go on.

Curiad.

Dada   Pedwar deg naw.

Gavin   Bloody hell. Ti *yn* digon hen i fod yn dad fi.

Dada   Charming.

Gavin   Ond ti'n edrych yn good, though. Beth yw secret ti?

Dada   *Oil of Olay.*

Gavin   Serious?

Dada   Serious. And I drink my own pee.

Gavin   SHUT UP!

Dada   Dwi'n jocan, Gavin bach.

Gavin   O, reit.

Saib.

Gavin   Falle bod ti'r un age ond ti ddim yn cock though.

Dada   Pardwn?

Gavin   Dad fi. Oedd e'n right knob-end.

Dada   Iaith, Gavin.

Gavin   Sori. Pen pidyn oedd fy Dad.

Dada   Nage, Gavin. Sdim isie'r fath iaith frwnt.

Gavin   Ond oedd e! Oedd e'n right pen pidyn.

Dada   Falle o'dd e …

Gavin   Fucking bully.

Dada   Ond y'ch chi'n fonheddwr, a dyw bonheddwyr ddim yn rhegi.

Curiad.

Gavin   Sai'n bonheddwr.

Dada   Ydych. Ma' nhw 'di dweud, yn Burger King.

Curiad.

Gavin   Ie. Fi yn! Fi'n bonheddwr.

Curiad.

Gavin   Dad fi yw'r knob-end.

Curiad.

Gavin   Sori.

Curiad.

Gavin   So how come ti'n edrych mor ifanc? Botox?

Dada   Botox?! Who needs botox when you've got disco. Mae'n cadw fi'n ifanc. Mae'r ifanc yn fy nghadw i'n ifanc. A'r ddinas.

Gavin   Fi moyn mynd i Llunden.

Dada   Cerwch, fyddwch chi wrth eich bodd.

Gavin   So pam des di nôl 'te?

Curiad.

Dada   O'dd mam yn dost.

Gavin   Yw hi'n OK nawr?

Dada   Na, mae 'di marw.

Gavin   Fi'n sori.

Dada   Jiw, jiw, ma' sbel ers 'ny.

Gavin   Ond mae dal yn sad.

Dada   Odi, mae dal yn sad.

Saib.

Gavin   Ti'n colli Llundain?

Dada   Ddim o gwbwl. O'dd hi'n amser gadel. 'All good things must come to an end'.

Gavin   So what is there after all good things come to an end?

Curiad.

Dada   Caerdydd.

Gavin   How depressing.

Dada   O na, Gavin bach. There's no place like …

Mae Rhys a Gareth mewn rhan arall o'r clwb.

Gareth   Home?

Rhys   Glywes di fi.

Gareth   It's not time yet.

Rhys   Odi ma' fe.

Gareth   Duncan's having a party.

Rhys   Wel cer i hwnna, a a' i gytre'.

Gareth   Come with me.

Rhys   Gareth, I don't like them. They're pricks.

Gareth   Just for a bit.

Rhys   Wel os ti jyst moyn mynd am bit, 'run man i ni fynd gytre'. Gareth, stop gurning.

Gareth   I'm not gurning.

Rhys   Yes, you are. You're champing at the bit.

Gareth   Please. Dere.

Rhys   You only want their drugs.

Gareth   You weren't complaining earlier.

Rhys   That was before your face contracted Parkinsons.

Gareth   I'm off then. I'll see you tomorrow.

Rhys   Fine.

Gareth   Fine.

Rhys   Fine.

Gareth   Fine.

Curiad.

Gareth   Please. Dere.

Saib.

Rhys   Fine.

Mae Aneurin ar y balconi.

Aneurin:
Dacw Dada'n dŵad

Dros ben y Gavin wen.
Rhys bach yn pregethu
A'r piss 'di mynd i'w ben.

Yr ieuainc wrth yr hen,
A melltith ar fy ngwefus.

Mae Dada, wedi'i wisgo fel Margaret Williams, yn ymddangos.

Oh my God,
I think that's my mother climbing out of the cigarette machine.
I'm fucked.

– Hia Mami,

– Ti'n OK?

– Just look at what your little boy's up to.

– He's looking for cock.

And her tears fall like loose change.

Mae Dada'n canu pennill a chytgan olaf **O'r Fan Acw (From a Distance).**

Mae'r gerddoriaeth yn parhau'n dyner. Mae'n cymryd sigarét ac yn cynnig un i Aneurin.

Sigarét?

Aneurin   S'o ni'n ca'l smoco mewn fan hyn.

Mam   'Na drueni.

Aneurin   Mami, s'o ti'n lico smoco.

Mam   Ond mae'n special occasion. Yndyw hi?

Mae Rhys yn ymuno ag Aneurin ar y balconi.

Rhys   Aneurin? Aneurin?

Mae Aneurin yn chwerthin.

Rhys   Beth? Aneurin?

Aneurin   Oh my God, I'm tripping.

Rhys   (*gan ddynwared* Mama Fratelli *o'r ffilm* The Goonies)
Come to Mama.

Aneurin   Aww … (*gan ddynwared* Sloth) Mama!

Rhys   (*Heb ddynwared*) Mae Mama'n gorfod gad'el.

Aneurin   (*gan ddynwared* Sloth) Mama! No! Pam?

Rhys   Gareth moyn mynd i after-party Duncan. Ma' isie cadw
llygad arno fe.

Aneurin   Ma' isie cadw llygad arna i.

Rhys   Dere 'da ni …

Aneurin   Na, peidiwch mynd!

Rhys   (*gan ddynwared eto*) Aww, nawr, nawr, Slothi bach. (*Yn
canu*)
  'Rock a bye baby on the tree top
  When the wind blows the cradle will' …

Aneurin   (*Yn canu*)
  'Rhaid gwisgo cot,
  Rhaid gwisgo het
  Rhaid rhoddi maneg ar bob llaw' …

  Ti'n cofio?

Rhys   (*Yn canu*)
  'Dweud dabo i'n hysgol ni
  A dweud helo wrth mami'.

Aneurin/
Rhys   (*Y ddau yn canu*)
  'Helô, helô.   A dweud helo wrth mami'.

Curiad.

Aneurin   I've just seen my mother.

Rhys   Ble?

Aneurin   Dath hi mas o'r cigarette machine yn canu *O'r Fan
Acw.*

Curiad.

Aneurin   Gynigodd hi Marlborough light i fi. O'dd e'n beautiful.

Rhys   Cariad.

Saib.

Aneurin   Do you think they can smell it on me?

Rhys   Pwy?

Aneurin   Sometimes I think I don't sweat pheromones. I just excrete all those little pieces of men that I have ever loved. And everyone can smell it, it puts people off.

Rhys   Paid bod yn soft. 'Na'r peth mwyaf stupid 'wi erio'd 'di glywed.

Aneurin   Is it?

Curiad.

Rhys   Beth sy'n mynd 'mla'n?

Aneurin   Dim.

Rhys   Liar.

Saib.

Rhys   Dere nôl.

Aneurin   'Wi moyn aros 'ma.

Rhys   Na, i Gymru. For good.

Aneurin   Sa'i moyn.

Rhys   Ti 'di bod yn tempo am dair blynedd.

Aneurin   'Wi di bod yn sgwennu am dair blynedd.

Rhys   Alle ti 'di neud 'ny fan hyn.

Aneurin   No I couldn't. I fucking hate Cardiff.

Mae Gareth yn ymuno â nhw.

Gareth   How are we?

Aneurin   Brilliant. Never been better.

Curiad.

Rhys   Gareth, ti'n meindio os aroson ni am dym' bach …

Aneurin   And cramp my style? 'Scuse me Mr Thomas but I want to be naked by the end of the night.

Rhys   'Se fe'n ddim byd fi heb weld o'r bla'n.

Aneurin   Oh it would be – 'wi 'di dysgu cwpwl o bethe ers o'n i'n bymtheg.

Gareth   (*dim malais*) Like how to avoid premature ejaculation perhaps?

Aneurin   Cheeky. That wasn't premature ejaculation – that was your vigorous boyfriend!

Rhys   Yes, but we were on the school bus. You could have told me in time!

Gareth   Euuugh!

Aneurin   A Erfyl Clements, poor dab, what he must have thought when he put on his parka.

Gareth   Oh my god, you ming.

Aneurin   Boy's got to do what a boy's got to do. Talking of which, go on, cerwch!

Rhys   Sa'i moyn gad'el ti.

Aneurin   'Wi'n fine.

Rhys   S'o ti'n fine. He's hallucinating, Gareth.

Gareth   What you seeing?

Aneurin   Miracles. Go, please, go.

Rhys   Ti'n siŵr ti'n OK?

Aneurin   Oh God, ydw. The night is but young!

Rhys Wnawn ni gysgu yn fflat Dada as planned, though. Wnai frecwast i ni gyd.

Aneurin I might not come home.

Gareth Well make sure you come round for breakfast 'cause I'll want a full report.

Aneurin What if I'm in the arms of a handsome stranger?

Gareth I'll eat your sausage.

Rhys Right, come on Gareth Lloyd. Ta-ra, cariad.

Aneurin Ta-ra, twat.

Gareth a Rhys yn gadael.

Aneurin:
So this is it:
Isn't he sexy!
Isn't he clever!
Isn't he wonderful!
I'm a coked up cock.
My genes are leading me ar gyfeiliorn.
Dwi'n barod am gyflafan.

Mae Dada a Gavin mewn rhan arall o'r clwb.

Gavin Wel sai'n surprised 'nes di adel.

Dada Dim dewis nethon ni, o'dd rhaid i ni adel. Does dim byd yn bod 'da tai cyngor, Gavin.

Gavin Yes but you deserve better. I deserve better.

Dada Pwy sy'n dweud?

Gavin Fi. I'm made for great things. I'm going to where the streets are paved with gold!

Dada Peidiwch â chael eich denu gan y palmant aur. Ma' gymaint o bobol yn mynd 'na am yr un reswm mae'n bur debyg welwch chi ddim mohoni: gormod o draed.

Curiad.

Dada   Chi'n gweld, Gavin, yn y bôn yn y Billy Banks o'n i
hapusa. Gadel fynna o'dd dechrau'r diwedd i Mami. A chi'n
gw'bod beth sy'n neud fi'n fwy crac? 'Sei 'di gallu aros 'na tan
y diwedd. Nethon nhw ddim byd 'da'r lle tan yn ddiweddar. Jyst
gad'el iddo bydru 'da'r blodau gwyllt a'r chwyn. Cofiwch chi, fe
wrthododd pedwar teulu bach symud. Real pen-tost i'r cyngor.

Gavin   Dyle chi 'di gwrthod symud 'fyd 'te!

Dada   Dreion ni, Gavin bach, ond do'dd dim dewis. Nid ni o'dd
berchen y fflat. Billy Banks *vs.* Penarth Heights: Dafydd yn erbyn
Goliath.

Gavin   Mae fel y Golden yn erbyn John Lewis, yn dyw e? Mae'n
edrych mor funny next door i fe. Like a runt.

Dada   Yn union. Ch'wel – llathen o'r un brethyn y'n ni i gyd
really. (*Yn canu*)
   'Ry'n ni yma o hyd,
   Ry'n ni yma o hyd!'

Gavin   Dafydd Iwan?

Dada   Da iawn, Gavin!

Gavin   Dafydd Iwan sucks.

Curiad.

Gavin   Beth fi ddim yn deall yw pam o'n nhw moyn aros yna?
With the blodau gwyllt?

Dada   The best views in Cardiff.

Gavin   Dim o'r outside.

Dada   O Gavin bach, os ots beth sydd ar y tu fas pan o'r tu fewn
mae'r byd yn edrych yn brydferth?

Mae Aneurin yn ymuno â nhw.

Aneurin   Co fi!

Dada   The wanderer returns! Lle ti 'di bod?

Aneurin   Cruising.

Dada   Unrhyw sailors?

Aneurin   Digon.

Dada   Ti'n cofio Gavin?

Aneurin   Shwt allen i anghofio Gavin?

Gavin   Haia.

Aneurin   Hello sailor …

Dada   S'o fe'n ddigon hen i fod yn sailor.

Aneurin   How about a cabin boy?

Gavin   I don't like the sea.

Aneurin   But think of the fun we would have hunting together.

Gavin   Hunting?

Aneurin   Moby.

Gavin   Moby?

Aneurin   Dick.

Curiad.

Dada   Hoffech chi ddrink arall, Gavin? fennoch chi hwnna'n gloi …

Aneurin   And seamen.

Dada   'Na ddigon, Aneurin.

Gavin   Ti'n gross.

Aneurin   'Na beth ma' profiad yn neud i chi … a oedran.

Curiad.

Aneurin   That's why Dada's filthy.

Dada   Woah!

Aneurin   Jôc fach, Dada. Ti'n dod 'ma'n aml 'te, Gavin?

Gavin   Twice a month, fel. Does dim byd yn Bargoed. Fel arfer fi just yn mynd i Wow a Pulse.

Aneurin   Tro nesa ddei di lawr a'i â ti i *Come to Daddy*.

Gavin   *Come to Daddy*?!

Aneurin   They would *love* you there!

Gavin   Beth yw hwnna?

Aneurin   'A night for bears and their admirers'. Ti'n ormod o twink i fod yn cub but you could be a chaser.

Gavin   Sai'n really hoffi bears.

Aneurin   'Sen i ddim chwaith 'sen i'n byw fan hyn. Yn Llunden, Bears are real Bears: beefy, hairy, sexy. Yn Nghaerdydd, Bears are just men who've let themselves go.

Gavin   Sa'i 'di bod i Llunden 'to.

Aneurin   'Na le 'wi'n byw.

Gavin   Wow. Cool. Beth ti'n gwneud?

Dada   Tempo.

Aneurin   Sgwennu llyfr.

Gavin   Really?! Sa'i 'di cwrdd gyda real live author o'r blaen. Beth mae llyfr ti am?

Aneurin   O, dim byd sbesial: time travel, one night stands, hen fyddin Gymraeg yn llawn cwplau hoyw.

Gavin   Serious?!

Aneurin   Serious. O' nhw'n fwy ffyrning nag unrhyw fyddin arall because they fought for their … (*yn anwesu'r gair gyda'i dafod*) lovers.

Gavin   Wow. How sexy is that!

Aneurin   Very.

Dada   Dyw rhyfel ddim yn sexy.

Gavin   Mae soldiers yn.

Aneurin   With shiny great swords!

Gavin   And gorgeous bodies!

Dada   Often attached to no head.

Aneurin   Who needs a head when you've got an arse.

Dada   'Na hen ddigon, Aneurin.

Gavin   Ti *yn* gross.

Aneurin   You love it really. I think we're quite a match.

Dada   Pwy sydd isie diod?

Aneurin   'Wi'n iawn diolch.

Dada   Gavin? Ginsen arall.

Aneurin   Beth ti'n treial neud Dada, get the boy pissed?

Gavin   Sai'n pissed. Fi'n gallu dal drink fi.

Dada   Gwnewch ffafr i Dada, os rhoia'i arian i chi, wnewch chi fynd i'r bar?

Aneurin   A' i. Ga' i hwn.

Dada   'Wi'n siŵr neith Gavin …

Aneurin   A' i.

Dada   Fine. Cer di.

Aneurin   Beth ti moyn?

Curiad.

Aneurin   Chaser?

Curiad.

Dada   Actually, ti'n gw'bod be'? Dwi wedi blino. 'Wi'n credu a'i gytre'.

Gavin   Paid mynd gytre'.

Dada   It's past Dada's bedtime.

Gavin   It's past my bedtime!

Dada   Yn union, Gavin. Mi oedd hi'n bleser pur ca'l cwrdd â chi. R'ych chi'n ddyn bonheddig ac yn gredit i'ch mam. Aneurin, fydd yr allwedd yn y lle arferol.

Aneurin   Paid mynd, Dada. Sori.

Gavin   Chi 'di arguo?

Dada   Naddo, Gavin.

Gavin   Pam ti'n gweud sori?

Dada   Ma' Aneurin yn aml yn dweud sori.

Mae Dada'n gadael.

Gavin   Sai'n deall.

Aneurin   He's just pissed.

Gavin   O ti'n windo fe lan, nagot ti?

Aneurin   Nagon.

Gavin   Pam ti'n windo ffrindiau ti lan?

Curiad.

Aneurin   Shut up and dance with me.

Golygfa Chwech

Tŷ Duncan Colefield.
Mae Gareth a Rhys yn cyrraedd.

Terry   Gar!

Gareth   Terr!

Terry   And Rudolph!

Rhys   Wedes i.

Gareth   Don't call him Rudolph, Terr.

Terry   Rhys!

Rhys   (*yn wawdlyd*) Terr!

Gareth   (*yn ceryddu*) Rhys …

Daw Duncan i mewn.

Duncan   Gar!

Gareth   Dunc!

Duncan   Rudolph!

Rhys   (*yn yr un cywair*) Twat!

Duncan   What d'you say?

Gareth   Don't call him Rudolph, Dunc. He's sensitive.

Rhys   I'm not sensitive. I'm nearly thirty. Gareth, ni'n mynd.

Gareth   We're not going, we've only just got here.

Duncan   Come on, mate, I was only joking. I can be sensitive too.

Terry   That's 'cause you're circumcised.

Duncan   Fuck off.

Gareth   You Jewish?

Duncan   Do I look Jewish?

Rhys   Well, now that you mention it, ma' 'na debygrwydd rhwng ti a Anne Frank.

Duncan   Who's Frank?

Mae pawb yn chwerthin.

Duncan   Who's fucking Frank? Don't speak that fucking Welsh shit. Who's fucking Frank?

Terry   It's alright Dunc – have a tequila.

Aneurin:
Tequilas yn tywallt.
Elicsir alcohol
Yn gwasgaru'r sgyrnygu.
Dau dîm yn un am ennyd.

Club X.

Gavin   Aneurin?

Aneurin   Ie?

Gavin   Ble ti wedi bod? Ti'n totally zono mas, fel.

Aneurin   Dunno. I was away with the fairies.

Curiad.

Aneurin   Ti moyn dod nôl 'da fi, Gavin?

Gavin   Ie. Ie, bydd hwnna'n cŵl.

Charles Street.
A minnau a Gavin yn esgyn o uffern
I nefoedd y stryd.
Duwiau ac angylion
Yn chwilio am adennydd.
Llygaid gwydrog
Yn ysu am adlewyrchiad,
Unrhyw fath o adlewyrchiad,
Rhyw fymryn o adlais:
Plîs, plîs, plîs
Gwêl fi, gwêl fi;
Nid yr wyneb gorffwyll,
Ond yr enaid pur.
Gorffwylltra chwant
Mor amlwg yn y gofyn.

Aneurin   OK?

Gavin   Yeah.

Aneurin:
Tacsi o wyrth

Fel seren yn y tywyllwch,

   – You free, mate?

Yn ein tywys,
Ni,
Y nefol rai,
Yn ôl i

   – Celestia, cheers pal.

Curiad.

Aneurin   *– Ie, good. Cheers, mate.*

   – Busy tonight?

   – Been out long?

   – Finishing late?

   – Didn't think we'd get a taxi.

   – Nah, I didn't watch it.

   – No I like Rugby. I just don't like Wales.

Ac wrth i'r car wibio
Lawr heol Bute i'r bae,
Mae Gavin yn gafael:
Llaw yn lleddfu'r ing nas ynganwyd.
Bachgen
Yn dangos beth yw e,
I fod yn ddyn.

   – Here's fine, drive.

Fflat Dada, Celestia.

Gavin   Wow! Ma'r lle 'ma'n lysh.

Aneurin   Yndyw e?

Gavin   Mae mor tidy. Mor …

Aneurin   Let's have a drink. Ti isie drink?

Yn sydyn.

Gavin   Oh my God, nath e ddim dweud fod e 'di cwrdd â Liza Minnelli.

Aneurin   O, s'o hwnna'n ddim byd. Ma' llun o fe 'da Joan Collins yn y bathroom.

Gavin   No way!

Aneurin   A weda'i beth arall sy' 'da fe yn y bathroom – un o'r knitted ladies 'na yn sgwoto dros y bog roll yn cadw fe'n gynnes.

Gavin   Posh!

Aneurin   O ie. Dada's done very well for himself. Ddylet ti 'di weld lle o'dd e'n arfer byw.

Gavin   Billy Banks?

Aneurin   Shwt ti'n gw'bod ymbiti'r Billy Banks?

Gavin   Wedodd e wrtha'i.

Curiad.

Aneurin   Absolute hellhole but it had the most amazing view of Cardiff. Fel bod yn uffern yn edrych mas ar y nefodd.

Gavin   O'dd Dada'n hoffi fe, nagodd e?

Aneurin   O'dd. Dwli arno fe. Nath e ffws mawr yn gadel: ganodd e *Don't Cry for me Argentina* a chaino'i hunan i'r railings. Terribly dramatic.

Gavin   Wow.

Aneurin   'Na le fenno' ni lan y noson netho' ni gyd gwrdd. Wedodd e 'na wrthot ti?

Gavin   Ie, a bod Mr Thomas wedi ennill karaoke competition yn y Golden yn canu'r song yna o *Moulin Rouge* a bod boyfriend e wedi cwympo mewn cariad gyda fe 'cause mae'n amazing yn canu.

Aneurin   Ti 'di ca'l y life story?

Gavin   Ie. Fi'n credu bod e more cute bod Geraint byth wedi bod allan ar y scene o'r blaen …

Aneurin   Gareth.

Gavin   … Ie, Gareth, a bod e wedi cwrdd gyda chi lot a bod Mr Thomas wedi canu favourite cân fi o *Moulin Rouge* a dyna beth oedd wedi gwneud Geraint …

Aneurin   … Gareth.

Gavin   Gareth yn gay.

Curiad.

Aneurin   Ti'n nervous?

Gavin   Na.

Curiad.

Aneurin   Breathe.

Gavin   Ok.

Curiad.

Aneurin   Y Billy Banks is where they first snogged. Nath Dada mynnu mynd â ni 'na achos o'dd hi'n ten year anniversary ers i fe gael ei dywlu mas. Ma' Gareth a Rhys yn dal yn mynd nôl 'na bob blwyddyn. Ma' nhw'n credu bod 'da'r lle mystical powers. Twats.

Gavin   Mae fel the beginning of *Rent.*

Aneurin   Rent?

Gavin   Ie. Y musical. 'Forces are gathering' mae'r cân cyntaf yn dweud … Loads o bobol cool yn dod at ei gilydd ac yn …

Aneurin   Marw o AIDS?

Gavin   S'o nhw gyd yn marw o AIDS.

Aneurin   Singing with too much vibrato?

Gavin   S'o ti'n hoffi musicals?

Aneurin   Na. They're ridiculous.

Gavin   Life is ridiculous!

Aneurin   Well don't make it worse by singing about it.

Curiad.

Gavin   Ma' canu'n cool.

Saib.

Aneurin   By the way, paid ti â galw e'n Dada. I don't think he'd like it. Dim ond ni sy'n galw e'n Dada.

Gavin   Oh, OK.

Saib.

Gavin   Mae Mr Thomas a Gareth eitha different, yndyn nhw?

Aneurin   Odyn.

Gavin   But it works.

Aneurin   Ambell waith.

Gavin   Pwy mor hir mae nhw wedi bod together?

Aneurin   Tair blynedd.

Curiad.

Gavin   I can't believe this place!

Aneurin   Indeed. I blame Elaine Page – she gave him ideas above his station.

Gavin   Beth mae job fe?

Aneurin   Singing teacher.

Gavin   Really? Ti'n credu bydd e moyn rhoi gwersi i fi?

Aneurin   Fi'n siŵr bydde fe moyn rhoi gwersi i ti. Drink?

Gavin   Cool.

Mae Aneurin yn estyn potel champagne a dau wydr.

Curiad.

Gavin   Ydi hwn yn iawn?

Aneurin   Beth?

Gavin   Fi fan hyn.

Aneurin   Wrth gwrs bod e. Dyw Dada byth yn meindo fi'n dod â pobol nôl.

Gavin   Slag! A fi'n meddwl bod fi'n special.

Aneurin   Mi wyt ti, Gavin bach. mi wyt ti.

Mae Aneurin yn dangos y botel i Gavin.

  Bollinger?

Gavin   Oh my God! There's posh! Beth ni'n celebrato?

Curiad.

Aneurin   Ti.

Mae'n tywallt dau gwydraid ac yn cynnig un i Gavin.

Aneurin   Llwncdestun … i Gavin.

Gavin   I fi.

Aneurin   Good boy.

Gavin   Wow. Ma' hwn yn blydi lysh. Ti'n spoilo fi.

Aneurin   Wedes i dy fod ti'n special. Take a bump with me?

Gavin   Bump?

Aneurin   Of coke. 'Na gyd sy' 'da fi ar ôl.

Gavin   Fydda'i off face fi!

Aneurin   And what a beautiful face it is too. Co ti.

Maent yn cymryd 'bump' o cocaine.

Gavin   Woah!

Aneurin   Ie, woah … here we go …

Tŷ Duncan Colefield.
Curiadau Techno.

Duncan   Turn it up! I loves this tune.

Gareth   Me too.

Terry   Me three.

Duncan   Pass the spliff.

Rhys   Gareth …

Gareth   Beth?

Rhys   Pass the spliff.

Gareth   Sorry. Yeah. Nice one.

Terry   Let's get mashed!

Curiad.

Terry   Rhys?

Rhys   Ie?

Terry   Ti'n mashed?

Rhys   Sa'i 'di ca'l dim.

Terry   Thought you were having a whitey. S'o ti'n dweud lot.

Rhys   'Wi'n shy.

Duncan   Turn it up!

Gareth   You're *not* shy! Rhys is *amazing*, right. He's got the most stunning voice. I get goose bumps, don't I, Rhys? He's touring Taiwan next week with his choir, singing solo. He could have been professional but he wanted to be a teacher and not even in music. In maths! Can you believe that? He's the cleverest person I know, serious. And all the kids love him.

Duncan   Not too much, I hope. I've 'eard about them Welsh schools.

Terry   Ti'n dysgu maths and all the kids love you?

Gareth   Too right. Thirty-three kids are doing A-level this year –
most ever.

Terry   Who'd want to do maths?

Rhys   Who'd want to play Rugby?

Terry   No offence, mate, but maths isn't better than Rugby.
Imagine scoring a try for your country in the Millennium stadium.

Rhys   If it wasn't for maths there wouldn't be a Millennium
Stadium.

Terry   Alright, but I bet you like looking at those nice legs, eh?
Those nice, firm, strong legs. You don't get *them* in maths.

Rhys   Yes you do – Carol Vorderman.

Curiad.

Duncan   Fancy Carol Vorderman do you?

Rhys   No.

Duncan   How about you, Gareth?

Gareth   What?

Duncan   Carol Vorderman or Richard Whiteley?

Rhys   Gareth, gawn ni fynd?

Gareth   That's a stupid question.

Terry   No it's not. If you had to shag one of them, who would
you shag? Carol Vorderman or Richard Whiteley?

Mae Duncan yn dawnsio'n afreolus.

Rhys   Gareth, ni'n mynd.

Duncan   Come on, Gar, tell us. It's not that hard. Carol
Vorderman's far hotter than Clare Riley and you screwed her.

Rhys   Ma' hwn yn blentynaidd. Come on, Gareth.

Duncan   Who's under the thumb then?

Rhys   Lle ma' dy got di?

Terry   O ie? Rhys sy'n gwisgo'r trowsus ife? Didn't expect that …

Rhys   Be' ti'n feddwl wrth 'ny?

Gareth   He doesn't wear the trousers.

Rhys   Be' ti'n feddwl wrth 'ny?

Terry   Just not what I expected.

Gareth   He doesn't wear the trousers.

Duncan   (*gan glosio at Gareth*) Gareth and Carol sitting in a tree …

Rhys   Get off him.

Duncan   (*yn esgus ei gusanu*) K-I-S-S-I-N-G.

Rhys   I said get off 'im.

Duncan   Don't speak to me like that, you poof.

Gareth   He didn't mean it.

Rhys   I bloody well did.

Gareth   Cool 'ead now, Rhys.

Rhys   Cool head? Glywes di beth alwodd e fi?

Terry   Woah, boys, 'na ddigon.

Duncan   'Boys', that's debatable!

Gareth   What's that supposed to mean, Duncan?

Duncan   I wasn't talking about you, man. I loves you.

Mae Duncan yn cusanu Gareth ar ei wefusau'n chwareus.

Rhys   (*yn ei wthio*) How many times do I have to tell you …

Duncan   Don't fucking touch me.

Rhys   You're the one kissing my boyfriend.

Gareth   Leave it, Dunc. He didn't mean it.

Duncan   You calling me a poof?

Terry   Come on now, Dunc, no harm done.

Duncan   (*yn gafael yn Rhys gyda gwir fygythiad*) Are you fucking calling me a poof?

Saib.

Duncan   You're not even worth my fist, you cock.

Mae Duncan yn gollwng Rhys.

Duncan   Now fuck off out of my house.

Mae Rhys yn gadael. Mae Gareth yn dechrau ei ddilyn.

Duncan   Not you, Gar. You don't have to go.

Curiad.

Gareth   In answer to your question. Richard Whiteley. Every time. And he's actually dead, Duncan.

Mae Gareth yn gadael.

Fflat Dada, Celestia.

Gavin   Seriously, right, ti yw un o'r pobol mwyaf cool fi wedi cwrdd.

Aneurin   Ti'n rhy garedig.

Gavin   Fi eisiau mynd i Llunden a stuff. Ti'n gwneud rhywbeth ti'n caru. Fi really eisiau gwneud work fi'n caru. Fi ddim eisiau bod fel mam. Or at least, fi eisiau bod fel hi, ond yn gwneud work fi'n caru.

Aneurin   A ti'n meddwl bod rhaid mynd i Lunden i neud 'na?

Gavin   Well I'm hardly going to get on *Pobol y Cwm* am I, and every time anyone from our school tries adrodd yn y 'steddfod we never get through the rhagbrofion. Dyw cynghanedd ddim yn soundo'n neis gyda Cwm Rhymni accent, apparently. Middle-class twats.

Aneurin   Gavin, cam a gafodd.

Gavin   Yw hwnnan'n cynghanedd?

Aneurin   Ydi.

Gavin   Wow. Ti *yn* cool.

Aneurin   Na. I'm a middle-class twat.

Mae ffôn Aneurin yn dirgrynu.

Aneurin   Oh just fuck off!

Mae Aneurin yn diffodd y ffôn.

Gavin   Pwy oedd hwnna? Jealous boyfriend?

Aneurin   Na, Dad.

Gavin   Oh my God, ydi mam ti'n OK?

Aneurin   Pam ti'n gofyn 'na?

Gavin   Dada 'di dweud bod ti nôl achos …

Aneurin   O'dd dim hawl 'da fe 'weud 'na wrthot ti.

Gavin   Sori. Oh my God. Oh my God.

Aneurin   Gavin. Mae'n fine. Honestly. Mae jyst yn ffono i weld lle odw i.

Gavin   Ti eisiau mynd?

Aneurin   Pam bydden i eisiau mynd?

Gavin   Achos …

Aneurin   Sdim point mynd.

Gavin   Ond …

Aneurin   Sdim point.

Curiad.

Gavin   Ti jyst yn bod yn really brave, yn dwyt ti? 'Se mam fi'n dost fel 'na, sai'n gw'bod beth bysen i'n neud.

Aneurin   Poppers?

Mae'n tynnu potel fechan o'i boced.

Gavin   Poppers?

Aneurin   Ti'n teimlo'n neis?

Gavin   Fi'n teimlo'n lysh.

Aneurin   Os ti moyn teimlo'n fwy lysh, have some of these.

Gavin   Beth mae'n neud i ti?

Aneurin   Neud ti'n horny.

Curiad.

Gavin   Ni'n like totally flirto nagyn ni?

Aneurin   Ydyn.

Maent yn arogli'r poppers. Mae'r effaith yn eu taro'n syth.

Gavin   (*Yn awchu am gusan*) O!

Curiad.

Aneurin   Gavin?

Gavin   Ie?

Aneurin   S'o ti di bod 'da bachgen o'r bla'n wyt ti?

Gavin   Fi wedi.

Aneurin   Liar.

Gavin   Fi wedi.

Aneurin   Ti ddim. Alla'i 'weud. I can smell your fear.

Gavin   Fi wedi. I just haven't been with a man.

Aneurin   A ti isie?

Gavin   I'd like that very much.

Saib.

Aneurin   Cult yw e beth bynnag,

Gavin   What?

Aneurin   Y 'Steddfod. Yr Urdd a pethe. Freaky cult yw e.

Gavin   Cult?

Aneurin   Seriously. I Gymry, i Gyd-ddyn, i Grist …

Gavin   O, reit. Ie.

Aneurin   … and there's that fucking weird triangle banner thing mae'r plant yn gorfod sefyll o dan tra bod nhw'n adrodd geiriau s'o nhw'n really ddeall ac yn esgus chwarae emosiwn s'o nhw'n really teimlo. I mean mae'r cystadleuthau adrodd 'na dan ddeg – they're the ugliest things I've ever seen. It's like watching robots having a spaz out. (*Yn dynwared*) Y Mwnci!

Gavin   (*yn dynwared*) Y Bwdgi!

Aneurin   And that cerdd dant stuff. Fuck! U-GLY! And all those parents, cheering for their offspring, their devil's spawn. It's just like a fascist rally.

Curiad.

Aneurin   God. I'm bitter about something aren't I?

Gavin   Ha, ha, wyt. Ges di cam yr yr Eisteddfod?

Aneurin   Every bloody year. But that's got nothing to do with it.

Curiad.

Gavin   Beth yw cult anyway?

Aneurin   (*wedi meddwl*) Rhywbeth sy'n neud sens o'r tu fewn ond ddim o'r tu fas.

Saib.

Gavin   Mae pob iaith yn cult then.

Aneurin   Ie, I suppose so.

Gavin   Mr Urdd's got a lot to answer for.

Chwerthin.

Aneurin   Ti'n bert pan ti'n werthin.

Curiad.

Aneurin   Tri chynnig i Gymro.

Gavin   Beth?

Aneurin   Ma' 'da fi tym' bach o 'K'? I fennu'r noson.

Gavin   'K'?

Aneurin   Special 'K'?

Gavin   Not my thing. Oes gyda ti Rice Krispies yn lle?

Aneurin   Na, you fool, *Ketamin.*

Gavin   Oh, oh right! Ie. God, stupid fi. Right. Ie. Um, sai di neud hwnna o'r blaen. Chanise wedi. Nagyw e'n horse tranquilizer neu rhywbeth? Hi'n dweud bod e'n cool though. Ie. 'Se hwnna'n cool. Just tipyn, though, I suppose.

Aneurin   Falle ddylen ni ddim os nag 'yt ti 'di …

Gavin   O na, bydd e'n fine. I've done everything else. Bydd tipyn bach yn fine.

Aneurin   Sdim lot 'da fi ar ôl anyway.

Gavin   Wicked.

Mae Aneurin a Gavin yn cymryd Ketamin.

Aneurin   Alli di gadw cyfrinach?

Gavin   Ie.

Aneurin   Ti 'di clywed am gystadleuaeth y goron yn yr Eisteddfod?

Gavin   Yr urdd?

Aneurin   Na'r Genedlaethol. Gwobr am ysgrifennu. 'Wi'n mynd i gystadlu.

Gavin   Nofel ti?

Aneurin   Na, cerdd sy'n ennill y goron. Dwi'n sgwennu cerdd.

Gavin   Mewn cynghanedd?

Aneurin   Na. I hate cynghanedd.

Gavin   Beth mae am?

Aneurin   Gays.

Gavin   Gays?!

Aneurin   Ie. Fi, a Dada, a Gareth a Mr Thomas.

Gavin   Ti wedi ysgrifennu poem am Mr Thomas yn bod yn gay. Mae hwnna'n hilarious! Ydi e'n rude?

Aneurin   More cocks than you can shake an archdderwydd at.

Gavin   Oh my god! Nagyn nhw'n becso? Bydd Mr Thomas yn cael mewn so much trouble.

Aneurin   Dyw Mr Thomas ddim yn gwybod.

Gavin   Ond mae'n teacher. Beth sy'n digwydd os mae'n ennill?

Aneurin   S'o fe'n mynd i ennill, Gavin. They wouldn't dare.

Gavin   Fi moyn clywed peth!

Aneurin   Llanc hardd,
Mor lân, mor loyw.
Diniwed heb gelwydd na chas:
'Greddf gŵr, oed gwas'.

Gavin   Oh my god, mae hwnna'n brilliant. Ti'n so going to win.

Aneurin   It's not about winning, Gavin.

Gavin   Beth mae am 'te?

Aneurin   Revenge.

Gavin   Ooh … scary.

Aneurin   'Wi yn scary.

Gavin   Fel cult leader.

Aneurin   'Wi yn cult leader.

Curiad.

Gavin   Lead me then.

Saib.

Aneurin   You're a precocious little cunt, aren't you?

Gavin   Beth mae 'precocious' yn meddwl?

Mae Aneurin yn syllu arno am ychydig cyn plygu ymlaen i'w gusanu. Mae cusanu amhrofiadol Gavin yn or-awchus. Mae Aneurin yn tynnu nôl.

Aneurin   Dwylo lan.

Mae Gavin yn gwneud ac mae Aneurin yn tynnu ei grys dros ei ben.

Aneurin   Dwylo lawr.

Mae Gavin yn gwneud.

Golygfa Saith

Stryd yn yr Waun Ddyfal.

Gareth   Woah, slow down, Rhys.

Curiad.

   Rhys!

Rhys   Beth?

Gareth   Wait for me.

Rhys   Pam?

Gareth   Don't be like this.

Rhys   Fel beth, Gareth fucking Lloyd? Fel beth? What am I being like, go on, dwed wrtha'i, what am I being like?

Gareth   Just cool down. Please. I'm sorry. I'm sorry we went.

Rhys   Neu ti'n sori est di 'na 'da fi. 'Se ti di bod yn fine 'na ar ben dy hunan, yn byse ti? You and your boys.

Gareth   That's just silly.

Rhys   Oh yes, silly, girly little Rhys. Rhys is silly. Rhys is just bloody silly. Gareth is not silly. Gareth is all fucking man.

Gareth   You what?

Rhys   'Nes di ddim byd, Gareth. Dim byd. O'n i'n sefyll mewn stafell llawn pobol a 'wi erio'd 'di teimlo mor unig. Hyd yn oed 'da'r person 'wi'n ei garu yn sefyll wrth yn ochor i. 'Run man i ti fod yn un ohonyn nhw ... For fuck's sake, ti *yn* un ohonyn nhw.

Gareth   I don't understand! I'm not following!

Rhys   Exactly. You left me out there on my fucking own.

Gareth   No I didn't!

Rhys   Yes you did! 'Nes di ddim. 'Nes di jyst 'weud bod fi ddim yn meddwl beth o'n i'n 'weud. You tried to pacify him. You didn't defend me. You should have fought for me. You should have punched him in the face, you should have made his nose bleed, you should have made his eyes come out of their sockets, you should have bloody dangos i fe bod e'n werth dim byd a bod fi'n werth popeth, bod fi yn werth dwrn, bod fi'n werth dy ddwrn di, Gareth.

Gareth   No you don't. You hate that. You hate that behaviour. You're the one always complaining about going out on Saturday night because there's too many drunk and violent straights. You're such a bloody hypocrite, Rhys. You can't stand the fact that I like to go out with the boys but you still want me to fight like one.

Rhys   'Wi am i ti ymladd fel dau.

Gareth   I'm always fighting. You. You! I'm always fighting –
you. It's exhausting …

Rhys   I just want you to …

Gareth   … what do you want, Rhys?

Curiad.

Gareth   It's always a drama with you, isn't it. You always have
to go over the top.

Rhys   Too much for you am I?

Curiad.

Gareth   Dunno, Rhys. Maybe you are.

Mae Gareth yn gadael.

Rhys   Gareth. Gareth!

Curiad.

Rhys   Plîs.

Curiad.

Rhys   Plîs.

Daw Aneurin ymlaen. Mae'r awyrgylch yn newid.

Aneurin   Gad e fynd.

Rhys   Na.

Aneurin   Gad e fynd.

Rhys   Oh my god. Oh my god. Alla'i ddim neud hyn ar ben fy
hun.

Aneurin   Sdim rhaid i ti. 'Wi 'ma. We can take them on. We can
take them all on.

Rhys   Ond s'o ti 'ma, Aneurin. Alli di ddim bod yma. Ni 'di
symud 'mla'n. Fel 'na o'dd hi, ond ddim nawr.

Aneurin   Ond all e fod mor brydferth. Grynda – angylion!

Clywir angylion yn canu.

Rhys   Yn canu!

Aneurin   Ie, yn canu.

Rhys   'Wi'n lico canu.

Aneurin   'Wi'n gw'bod, they're all for you.

Mae'r angylion yn dechrau canu **Fedrai m'ond dy garu di o bell** *o'r ffilm* **Ibiza, Ibiza.**

Rhys   Nagyw hwn bach yn od?

Aneurin   Beth?

Rhys   Shwt ma' nhw'n gw'bod y love song o *Ibiza, Ibiza*?

Aneurin   God works in mysterious ways.

Curiad.

Rhys   Ond s'o ti'n credu mewn Duw.

Aneurin   I've met him.

Curiad.

Aneurin   He looks like Beti George and Hywel Gwynfryn.

Rhys   Shwt all e edrych fel y ddau?

Aneurin   He's got two heads. Beti ar y chwith, Hywel ar y dde. They don't half argue.

Curiad.

Rhys   God, dwi'n caru'r gân 'ma.

Aneurin   Gei di beth wyt ti moyn.

Rhys   Really.

Aneurin   Really. Try it. Unrhywbeth.

Rhys   Beth am *Wind of Change*?

Aneurin   Unrhyw beth i ti.

Mae'r angylion yn canu **Wind of Change** *gan y Scorpions.*

Aneurin Co ti.

Rhys Wow. This is our soundtrack.

Aneurin This is our soundtrack. Our time.

Rhys Our time.

Saib.

Rhys Dros beth ydyn ni'n ymladd? Dros Gymru?

Aneurin Dros gyd-ddyn.

Rhys Beth am Grist?

Aneurin He can go to hell.

Rhys S'o ti'n ca'l dweud 'na. Ti'n fab i weinidog!

Aneurin I can say what I like.

Mae **Wind of Change** *wedi newid i'r emyn-dôn* Rhys.

Rhys Ma' nhw'n canu'n emyn i!

Aneurin *Rhys*. It's all for you.

Rhys Ti'n cofio ni'n canu hon yn Neuadd Dewi Sant yng nghymanfa'r Arglwydd Faer?

Aneurin A ti'n cofio ni'n cyfri'r pennau moel yng nghôr meibion Pendyrus?

Rhys A cael stŵr gan Miss Jones am werthin ar ffrog y soprano …

Aneurin/
Rhys Achos bod hi'n edrych fel meringue.

Rhys A dy Dad di'n rhoi crasfa massive i ni achos bod ti'n fab y capel a bod ti 'di embaraso fe o flaen y Maer?

Aneurin A ti'n cofio fi'n dweud 'se bywyd lot yn haws 'sen rhieni'n farw achos wedyn bydden i'n gwbwl rhydd?

Saib.

Aneurin   I wished for this.

Rhys   Nid dy fai di yw e.

Aneurin   Nag ife?

Rhys   Nage.

Curiad.

Aneurin   Well i ni newid yr emyn yfe? Mae bach yn depressing.

Rhys   Mae'n neis bod ti gytre' gyda hi. Mae'n neis bod ti 'di dod nôl am dym' bach.

Aneurin   Beth ti moyn yn lle. *Eternal Flame*?

Rhys   Aneurin …

Aneurin   Ti'n lico *Eternal Flame*, yn dwyt ti? Ti'n cofio ni'n treial slow danso i fe yn disco Melin Gruffydd a cael row gan …

Rhys   Aneurin …

Aneurin   Na, *Ysbryd y Nos*. Ti'n lico *Ysbryd y Nos*.

Mae'r emyn-dôn **Rhys** *yn newid i* **Ysbryd y Nos.**

Aneurin   'Na welliant.

Curiad.

Aneurin   Cana, Rhys.

Rhys   Cana gyda fi.

Aneurin   Na.

Rhys   Go on.

Aneurin   Na! This is not a musical.

Rhys   Just let yourself go, Aneurin.

Aneurin   'Getting lost; letting go' …

Rhys   Na, nid fel 'na.

Aneurin Fel be'?

Rhys Cuddio yw hwnna. Yn y tywyllwch, yn y dark rooms 'da dynion di-enw – Rhedeg bant. 'Wi'n siarad am fod yn honest.

Mae'r angylion wedi newid yn ôl i ganu'r emyn-dôn **Rhys.**

Aneurin Pam newides di'r gân?

Rhys Sa'i di newid y gân.

Aneurin Do. Dim ond fi sy'n ca'l neud. Dim nawr!

Rhys Naddo!

Aneurin Dal fi.

Rhys Beth sy'n bod, cariad?

Aneurin Wnei di aros 'da fi, 'nei di?

Rhys Wel …

Aneurin Plîs …

Rhys Nagodd … nagodd rhywbeth o'dd rhaid i fi neud?

Aneurin Nagodd.

Rhys Mi o'dd. Beth o'dd rhaid i fi neud?

Aneurin Sdim gwahaniaeth. Aros 'da fi.

Rhys Na, alla'i ddim, o'dd rhywun, o'dd rhywun …

Mae'r angylion yn canu'r hwiangerdd **Cysga di fy mhlentyn tlws.**

Aneurin But I'll sing! I'll sing for you. Whatever you want. All e fod mor brydferth. Allwn ni fod mor brydferth.

Rhys Prydferth? Fyse fe ddim yn brydferth. 'Se fe ddim yn gweitho.

Aneurin Pam?

Rhys We don't fancy each other!

Aneurin Come on, Rhys! It's war. Survival of the fittest. Let's take them all on. Ti a fi?

Rhys   Dyw rhyfel ddim yn brydferth. Ma' rhyfel yn hyll uffernol. Drycha.

Curiad.

Casualties yn barod.

Mae'r golau'n codi ar Gavin.

Aneurin   Cysgu ma' fe. (*Gan fynd ato*) Ti'n cysgu yn dwyt ti, fy nghariad bach i?

Mae Aneurin yn cymryd Gavin yn ei freichiau.

'Cysga di fy mhlentyn tlws,
Cysga di fy mhlentyn tlws,
Cysga di fy mhlentyn tlws,
Cei gysgu tan y bore,
Cei gysgu tan y bore.'

Mae Rhys yn gadael. Mae'r angylion yn peidio canu ond mae'r gerddoriaeth yn parhau.

Tirwedd esmwyth ieuenctid
Yn ddolur yn fy nwylo.
Hedfan Icarus

I haul dy ogoniant:
Disglair ddyfodol
Heb ddisgyn,
Fel gwnes i,
I ddyfnder y dŵr du.
Dwi'n dal i ddisgyn.
Mor dywyll.
Mor dywyll.
I'r chwant y rhêd y dŵr
O fôr nostalgia.

Llais Dada   Aneurin.

Aneurin:
Ti moyn fi yndwyt?
Bychan.

Ti moyn fi?
Fi moyn ti.
Fi moyn ti.

Mae'r golau'n codi ar Dada a'r gerddoriaeth yn dod i ben yn sydyn.

Dada   Aneurin. Aneurin.

Mae'r golau'n newid. Fflat Dada. Mae Gavin yn griddfan yng ngafael tynn Aneurin.

Dada   Aneurin.

Aneurin   Dada?

Dada   Dere fan hyn, Gavin bach.

Mae Gavin yn mynd at Dada.

Dada   Co ti. Dere di.

Curiad.

Dada   Beth 'nes di?

Aneurin   Sa'i di neud dim byd.

Dada   'Na ti, Gavin bach, mae'n olreit. (*Wrth Aneurin*) Be' mae 'di gymryd? (*Wrth Gavin*) Ti'n olreit. 'Na ni. 'Na ni, cariad bach.

Aneurin   Gad e fynd. Gad e fynd.

Dada   Aneurin, 'stedda lawr, ti off dy ben.

Aneurin   Gad e fod!

Dada   O'dd e'n sgrechen!

Curiad.

Dada   Pam o'dd e'n sgrechen, Aneurin?

Curiad.

Aneurin   O'dd e ddim.

Dada   Beth 'nes di?

Aneurin   'Nes i ddim byd.

Dada   Sai'n rhoi cyfle arall i ti, Aneurin. Dwi'n cyfri i dri a ti naill ai'n dweud wrtha'i beth ddigwyddodd neu ti'n gadel.

Curiad.

Dada   Un …

Aneurin   Oh for fuck's sake …

Dada   Dau …

Aneurin   … ti'm yn Dad i fi.

Curiad.

Dada   Tri.

Aneurin   Ti'n meddwl fi jyst yn mynd i adel, and let you have your wicked way gyda fe?

Dada   Paid bod yn ridiculous, Aneurin.

Aneurin   Ti'n ddigon hen i fod yn Ddadcu iddo fe.

Dada   Mas.

Aneurin   Jyst achos bod ti'n lonely old queen s'o fe'n esgus i neud yn siwr fod pawb arall yn bennu lan yr un ffordd a ti.

Saib.

Aneurin   Oh my God. Oh my God.

Curiad.

Aneurin   Sori.

Saib.

Aneurin   Dada, 'wi mor sori. Dada?

Gavin   I want my Mam. I want to go home.

Dada   Dere di. Dere di, 'machgen i.

Mae Dada'n ei dywys o'r ystafell.

Golygfa Wyth

Y Billy Banks.
Mae Gareth yn edrych allan ar yr olygfa.
Mae Rhys yn ymddangos tu ôl iddo.

Gareth   It looks a bit like LA.

Rhys   Na dyw e ddim.

Curiad.

Gareth   How did you know I'd be here?

Rhys   Just a hunch. A place for anniversaries. And break ups.

Curiad.

Gareth   It *does* look a bit like LA.

Golygfa Naw

Tŷ Bach Dada.

Gavin   Fi'n sori. Fi'n really sori.

Dada   Peidiwch â phoeni nawr.

Gavin   Ond mae'n so neis yma. Fi wedi neud mess.

Dada   Sdim gwahani'eth.

Gavin   Splashes i hi …

Dada   Lavinia? Ma' Lavinia 'di gweld gwaeth.

Gavin   Lavinia?

Dada   Ie, am ei bod hi'n eistedd ar y lavatory.

Mae Gavin yn chwerthin.

Gavin   O … paid neud fi chwerthin. Mae'n brifo pan fi'n chwerthin. (*Chwerthin yn troi'n grio*).

Dada   Jiw, jiw, beth sy'n bod, Gavin bach?

Gavin   Ti jyst mor neis i fi. Sai'n deall pam ti mor neis i fi.

Dada   Why ever not, cariad bach?

Gavin   Ti ddim yn nabod fi.

Dada   Nagw i?

Gavin   Dim really. Dim fel ffrindiau ti. Ti'n gwybod. Like adnabod. Like adnabod pethau am rywun sy'n neud nhw'n hapus neu'n scared. Cael memories gyda nhw.

Dada   Wel dyma chi atgof, Gavin. Atgof penigamp. Chi, fi a Lavinia.

Curiad.

Gavin   Ti'n gw'bod beth sy'n neud fi'n scared?

Dada   Beth?

Gavin   Yvette Fielding's *Most Haunted.*

Curiad.

Dada   Beth ddigwyddodd?

Gavin   Mae'n OK. Nid bai fe oedd e.

Dada   Gavin …

Gavin   Nid bai fe oedd e.

Curiad.

Gavin   Fi'n really hoffi Aneurin, Dada. Fi moyn bod fel fe.

Dada   Alla'i ddeall 'ny bach, alla'i ddeall pam. Ond dyw …

Gavin   Mae'n different. Mae'n neud pethau interesting. Like poem fe am chi.

Dada   Beth?

Saib.

Dada   Be' chi'n feddwl, Gavin?

Gavin   Dim byd.

Dada   Gavin.

Gavin   Fi ddim fod dweud. Mae'n secret.

Dada   O, OK.

Curiad.

Gavin   Mae'n rhaid ti addo peidio dweud. Addo?

Dada   Gaddo.

Gavin   Ar mam's life ti.

Dada   Wel …

Gavin   Oh my god. Fi'n sori. Fi'n totally trusto ti anyway. Totally, totally, totally.

Curiad.

Mae Aneurin yn ysgrifennu poem am chi, i'r Eisteddfod. Nagyw hwnna'n cool? Mae'n really caru chi, nagyw e?

Dada   Ydi e?

Gavin   Ydi. Mae'n brilliant, fi wedi clywed peth o fe. Mae am ti a Mr Thomas a Geraint …

Dada   Gareth?

Gavin   Ie, Gareth. Fi'n gobeithio bydd rhywun yn caru fi gymaint i ysgrifennu poem am fi un diwrnod.

Curiad.

Gavin   Diolch, diolch am fod mor neis i fi.

Dada   Ma' pawb yn haeddu maldod.

Gavin   Beth yw maldod?

Dada   Bach o gariad. Tyco ti lan yn gynnes neis ar y soffa pan y't ti'n dost a bwydo rich tea i ti wedi dynco mewn te. 'Na beth yw maldod.

Gavin   Ife 'na beth o'dd mam ti'n arfer neud?

Dada   Ie.

Saib.

Gavin   'Wi'n lico maldod.

Dada ⸱ A fi, Gavin bach. A fi.

Golygfa Deg

Y Billy Banks.

Rhys   Ddylet ti ddim 'di gyrru 'ma.

Gareth   I can do what I want.

Rhys   Not when you're in prison.

Gareth   I wanted to come here.

Rhys   Ddim 'na'r pwynt.

Gareth   Leave it.

Rhys   Ond mae'n really stupid.

Gareth   I'm not stupid!

Rhys   Ddim 'na beth wedes i.

Curiad.

Gareth   For fuck's sake, Rhys.

Rhys   Ddim 'na beth wedes i!

Gareth   You think you're fucking it. You think you're always right.

Rhys   Na fi ddim.

Gareth   Yes you do. Everything's your choice. Your decision. I'm not even in the bloody equation am I? I just happen to be here because you were kind enough to let me in. Wel diolch yn fawr, sir! Diolch, for allowing me into such a privileged life. I come away a richer man for it.

Rhys   Ti 'di gweud 'ny dy hunan. Sawl tro.

Curiad.

Gareth   Oh my God, you really believe that! You really think I'd be nothing without you.

Rhys   I'm just saying that you always say how much your life has changed. How you've grown as a person since meeting my friends, learning my language.

Gareth   *Your* friends. Oh for Christ's sake!

Rhys   'Na beth wedes di.

Gareth   Change is a good thing. You couldn't change if you tried. You're a fucking stubborn ass.

Curiad.

Rhys   Gareth.

Gareth   I don't need you.

Rhys   Awn ni gytre'.

Gareth   Na.

Rhys   OK.

Gareth   I said I don't need you.

Rhys   I know.

Curiad.

Gareth   I don't get it Rhys. I really don't get it. Where have you gone? I know you're still there because I see it, I've seen it tonight. I see the way you are with Aneurin and even with that kid, that kid on St Mary's street. Your fucking kids get to spend more time with the Rhys I met and fell in love with, and I don't anymore, ever. Ever. So there's something really wrong here or I'm really wrong here.

Rhys   Ti ddim yn wrong. Ti ddim. Ti'n …

Gareth   Patronized, shouted at, never good enough.

Rhys   Dwi'n genfigennus.

Gareth   No, Rhys. No. No drama. Plain, simple, no drama.

Rhys   That was Welsh!

Gareth   No. That was drama.

Curiad.

Rhys   I just don't want you to die.

Gareth   What?

Rhys   Yn y car. You were off your face, you always get off your face, and you got in the car a 'nes di ddreifo mas 'ma, ar ben dy hunan yn y tywyllwch. Off your face. Alle unrhyw beth 'di digwydd i ti. A ti jyst yn sefyll 'na, yn sefyll 'na fel 'se hwnna'n OK. But it's not OK, OK? You could have died, or you could have killed someone and you could have gone to jail a 'se hwnna'n neud fi'n …

Gareth   Woah … slow down, bach, what's going on?

Rhys   A falle bo fi'n stwbwrn, a falle bo fi'n bossy, but I don't get into a car off my face and drive, do I?

Gareth   What's that got to do with anything?

Rhys   Popeth, Gareth, popeth. 'Cause I need you, you twat. I need you. I love you.

Saib.

   Fi'n meddwl ti'n blydi brilliant.

Saib.

Gareth   I chose Richard Whiteley.

Rhys   I would have so gone with Carol Vorderman.

Curiad.

Rhys   It *does* look a bit like LA.

Golygfa Unarddeg

Lolfa Dada.

Dada   Wnes i ofyn i ti adel.

Aneurin   Ydi e'n iawn?

Dada   Mae'n cysgu. Nawr cer.

Aneurin   Ond fydd e'n iawn, yn bydd?

Dada   Ddim 'na'r pwynt.

Mae Dada'n edrych ar y botel Bollinger gwag ar y bwrdd.

Aneurin   Bryna'i un arall.

Dada   Ddim 'na'r pwynt chwaith.

Curiad.

Aneurin   Na, ond bryna'i un arall.

Saib.

Dada   S'o ti'n 'y mharchu i wyt ti?

Aneurin   Wrth gwrs bo fi.

Dada   Nagwyt. Neu 'set ti ddim di dod â fe gytre' 'da ti.

Aneurin   Ond wedes di nad o't ti'n lico fe yn y ffordd 'na.

Dada   Dwi ddim, Aneurin. Ond mi o't ti'n meddwl o'n i. Dyna'r pwynt.

Curiad.

Dada   Dim stori odw i, t'wel. Dim rhyw gymeriad yn dy waith di, dy nofel di neu pa bynnag 'epic' ti'n digwydd bod yn scriblo. Dwi ddim yn rhyw ddrychiolaeth hanesyddol. Dwi'n gig a gwaed. Dwi'n teimlo. Dwi'n werthin. Dwi'n llefen. Dwi'n caru.

Aneurin   Dwi'n caru. 'Wi yn, Dada, 'wi yn. 'Wi'n sori. 'Wi'n caru ti.

Dada   Wyt ti? Ma' 'caru' yn ferf, t'wel. Rhywbeth ti'n neud. Rhywbeth ti'n ddangos. Nid rhywbeth ti'n ddweud. Mae'n golygu commitment, Aneurin. When the shit hits the fan, ti ddim yn rhedeg, ti ddim yn dewis rhywbeth neu rywun arall. Mae cariad yn golygu ti 'di neud dy ddewis yn barod.

Aneurin   Dim cariad yw hwnna, teyrngarwch yw hwnna.

Dada   For Christ's sake, Aneurin, 'na beth yw cariad.

Aneurin   That's so old fashioned.

Dada   Ma' bod yn ffyddlon yn hen ffasiwn?

Aneurin   Sdim rhaid i ni ddilyn y rheolau …

Dada   Oh for God's sake, Aneurin, you have to commit to something!

Aneurin   No I don't.

Dada   Ti ffili rhedeg o hyd – o dy deulu, o Gymru …

Aneurin   Sai'n Gymro!

Dada   Wyt mi wyt ti.

Aneurin   I can be who I want to be.

Dada   Dyw hynny ddim yn fater o ddewis, Aneurin. Enjoy the contradictions. Enjoy the mess.

Aneurin   Or rewrite who I am. I can do that.

Dada   Ti ddim yn special, Aneurin. Fi wastad 'di meddwl bod ti. Achos mi o't ti'n exciting! O't ti fel chwa o awyr iach bob tro o't ti'n dod nôl drwy'r drws 'na. Ond nid awyr iach wyt ti, ti'n ddim byd ond hen ddrafft. Ti'n fachgen bach sy'n gwrthod tyfu lan. You're just fucking as many holes as you can, to try and avoid thinking about the gaping one in your life, and you're fucking up everything else in the process.

Mae Rhys a Gareth yn cyrraedd.

Aneurin   I'm going home.

Dada   S'o ti'n gw'bod ystyr y gair.

Curiad.

Gareth   What's going on?

Rhys   Aneurin?

Dada   Mae Aneurin jyst yn gadel.

Rhys   O's rhywun yn mynd i 'weud wrtho ni?

Gareth   What the hell's been going on?

Mae Gavin yn dod i mewn.

Gavin   Mr Thomas?

Curiad.

Rhys   Beth ma' fe'n neud 'ma? Dada?

Dada   Gofyn i Aneurin.

Gavin   Dim bai fe yw e. Fi'n digon hen i gwybod be' fi'n gwneud.

Rhys   Beth?

Aneurin   It's all fine, honestly.

Rhys   You twat. Shwt allet ti fod mor dwp!

Aneurin   Sdim problem, honestly.

Rhys   Sdim problem? Sdim problem?! Allen i golli'n swydd.

Gavin   Sai'n mynd i dweud.

Aneurin   Paid bod yn sofft. S'o fe ddim byd i neud 'da'r ysgol.

Rhys   Mae'n blydi disgybl yn yr ysgol.

Aneurin   Cyn-ddisgybl. S'o ti'n dysgu e rhagor!

Rhys   Ie, achos o'dd rhaid i fi symud e *lawr* set. Blwyddyn unarddeg yw e. Pymtheg mlwydd o'd yw e!

Aneurin   So what? O'n ni'n bymtheg. Ti'n cofio?

Saib.

Gavin   Mr Thomas?

Curiad.

Rhys   Gavin.

Gavin   Mae'n OK. Fi'n addo. Fydda i'n neud e'n OK.

Saib.

Gavin   Ma' pen fi'n teimlo fel car crash.

Dada   A'i nôl dŵr i chi, bach.

Gavin   Oh fuck, fi mynd i fod yn sick.

Dada   Dere 'da fi.

Gavin   Oh fuck …

Dada   Mae'n olreit, dere'n gloi, bach.

Mae Dada a Gavin yn gadael.

Rhys   That's it.

Aneurin   O'n i ddim yn gw'bod!

Rhys   Ti 'di mynd rhy bell tro 'ma. Mae'n fess. Complete and utter mess.

Curiad.

Rhys   'Yn job i, Aneurin. My bloody job.

Aneurin   Paid bod yn silly.

Rhys   Ti'n gwbod beth, Aneurin, you actually repulse me. Ti'n disgusting. Beth o'dd hwn i fod? Stori arall i ti 'weud? Ti 'di bod 'da vicar, ti 'di bod 'da superman. Might as well score a hatrick with a schoolboy.

Aneurin   S'o fe'n ddim byd gwahanol i beth ti'n neud 'da Gareth.

Rhys   Beth?

Gareth What the fuck does that mean?

Aneurin Ti jyst yn llenwi dy fywyd di 'da fe achos mae'n neud ti'n teimlo'n special. Ti wastad yn mynd mas 'da pobol ti'n meddwl ti'n well na nhw.

Gareth I'm here you know, I can understand you.

Aneurin You would never, ever, go out with anyone who could challenge you.

Gareth You think Rhys is better than me?

Aneurin No, I think Rhys is cleverer than you. But it's OK because you're younger and hotter than he is.

Daw Dada nôl i mewn.

Dada Bydden i'n gadel 'sen i'n ti.

Aneurin Why, have I pulled?

Dada Cer, cyn i fi ffono'r police …

Aneurin Rubbed him better?

Dada Paid ti â meiddio …

Aneurin Oh come on! Come on! Don't play innocent, Dada. We all know how it is.

Dada Grow up, Aneurin.

Aneurin You're the one who refuses to grow up. Ti byth yn ware 'da unrhyw un dy oedran di wyt ti. Daddy? You like your boys, don't you? Your lost boys. Ni'n cadw ti'n ifanc, or do we turn you on? We're all your lost boys. A 'na beth o'dd Gavin i fod ife? Recruit bach arall? To make you feel loved, wanted.

Rhys Stopa'i, Aneurin, plîs stopa'i …

Aneurin Achos 'na pam ma' pobol yn ca'l plant yndyfe? Because deep down they know there is no meaning to life. It's ridiculous! Ni'n sefyll ar blaned mewn bydysawd sy' byth yn gorffen. It's absolutely absurd. Does 'na ddim Duw. Does 'na ddim gwyrthiau. And so some people fuck, and some people

become gym managers and some, teachers and, and ... You're
bored! You're all bored. 'Cause it's shit here. You're jealous.
'Cause it's shit here and
... and ... I write and I fuck. I write and I fuck achos does dim
byd yn digwydd i ni wedyn – that's it, we just die – and so I might
as well just write and fuck, and other people, other people have
children, and other people who can't have them, just surround
themselves with them because they want to fuck them instead.

Mae Gareth yn taro Aneurin yn ei wyneb â'i ddwrn. Mae
Aneurin yn syrthio.

Aneurin   Mae 'di marw.

Saib hir. Mae Aneurin mewn dagrau. Maent yn syllu arno am
gyfnod, neb yn medru symud.

Mae Rhys yn mynd ato.

Rhys   Dere fan hyn.

Aneurin   I ... I ... I ...

Rhys   Sssh nawr.

Aneurin   Ma' Mami 'di marw.

Mae Aneurin yn beichio crio.

Rhys   Sssh. Gareth, get some ice.

Dada   Drawer waelod, bach.

Mae Gareth yn mynd i nôl iâ.

Saib.

Aneurin   She died and I wasn't there.

Rhys   Gad fi rhoi hwn arnat ti (*sef y iâ*).

Aneurin   I didn't go.

Rhys   Ca' dy lygaid, bach.

Aneurin   Aw.

Rhys   'Na ni. Dal e i fi.

Aneurin   Pam ti'n bod mor neis i fi? I'm horrible. I'm so horrible.

Rhys   Co ti.

Aneurin   'Wi mor sorry.

Curiad.

Dada   A fi, bach.

Curiad.

Rhys   Pam na wedes di?

Aneurin   I said all those things.

Curiad.

Aneurin   Rhaid i fi fynd gytre'.

Rhys   Ddim 'to, s'o ti mewn unrhyw stad.

Aneurin   Ond s'o nhw'n gw'bod lle odw i. O'n i fod mynd gytre' ddo', a 'nes i jyst ddim mynd.
A nawr mae 'di marw. And I was being fucked on Hampstead Heath.

Curiad.

Aneurin   'Raar, I just died in your arms tonight' ...

Mae Aneurin yn dechrau chwerthin.

Rhys   Twat.

Aneurin   Knob.

Curiad.

Aneurin   'Wi ofn mynd gytre.

Rhys   Sdim ise ti bod ofn.

Aneurin   I just want to be a little boy again.

Rhys   Na ti ddim.

Aneurin   It was easier then.

Rhys   Nagodd e ddim.

Aneurin   Ni yn erbyn y byd.

Rhys   Dyw'r byd ddim yn ein herbyn ni, Aneurin. Ddim rhagor. Mae 'di newid, ti jyst ddim 'di sylwi. Dyw dy deulu di definitely ddim yn dy erbyn di.

Aneurin   They would be if they knew the whole truth.

Saib.

Rhys   Ma' jyst ise ti fod yn onest. Gwed wrtho fe.

Aneurin   Y gwir yn erbyn y byd?

Rhys   Sdim shwd beth â'r gwir yn erbyn y byd.

Aneurin   Sdim shwd beth â heddwch 'te, oes 'na?

Curiad.

Rhys   Oes.

Curiad.

Aneurin   'Nes i ddim byd iddo fe. 'Wi'n addo. Jyst dal e. Ond o'n i'n dal e'n really dynn. Yn really, really dynn. A ga'th e ofn. Ond o'n i jyst ddim moyn gadel e fynd.

Golygfa Deuddeg

Amlosgfa Thornhill.

Aneurin:
Haul braf y gwanwyn.
Llwyth o ddynion,
Llwyth o deulu,
Llwyth o gyfeillion,
Tylwyth.
Oll yn eu lifrau duon …

Rhys   (*Wrth Gareth*) S'o fe 'di gweud dim byd drwy'r bore.

Aneurin:
Dad yn llefen.
Dwi'n gafael yn ei law,
Heb feddwl.
Un eiliad tragwyddol.
Dau ddyn yn gwlwm o gariad:
Ac mae'n gwasgu.

A'i waed sy'n gynnes.

'Rhaid gwisgo cot,
Rhaid gwisgo het,
Rhaid rhoddi maneg ar bob llaw.
Dweud dabo i'n hysgol ni'
A dweud dabo wrth mami,
A dweud dabo wrth mami.

Rhys   Ti'n olreit?

Curiad.

Aneurin   Shit, ti fod yn Taiwan. Nagywt ti fod yn …

Rhys   Sai'n mynd.

Aneurin   Beth am dy solo di?

Rhys   It's sorted. Ti sy'n bwysig.

Curiad.

Aneurin   Diolch.

*Mae'r côr yn ymddangos. Gavin sy'n canu unawd Rhys. Mae'n canu pennill cynta **Ysbryd y Nos**, ac yna mae'r gerddoriaeth yn parhau.*

Aneurin   Chi'n gw'bod lle 'wi moyn mynd?

Curiad.

Aneurin:
Ymlwybro'n araf o'r amlosgfa,

Car yn cruiso'r ddinas.
I lawr heol Penarth
Hyd nes cyrraedd y dibyn,
Lle saif y Billy Banks,
Creithiau brwydr
Yn dyst ar ei dalcen.

Dada   We've both seen better days.

Aneurin:
Y bae oddi tanom,
Gwesty Dewi Sant,
Stadiwm y Mileniwm –
Brwydr cynnydd a brad y bobol:
Make way, make way for progress.

Dada   I feddwl bo fi'n byw 'ma unwaith.

Rhys   Y Cwîn yn erbyn y byd!

Dada   Rhoison nhw'r 'Danger Keep Out' 'na i rybuddio pobol amdana i.

Aneurin   It's where it all began …

Rhys   Fan hyn nethon ni bron bennu.

Aneurin:
Rhys a Gareth.
Dau enaid hoff gytun
Yn cydio'n dynn,
A Chaerdydd yn ei gogoniant
Yn chwerthin yng ngolau'r haul.

Dada   Ni yn lwcus, yndyn ni?

Curiad.

Aneurin   Wedes i wrtho fe, chi'n gw'bod.

Rhys   Dy dad?

Aneurin   (*Yn drist*) O'dd e'n OK.

Curiad

Aneurin   Gynigodd e Welsh cake i fi.

Dada   Wel, co ti special occasion! Trueni bod ti …

Mae Aneurin yn datguddio potel o Bollinger.

Saib hir.

Dada   'I am what I am, I am my own special creation' …

Mae'r côr yn ymddangos yn canu plethwaith o **Ysbryd y Nos, Chwarae'n Troi'n Chwerw** *ac* **I am what I am** *yn gyfeiliant i'r ddeialog ganlynol.*

Gareth   God, how cheesy is this?

Rhys   Ddyle rhywun dynnu llun!

Gareth   Or sing a song. It's beginning to feel like a musical.

Aneurin   Oh my god, Dada, beth sy'n bod 'da ti?

Dada   Dwi just yn browd ohonot ti.

Aneurin   Ti jyst yn walking cliché!

Rhys   (*Gyda'r côr*) 'Ac mae chwarae'n troi'n chwerw' …

Aneurin   Nid ti 'fyd!

Rhys   Come on, o't ti'n arfer dwli canu hon …

Mae Rhys yn parhau gyda'r gân.

Aneurin   Rhys Thomas, if you don't shut up this second I will put this bottle lle dyw'r haul ddim yn gwenu.

Gareth   I better start singing then, I'd enjoy that!

Mae Gareth yn canu llinell olaf cytgan **Ysbryd y Nos.**

Aneurin   Oh my god, this is ridiculous!

Mae'r gerddoriaeth yn parhau: cyfuniad o gytgan **Y Cwm** *a chytgan* **O'r Fan Acw.**

Dada   Os ti ddim moyn canu alli di wastad sgwennu cerdd …

Curiad.

Aneurin   Sai'n really mynd i anfon hi mewn.

Dada   Well i ti fennu hi, gw' boi. I want to be immortalised!

Aneurin   Na, 'wi'n mynd i fennu hi, 'wi jyst ddim moyn anfon hi mewn.

Curiad.

  I'm no Hedd Wyn.

Gareth   You going to open that before I sit on it?

Mae Aneurin yn gwenu.

Mae'r côr yn ail-ymuno: cyfieithiad Cymraeg o **Come what may** *wedi ei chyfuno gyda* **Y Cwm.**

Maent yn agor y Bollinger ac yn yfed o'r botel.

Mae'r gerddoriaeth yn cyrraedd uchafbwynt, yna'n parhau yn dawel.

Gareth   Do you think it looks like LA?

Aneurin:
A co ni'n edrych am eiliad.
Y Golden Girls,
Fi, Dada, Gareth a Rhys.
Yn herio'r gorwel,
A'r haul yn wenfflam.

Y Diwedd.

Parallel Lines

Katherine Chandler

Parallel Lines received its world premiere on 20 November 2013 at Chapter Arts Centre, Cardiff, and won the inaugural Wales Drama Award. The production featured the following cast:

Steph	Rachel Redford
Melissa	Jan Anderson
Julia	Lisa Diveney
Simon	Gareth Pierce
Director	Catherine Paskell
Designer	Signe Beckmann
Lighting Designer	Jason Osterman
Sound Designer	Dan Lawrence
Fight Director	Kev McCurdy
Assistant Director	Anna Poole

'If anyone injures his neighbour, whatever he has done must be done to him: fracture for fracture, eye for eye, tooth for tooth. As he has injured the other, so he is to be injured.'

Leviticus, Old Testament

Notes

Parallel lines: Two lines that are parallel never meet, never cross over one another. This should be reflected in the staging of the two worlds within the play.

There is a feeling of symmetry in the play. Both women are thiry-five, both families are affected by the events.

Melissa and Steph's relationship is fiery and physical and immediate. Zero to a hundred and back again in a matter of seconds.

Movement and physicality is important for this play in order to express the symmetry of the piece and the emotion and narrative of the scenes, where there is no dialogue.

*denotes when action should be simultaneous.

Scene One

A sparse kitchen. Morning.

Steph, fifteen, looks through the cupboards for something to eat. Pulls out a bowl for cereal. Gives it a wipe with her t-shirt. Picks at something stuck in the bowl. Grabs a lonely packet of supermarket own brand sugary cereal. The dregs of the packet spill out. She hunts for milk. None in the fridge. Looks at the kitchen table at a carton of milk that's been sitting there overnight. She sniffs it. Stinks. Dips her finger in the dregs of a sugar packet. Sucks her finger. Looks around for something else to eat. There's nothing. Starts to eat the dry cereal leaning against the units.

Melissa thiry-five, with a banging hangover enters.

Repeats the same actions as her daughter. Looks through the cupboards for something to eat. Grabs the same lonely packet of supermarket own brand sugary cereal looks inside. Empty...

Steph   There's nothing.

Melissa   What you eating then?

Steph   Nothing.

Melissa flicks the switch on the kettle. Grabs a packet of fags from the side. Lights it. Looks for the milk.

Sniffs the milk. Recoils. Pauses. Bites the bullet.

Melissa   Go down the shop for me, Steph.

Steph   No.

Melissa   Get us some milk. Some bread.

Reaches for her handbag on the table, takes out her purse. No luck.

Steph   No.

Goes back to the bag. Empties it out. A fiver wrapped in a receipt.

Melissa   Get yourself some sweets.

Steph   For fucks sake.

Melissa   Fags then. Cider, crack cocaine.

Nothing. Exchange a glare.

Steph   Shut up.

Melissa   Get some clothes on and get your arse down the shop.

A look.

You're going back, Monday. They said.

Steph   Is that what they said, is it.

Melissa puts out two cups, adds two tea bags. Steph notices.
Melissa looks at her. Drags on her fag.

Melissa   I got a letter. From school. They're on my case Steph. It says you gotta go back.

Steph   I ain't going back.

Melissa   Monday.
They wants you in Monday morning. See how you goes.

Steph   See how I goes?

Melissa   You can't just sit on your arse, day in day out.

Steph   Like you.

Drags her fag.

Melissa   You needs to get out.

Steph   I likes to sit on my arse.

Melissa   Needs to put it behind you.

Steph   I likes it in.

Melissa   You've had long enough.

Steph   On my own. It's what I'm used to, ain't it.

Melissa   I was talking to Stacey Lee's Mam in the Lion last night. She works for social services don't she. She says you have to go back. It's the law. Says they'll be getting on me for keeping you off.

Steph   Stacey Lee's Mam knows shit all.

Melissa   Yeah well.

Eyes up Steph.

Drags her fag.

She's pregnant again, Steph. forty-four, she is. To a man called Hilary. Can you imagine.
A fucking man. Hilary. Why, for fucks sake. Janine reckons he's only twenty-seven?

Steph   I'm not going back.

Melissa   It was one of them nights, you know Steph. My sides cramped right up with laughing. Hilary, though.
'I'm a community van driver, in the community' he had one of them little high pitched voice like that. 'I got my own van'.
Sounds like that one of the Muppet show. What was his name.
You know, that doctor one with the ginger hair.
And the nose. What's he called?

Steph   You said you wasn't going out. Last night.

Melissa   We watches them leave cos we can see the car park from the window and we're thinking where's this van then. Janine's thinking it's one of them Beetles campers things. The only thing we can see Steph, is a sprayed ambulance you know one of them old ones they sell off. I didn't even notice it cos I'm thinking it's a wreck that's been left there. Anyway they only gets in this ambulance don't they. Laugh. Janine's pissed herself. She's grabbing herself and saying it's all down my leg and that's before we even seen the side of the van, you'll love this Steph, on the side he's painted 'give the old a sporting chance'. And she's sat there smiling at us out of the window.
What a night.

Melissa grabs an near empty pack of sugar and sucks her finger then dips it into the packet. She eats the sugar.

Melissa   I'm paying for it now though. Jesus.

Melissa rubs her head.

Melissa   Go down the shop Steph, my head's banging.

Steph   No.

Melissa   You're going back.

Steph   Am I.

Pours water in the cups.

Melissa   Get some exams. Get a good job.

Steph   Don't give me all that. Don't give me all that, like you gives a shit about me getting a good job an that. You wants me back in school so they don't come round yer again. So they don't start giving you any shit.
You're so full of it.
So fucking transparent.

Melissa   Transparent. Transparent am I. You didn't learn words like that from me. I gave you the shit and the fuck but transparent. Well. Now we knows. You're definitely going back, you.
Learn yourself some more of them words.

Steph   You don't care about what I learns.

Melissa   No.

Steph   You don't care about nothing except when it affects you.

Melissa   Stop banging on Steph. Like a broken record. I don't want no one coming yer.

Steph   And finally the truth.

Melissa   Don't want them yer telling us how to be. Looking down their noses at us.
It'll be all that twitching and sniffing and looking like they don't wanna sit down in case they catches something.

It'll be all forms and whispers and briefcases. I'm not having that, Steph.

Steph   I'll leave. Go to a different school.

Melissa   D'you think I got the money to be putting you on a bus every day, getting you new uniform an all that.

Steph   Will he be there?

Melissa   I don't know. What if he is?

Steph   I don't wanna see him.

Melissa   You got nothing to hide. You got nothing to be ashamed of.
Him. That Simon. He's the one.
They should've pressed charges. But they looks after their own, that lot. That headmaster.
And in his eyes you ain't worth the paperwork. They should've gone to the police when they found that diary. Straight away.
That's what they should've done.
Straight to the police.

Steph   Oh yeah? You wouldn't go to the police.

Melissa   *They* Steph, when it all came out, they should've done something.
I would though. I would, if it's what you wanted.

Steph   Let's go to the police.

Melissa   If that's what you want, that's fine with me. Is that what you want?
Cos I would, you know … I dunno, the police an that though Steph. They said didn't they, the school, they said they sorted it, didn't they?
They said it was nothing.

Steph   It weren't *nothing*.

Melissa   I know that … we know, don't we.
What happened.
The police mind.

We could Steph but, you know.
That's a right can of worms that is.

Steph   He'll be there. Simon. On Monday.

Melissa   I'll tell the head.
I'll say she don't want no contact. I'll say there'll be no contact at all.

Steph   I'm not sitting there with the head. Talking about it all.

Melissa   I'll say that.
I'll say she's not coming in yer, talking about nothing.
Anyway, his room stinks.

Steph   He stinks.

Melissa   He fucking hums, Steph.
Shall I say that to him Steph, shall I? I'll say she ain't coming in here cos you fucking hum, mate.
I could say that Steph, cos he wouldn't dare say nothing back, in the circumstances like.

Melissa laughs then spoons the tea bags out of the two cups and chucks them into the sink.

Steph   You weren't going out. That's what you said.

Melissa   It'll be good to see your friends though, won't it?

Steph   You said you'd stay with me.

Melissa   Good to be back in a routine.

Steph   Said we'd watch the telly.

Melissa   You gotta stop this Steph. You can't stay in forever.

Steph   I watched this thing about the soldiers from Iraq.

Melissa   You watched about Iraq?

Melissa grabs an near empty pack of sugar and sucks her finger then dips it into the packet. She eats the sugar.

Steph   When you was out.

Melissa   What are you watching stuff about Iraq for?

Steph   About the soldiers when they come home it was. Got post-traumatic stress and all that.

Melissa   There's other stuff on – good stuff.

Steph   They went to this hospital but it weren't a hospital, you know, they were just all there …

Melissa   You should've seen Janine's dress.

Steph   … This big old house in the country.

Melissa   You'd have loved it, you would. Like an emerald green.

Steph   Some of them were just lying there like they was in cots.

Melissa   Green it was.

Steph   Cos the beds had bars.

Melissa   She's dark in' she.

Steph   Rails like if they was going to fall out.

Melissa   She can take all them lovely colours.

Steph   They was lying there and looking through the rails and I was thinking that it looked like they was in prison.

Melissa   Oh, happy days.

Steph   I thought to myself that they was.

Melissa   Can't you watch something normal.

Steph   I watched it. You was out.

Melissa   Christ d'you blame me? Watching that shit.

Steph   They're gonna close it. The hospital.

Melissa   Good.

Steph   Where did she go?

Melissa   Who?

Steph   Where did Janine go?

Melissa   Janine? What about Janine?

Steph   Where did she go?

Melissa   What you talking about?

Steph   Last night.
I'm talking about last night.

Melissa   What about last night?

Steph   Where did Janine go?

Melissa   I don't know. Home I s'pose.
Ain't that where people go.
After a night out.

Steph   He didn't go home.

Melissa   Who?

Steph   Him in your bed.

Melissa   Look at each other for as long as can get away with.

Steph   Probably haven't got a home.
Some pisshead looked at you longer than five seconds was it.

Melissa   He did go home.
My home.
My bed.

Steph   You said you wouldn't do that.

Melissa   Shut it, will you.

Steph   You said that wasn't gonna happen no more.

Melissa   Says a lot of things, don't I.

Steph   You said, Mam.

Melissa   Don't start *(wants to shout but aware of bloke upstairs)*.
Fucking going on. Just keep it down.

Steph   You said it would be different.

Melissa   Just fucking shut it.

Silence.

Melissa   Anyway you'd like him.
He was in Iraq.

Steph   He deserves better than you then.

Melissa   You're going to the shop.
And then you're going to make yourself scarce.
So you can stay in your room or better still get out.

Steph   I'm not going back.

Melissa   You're going back on Monday. And that's the last I
wants to hear about it.

Steph   Mam. Please.

Melissa   You're going back.

Steph   I can't Mam.

Melissa   You starts back Monday.

*Steph launches at her Mam, screams at her with such ferocity that
Melissa feels attacked.*

After a while.

Melissa   What is wrong with you.

Beat.

Melissa   Jesus Christ.

Beat.

Melissa   Get your arse down the shop.

*Melissa pulls leggings out of a laundry pile and chucks them and
the fiver at Steph.*

Steph picks up the fiver.

Looks at her mother.

Leaves.

Melissa *shocked in the kitchen.*

*Puts her head in her hands.

Takes a minute.

Gathers herself.

Picks up the two cups and heads with them back to the bedroom.

*****Julia*** *thirty-five, enters her modern mod cons kitchen.*

Makes a cup of fruit tea.

Takes her bag.

Takes out a make-up bag and checks her face.

Touches up her makeup.

Fusses around the kitchen, morning routine.

Simon thirty-five, enters.

Drying his hair with a towel.

Casual, t-shirt, jeans.

Simon   Bloody shower.

Julia   Oh god. Not again.

Simon   We'll have to get it resealed because it's every time now.

Julia   Not every time.

Simon   I could do it?

Julia   If you like.

Simon   I think it's bowing, the ceiling.

Julia   It's not bowing.

Simon   Well, there's a patch. There's definitely a patch.

Julia   You need a hobby.

Simon   And it's right above where I sit. I keep thinking one day the whole bloody roof will cave in on me. And I'll be sat there in a mound of dust and plaster and floorboards and ceiling stuff.

Julia   That won't happen.

Simon   Or the water will get into the electrics and god, then what.
You'll have to go to B&Q and get something.

Julia   You really do need a hobby.

Julia sips her herbal tea. Grimaces slightly.

Simon   Coffee?

Julia looks at her cup. Sniffs it. Recoils.

Julia   I should give it a chance.

Simon starts to make coffee.

Simon   Never drink anything that you have to hang in your cup. It always tastes like shit.

Julia   Yeah, well.

Simon   What do you want for dinner?

Julia   Dinner?

Julia   It's twenty to eight in the morning. I don't know what I want for my dinner. I can just about stomach this ... (pause) Pasta's fine. It's fine.

Simon   I was thinking of pasta. But then I thought with that carb diet you go on? Are you on it today? I could do salmon? I'll go shopping ...

Simon   I'll make a pudding.

Julia   Not after pasta.

Simon   I'll make crumble?

Julia   I won't want it.

Simon   I'll get some wine?

Julia   I've got book club tomorrow.
I need a clear head, because I've not even started the book yet.
I've read the cover. Talking of which I need to bloody well find it
now. I'm sure I put it down on the table.

Simon   I've not seen it.

Looks at her watch, takes a gulp of her tea, grimaces.

Julia   Fucking 10S.

Simon   Fucking 10S.

Julia   Fucking Tyler Banks.

Simon   Fucking Tyler Banks.

Julia   He's an idiot and it's not like I haven't tried.

Simon   No.

Julia   I just want to kick his head in. Actually kick his head in.

Simon   I'll kick his head in. I'll follow him home.

Julia   I don't think …

Simon   I was joking.

Pause.

Julia   Pity.

Simon   In eight hours you'll be home.

Julia   I've got that thing.
That poetry slam. After school.

Simon   In nine hours you'll be home.

Julia   Yes.

Simon   And you can sit down and eat pasta and pretend to read
the book.
I'll print you off some reviews from Amazon so you can talk
about it tomorrow.

Julia   You'd do that for me.

Simon   I would, yes.

Julia   What are you doing today?

Simon   I thought I might go to the gym.

Julia   Right.

Simon   There are lots of old people at the gym I noticed. They have good trainers. Their clothes are ironed. When I say old I'm thinking over sixty-five.

Julia   Grey days they call them. You've gone on a grey day.

Simon   There's a difference that isn't obvious.
Not wrinkles and grey and obvious physicalities. Ironed tracksuits and brushed hair.

Julia   Ironed tracksuits!

Simon   It's true.
Signs that they're from a different time.

Julia   Okay.

Simon   There's this old guy. He's there all the time. He changes his shoes. So. He comes to the gym in his tracksuit and his shoes. Then he sits and he puts on his trainers. He works out a bit. Then he sits and puts his shoes back on.

Julia   With his ironed tracksuit.

Simon   Yes.
And I'm thinking. Just leave the trainers on. Don't worry about the trainers.

Julia   You definitely need a hobby.

Simon   But he's from an age that don't wear trainers.

Julia   That iron their tracksuits and brush their hair.

Simon   I don't think it's like that anymore. There aren't those clues.

Julia   You say that because you're thirty-five.

Simon   I say that because I noticed it.

Julia   You think you're twenty.

Simon   I notice things. I have time to notice things. Things I never noticed before. Like nature.

Julia   Nature?

Simon   I've started to notice nature.

Julia   You'll be ironing your tracksuit, soon.

Simon   I like its patience. It doesn't rush. In a world that's in a rush.
Nature happens when it's ready. In it's own time. I was thinking this because last year April was warm. When I was off? Do you remember?
And the April before that was warm. And so everyone thought 'Oh here we go, this is it, global warming'. And then we had the coldest June in the entire history of June. Do you remember? Last year.

Julia   I do, yes.

Simon   But the poppies were out in April.

Julia   I remember.

Simon   I remember thinking they were magnificent. That's not a word to use lightly but they were.
For a short time.
They were magnificent.

Julia   They were.

Simon   How things can change in a year because now it's June and the poppies are only just budding. They've thought 'April's a bit shit this year, we'll sit it out.'
And that's what they've done.

Julia   God, they're not dead are they.

Simon   They'll come when they're ready.

Julia   Yes.
And they'll be magnificent.

Simon   They want me in for two days.

Julia   What?

Simon   A phased return. They like to get you back. Quickly.

Julia   They want you in?

Simon   They want it all dealt with.
It's within a month. They want you back and. Everything back to normal. So.

Julia   When? What did he say?

Simon   He phoned me. Yesterday.

Julia   You didn't say.
He phoned you yesterday?

Simon   Yes. Two days a week he said. To start.

Julia   This week?

Simon   Next

Julia   Two days. For now.

Simon   Then within the month.

Julia   Back full time?

Simon   Yes.

Julia   Back to normal within the month.

Simon   That's how they do it.
When it's unsubstantiated so.
Everything forgotten.
Getting back to normal.

Julia   Back to normal.

Simon   I said, didn't I? I said it would be fine.

Julia   You did, yes.

Simon   I'm ready. I feel ready.

Julia   Will she be there?

Simon   Please Julia.

Julia   No. I know but it's –, but it just seems.
A month and then it's all done.

Simon   It's how they do it. To the letter he said.
Everything done – followed the book, so to speak.

Julia   That's great. It's great. It is. It's great.
It just seems quick but if that's how they do it.

Simon   That's how they do it.

Julia   Simon.

Simon   It feels like it's a start. Don't you think?

Julia   Simon ...

Simon   I feel like we've turned a corner.

Julia   I can't find my book.

Simon   It'll turn up. And if it doesn't I'll buy you a new one.
We'll go into town and I'll treat you. We'll have dinner and
something fizzy.

Julia   Things are moving.

Simon   Yes. They are. We're moving on.

Julia   No.
Not that. Not you.

Pause.

Looks at Simon.

Starts packing her bag ready for work.

Julia   It doesn't matter.

Julia looks at her watch.

Julia   I should go.

Pauses.

Julia   I hope something happened to him on the way home from school last night. A hit and run. On a life support. I hope he's ill. Hope he's got something terminal.

Simon   He might have.

Julia   He won't see thirty. Possibly not even twenty.

Simon   Nine hours, that's all.

Julia   I had to tell him to stop looking at my arse the other day. I worried all day that I had spoken inappropriately to a minor. A minor to whom I had a duty of care …

Simon   Don't Julia.

Julia   … He's fifteen.
He thinks I would and he's fifteen …

Simon   Please don't.

Julia   … And I thought, can you imagine – both of us. God, that's all we need. After you?

She looks at him. Moves past him to put her cup in the sink.

Starts to gather her things together for work.

Julia   It makes you wonder why we do it?
Why anyone does it.
When some – little – on a whim – or for a laugh or –
There was a time, it was respected.
Being a teacher – I thought it was decent.
A respectful profession.

Stops herself.

Takes a deep breath.

Julia   I have to go.

Puts last night's marking in a bag.

Exercise books.

Picks one up.

Flicks through it.

Looks at **Simon**.

Takes a moment.

Julia   Nine hours and counting.

Picks up her bags and leaves.

Simon takes a moment.

Looks around an empty kitchen.

*Tidies a few things away.

Leaves the kitchen in his own time.

*Melissa sits at table in darkness.

The sounds of late night radio in the background.

She sits smoking.

The light of the cigarette being dragged should be our only focus for a while.

We hear a key in a door and a door open and close. In darkness Steph enters the kitchen.

Melissa   Alright, Steph?

Steph   For fuck's sake.
What the fuck are you doing sat there …

Melissa   You alright?

Steph   … Like a ghost.
A smoking ghost.
Or a nutter, like sat there, in the dark.

Puts a lamp on.

Melissa   Just sat here.

Steph   What's that?

Goes to saucepan on the hob.

Steph   Is that tea is it? Chilli?
What is that?
Is it that …

Melissa   It's Chilli.

Steph   Hot is it? Spicy?

Melissa   No.

Steph   I like it hot.

Melissa   Where've you been Steph?

Steph   Nicey, spicy.

Melissa   Where?

Steph   Out.

Melissa   Out.

Steph   Just out.

Melissa   It's one o'clock in the morning.

Steph   Time flies!

Melissa   I been worried.

Steph   Christ! Right. Sorry about that. It's just normally …

Melissa   I wondered where you was.

Steph   … you wouldn't give a shit.

Melissa   Night after night you're in. Like some sort of hermit.
And then tonight? Tonight you decides to go out?
Where?

Steph   Nowhere special.

Melissa   Where?

Steph   I fancied a walk.

Melissa   You been acting weird, Steph. Proper weird like. Since you been back in school.

Steph   I like walking. Getting my exercise. There's an obesity epidemic, haven't you heard.
I. Can't. Sleep.
So I walks.

Pause.

Melissa   In the dark?

Steph   Dark don't frighten me.

Melissa   You'll end up dead.
There'll be a knock on my door …

Steph   It feels like home.

Melissa   You're talking shit, Steph.

Steph   I like its truth.

Melissa   Its truth?

Steph   It don't pretend to be anything other than what it is.

Melissa   D'you think I'm a fucking idiot.

Steph   Lovely as it's been, chatting with you Mother – I'm going to bed.

Melissa   Do I look like a fucking idiot to you?

Steph   Yes.

Melissa grabs at Steph looks for tracks on her arms. Her eyes. Melissa knows what to look for. Grabs Steph's bag roots through it. Empties it out onto the floor.

Steph   For fuck's sake. I'm not you. I'm not you yet am I.

She grabs her bag back. Scrambles her things back into it. As she puts things back in Melissa talks.

Melissa   Got all your things …

Steph   I have, yes.

Melissa … got your purse …
and your keys there … and your keyring – got that when we was
in Devon. I knew you'd have that.
Headphones.
They'll be in there somewhere.
I know.
I knows what you got in there.
Could have told you without looking.
I. Know. You.

Steph *has finished putting her things back in the bag.*

Steph   I'm going to bed.

Melissa   You don't keep a diary, Steph.

Steph   You what?

Melissa   When they said diary? At first I was like. It was – shock
and then …
But it was all confused cos there was this Simon and he was your
teacher and they was saying about you being fifteen like and then
I didn't think. But then I thought.
They had this diary. Your diary. That's what they said.

Steph   That's right.

Melissa   And they said that no one knew nothing about it, all this
stuff with that teacher but then they found this diary and they had
to. They had to act on it. Any implication they said.

Steph   What are you saying?

Melissa   You never had a diary.

Steph   You saw it.
The head. He had it. It was on his desk.

Melissa   First time I seen it. How did it get there?

Steph   Someone found it. Gave it to him. Cos of what was in it.
You knows this.

Melissa   I thinks you've done something.
I don't know what.
But you have, I can see it in you.
You've done something and you ain't telling me.
And I needs to know. Because I can't do nothing to help you
unless I knows.

Steph   Help me?

Melissa   Yes.

Steph   You? Help me? Jesus.

Melissa *looks at* **Steph**.

Steph   Remember Davey, Mam.

Melissa   What? Davey?

Steph   You remember Davey. Course you do.

Melissa   What d'you think you're doing?

Steph   How old was I then?

Melissa   What are you bringing all that up for?

Steph   I was eleven.

Melissa   Shut up.

Steph   He was an animal.

Melissa   D'you think I don't know that?
Is that what you think?

Steph   I found him.
After he left us.
I looked for him.
He was with someone.

Melissa   I know what you're doing.

Steph   What was he called, that one that took us to
Alton Towers?
Ritchie was it?
Something like that.

Melissa   I know what you think you're doing.

Steph   Truth Melissa.
How old was I?

Melissa   You was six. Seven, you was seven.

Steph   I was eight.

Melissa   That's right.

Steph   He took us there for my birthday. To Alton Towers. He
left us there.

Melissa   I wants to know where you been.

Steph   I saw him. About a week after.
Walking up the high street pushing a pram with some kids.

Melissa   I don't want to know.

Steph   One was about four or something walking behind him,
struggling to keep up.

Melissa   I'm not listening to this.

Steph   Other one about eight.

Melissa   I want you to tell me where you been.

Steph   A girl. Like me. Eight. Looked like me. An she was
looking at him all adoring. Like me.

Melissa   Where have you been, Stephanie?

Steph   I told you, I been walking.

Melissa   I don't believe you.

Steph   I been to the canal. Stormy's. Even went down as far as
the viaduct Mam.
That's where I been.

An I'll go there again, if I wants.

Melissa   I won't have you there.

Steph   It's dark there.
You can't see the ground in front of you it's so dark. Pitch black it is.
There's this street lamp down the Ash path, it buzzes. I think it's the oldest street lamp ever. That lamp have seen some things, I bet Mam.
It looked like a star, so I followed it.
Just at the end of the path, in the shadows. This man's stood there. He looks like he's part of the shadows, it's so dark. I can't see his face.

Melissa   You don't go there. You hear me. I don't want you there.

Steph   He's got his cock in his hand. Just stood there with it in his hand. I stares at him.
And then I walks on.
Who I used to be.
She would have screamed.
But me, I just looks at him and he knows not to fuck with me and I walks past him and he was right. He was right not to fuck with me.
I thought he was disappointed.
A disappointed man.
It's all in yer.
It's how you deal with it. I knows that now. I faced it.
I walks.
In the dark.
In the night. I goes wherever I wants.
People goes down Stormy's in their cars to fuck each other.
All sorts of people. All sorts of cars.
Police comes and everyone scarpers. They let them, the police, they don't do nothing.
Maybe it's truth, Mam. Maybe that's it.
You wants to talk about truth.
People wants to fuck each other, Isn't that the truth. In cars, in lanes, toilets, whatever, it's the truth of people.

The Via Duct is different though.
You knows about the Via Duct, Mam.

Melissa   *I don't.*
No, Steph. Don't say that. You don't say that.

Steph   Truth Melissa!
I think it's sad. A sad place.
Full of sad people with fucked up lives. And I thinks, how?
How did they get there? How did they get to this? What was it?
What happened that got them there? Cos you're not just born into
it, are you. You're not born into being fucked up?
Or is that it? Is that what it is, some of us – that's what we're
meant to be.

Melissa   You're not that. You're not. You're not that.

Steph   I went up the old railway line at the backs of them big
houses on Wordsworth court.
No one goes up there, not in the dark.
It started to rain so I sat under the trees and brambles and it was
like an umbrella.
Nature, it looks after you, don't it.
I liked sitting there in the dark and the rain. You can see in the
houses.
I goes in the gardens and they don't know I'm there.
I like it.
I likes watching them. People.
All doing the same things in different ways. Their houses all looks
the same, like hotels. Like they wears uniforms.
It's like they're showing off by not showing off nothing about
themselves.
But you know what Mam, when their doors are closed they're all
crying, shitting and fucking the same as the rest of us.
I went in to one of them.
The door was open and I went in.

Melissa   What did you do?

Steph   It was clean. Smelt like talc.

Melissa   What did you do, Steph?

Steph   I'm not afraid no more.
Not of nothing.
Not of the dark.
Not of the night.
Not of the shadows.
Nothing.

Melissa   Then God help you.

Melissa *leaves.*

Steph   He won't help me.

Steph *stands in the kitchen.*

*Breathing.

Breathing.

For a moment we see the child.

The music is on the radio.

She moves.

Dances.

Innocent.

The music slowly builds as she breathes.

She starts to really move to the music.

Dances.

Sexualized.

Abandoned.

Lights and music fades to darkness.

*Simon is in a shirt and trousers. A loosened tie.

He's sat at table with a carrier bag open and papers of some sort strewn over the table.

He has a pencil in his mouth.

He's looking at the papers.

Puts down the pencil.

Rubs his brow.

Rubs his temples.

Head in hands.

Deep breathes.

Leans back in chair, head back, closes his eyes, breathes.

Breathes.

Back to it.

Picks up the pencil.

Looks at the papers.

Pushes the papers off the table on to the floor.

Frustrated with himself.

Holds the pencil in fists.

Pencil bends, bends ...

Snaps.

We hear the front door close and Julia sigh.

Simon sits up quickly hides pencil and picks up papers from floor.

Julia enters the kitchen with bags for life full of food.

Simon   Bloody things. Had them piled and then once one goes, they all ...
I'll have to get another briefcase, replace that one I lost.

Julia hasn't noticed. She gets straight into emptying bags into fridge and cupboards.

Julia   Two birthdays and a new baby. Thirty quid. And the worst of it, is that the new baby is Sean Watts from the English

Dept. So Sue McGillis or should I say saint Sue says we should get a special something just from us because a new life is such a wonderful gift. I did this face (does face) and I was thinking if the new baby is such a wonderful gift then why am I forking out an extra twenty quid for another gift.

Simon   Did you say that?

Julia   I was thinking it.

Simon   It was always a fiver. That was the rule. Regardless of occasion.

Julia   Which is exactly what Jean Pritchard said. She said for a new baby she was only prepared to give a fiver. She's got four children and 16 grandchildren of her own to fork out for.

Simon   Fair comment.

Stops for a second.

Julia   How did it go?

Simon   Okay.

Julia   Okay?

Simon   Good. I don't know. Okay. It went.

Julia   Nothing happened?

Simon   No. It was fine.

Julia   No incidents?

Simon   Incident free. He said next week.

Julia   Full time?

Simon   Yes. Back to full time.

Julia   Right.
You're okay with that?

Simon   I am. Yes.
Yes, I think it'll be fine.

Back to unpacking bags.

Simon   He asked me to get his dry cleaning at lunchtime. I
wanted to tell him shove his job. I came this close. Of course
Seth Roberts saw me in the car park. His year eights have won
the under fourteens South West cup so he was 'up for the craic'
as they say. He sees that I'm carrying the Head's dry cleaning and
he hilariously takes to calling me 'Jeeves', for the rest of the day.
'Isn't that so, Jeeves,' 'What does Jeeves think about this'. I could
look at other jobs. I thought of gardening.

Julia   You're a teacher.

Simon   I thought of everything I put you through.

Julia   Head of department.

Simon   The way he looks at me. I wanted to walk out.

Julia   No talk of getting back into the classroom?

Simon   I'm still in the office. I've not yet been unleashed.
Although I've been given things to mark. I think it's a step up.

Julia   There's some soup in the fridge. Left over from yesterday.
I bought the bread you like.

Simon   Although I am good with systems and organisation so I
was a good filer, better than Ann Marie, I thought.
I walked from the office to the dinner hall. Third period.

Julia   A snack before this evening.

Simon   This evening?

Julia   We said we'd go. Max and Henry? We did say. Are you
sure today was okay?

Simon   It's come to my attention that a handful of the female
staff have made the decision to have no further contact with me.
Since my return I mean.
Which is entirely reprehensible all things considered.

Julia   Oh.

Julia stops.

Her mood has changed.

We physically see the change in Julia throughout this speech.

She listens to him.

Simon   I was in the Staff room, sat in my usual chair. Jennifer Hodge and her ridiculous tambourine and Grace Simons were sat opposite. I'd filled and turned on the kettle and was flicking through a holiday brochure one of the mid-day supes had left. Vanessa Harris came in and booms over 'Time for a Tetleys' and the others dutifully laugh even though I've heard it at least fifty times since I've been back and believe me it wasn't remotely funny the first time. So I lift my head and say, 'Milk no sugar thank you Vanessa'. I could visibly see them shuffle. They exchanged looks. So I think 'Let's let this one play itself out and see where they take it'. Vanessa is in the mug cupboard so I call over. 'Mines got a rose on,' I say. No response. She places four mugs next to the kettle. Jen's red and white polka dot, Gracey's floral china and Vanessa's piglet. Next to them is a Woolworth's general purpose, chipped and tannin stained, no sign of my rose. Before I know it, she's poured the water over the teabags and is looking for a spoon. I'm just about to rise to the bait when in bursts Seth Roberts singing some football chant from a five a side social they'd all been at on Sunday. They all fall about laughing as you can imagine. I look over to see Vanessa squashing the teabags against the side of the mugs and spooning them into the bin. All except mine that is. She hands the others out and then turns to me and says, and this is without eye contact, 'yours is on the side, I don't know how you have it'.

Julia   I see.

Simon   Which for the record is entirely untrue because I laminated a list of staff tea and coffee requirements and stuck it on the mug cupboard last week.

Julia sits.

Julia   I need five minutes.

Simon   Then Seth Roberts pipes up, 'Weak Vanessa, Jeeves likes it weak and watery.'
Are you alright Julia, you look wiped out.

Julia   I'm wiped out. I feel completely done in.

Simon   Have five minutes. A cup of tea?

Julia   I'm having five minutes.

Takes off her shoes.

Simon   You come to bed late.

Julia   I could be going down with something.

Simon   You never used to come to bed late.

Julia   I may have a virus.

Simon   Yesterday, you were in the bedroom getting dressed. The door was closed. I nearly knocked.

Julia *looks past* **Simon** *startled. Stands.*

Simon   And I thought ten years we've been together ten years and I felt I should knock. I stopped myself.

Julia *walks to the kitchen top.*

Frantically looks for something.

Lifts things, looks to the floor.

Julia   It's gone. I put it down.
I put it here.
Right here.

Simon   What?

Julia   My watch. I thought, I'll put it there. I'll leave it there and then I'll know.
Did you move it?

Simon   Your watch?

Julia   Yes, my bloody watch. Did you move it?

Simon   No. I haven't seen your watch.

Julia   It was there. That's where I put it. I put it there. Please
Simon.
Is this you?
Are you moving things?

Simon   Am I what? Moving things? What things?

Julia   Please, if it is you, please?

Simon   I don't know what you're talking about?

Julia   Something's not – there's something … Things are moving.

Simon   Moving?

Julia   I think someone's moving my things.

Simon   What?

Julia   Things are moving. Things. I put things down and then
they're not there.

Pause.

Simon   I don't understand.

Julia   My things. Some things have gone.

Simon   Gone!

Julia   I think.
I have a feeling.
I have a feeling that someone … and I know it sounds mental but
… It feels like someone is here. With us.
I can't shake the feeling that someone is here. I don't know.

Simon   There's no one here. You're being …

Julia   My things?

Simon   Right.

Pause. Thinks.

Simon   What things exactly?

Julia   My perfume. The one I got with that voucher from your sister.
And some of my pants.

Simon   Your pants?

Julia   My knickers.

Simon   Jesus Christ.

Julia   I don't know. I thought it was me. But then the window.

Simon   The window?

Julia   Last night. I closed it and I know it's a bit dodgy but that's how I know I closed it. Because it's the one I check.
And last night I checked it and then when we get back it's open?

Simon   Thing is.
Its all fine and this is fine to tell me but fucking hell
I'm like this (holds out his shaking hand to demonstrate flat line) and that's when I'm good. At the moment, at this point in my life – good is nothing.
Good is getting up, scratching my balls, getting dressed, going to work and absolutely nothing happening.
That is a good day.
So things moving and knickers and open windows and shit (shakes his flat-lining hand building to over-exaggerated shaking).

Julia   I know this, (demonstrates the shaking hand) but that window can't just open, can it.

Simon   'Gone' you said?

Julia   Not expensive stuff. It seems more sinister, not just stealing things but then also moving them.
Moving my things.
It's weird.

Simon   '*Your* things' you said.

Julia   I did, yes.

Simon   Just things you put down and then they're not there?

Julia   Yes, sort of, I think.

Simon   You're so busy.
That's what it'll be. You're tired. Forgetting where you put things.

Julia   I thought that. I did.
I thought 'Oh, it's me, I'm knackered. Dementia starting.'
That's what I thought.
Then the window.

Simon   It must have been open.
I think I remember it being open. I'm sure – almost certain – I looked up at it and thought 'Oh the window's open, shit.'

Julia   I put my watch there.
I put it there.
I did. I'm certain.

She sits back down.

Simon   You look exhausted.

Julia   I'm tired.
I don't seem to be able to switch off.

Simon   You're never in bed before one.

Julia   My head is spinning with it all. The last few months.

Simon   You're up at six.

Julia   I don't think I'll ever get back up.

Simon   You should come to bed the same time as me.

Julia   Over and over in my head.

Simon   Please Julia.

Julia   I can't shake it.

Simon   Please.

Julia   I'm sorry. I'm tired.

Simon   Unsubstantiated. Insubstantial evidence. No basis for further investigation. Jesus Christ. These things happen all the time to teachers.

Julia   It was poetry slam tonight. Attendance was low.
Actually no one came.
Sue McGillis took it upon herself to volunteer two lads she had in detention.
The potential for disaster was great.
In they come with attitude and intimidation. A fight broke out almost immediately.
Sue took Kai Riches off to the staff room with her and I was left with Tyler Banks.

Simon   Right.

Julia   Divide and conquer.
He worked. Quietly. For almost half an hour. He curled his arm around his book. Chewed his top lip.
Like a child.

Simon   You made progress. That's good.

Julia   I asked him to read out his work.

'Girl you know I like it when you climb on top
Love muscles feel tighter than a headlock
And you know I love the way you make the bed rock
Take me to ecstasy without taking Ecstacy.'

It's a rap. 50 cents. He was aggressive and frowning.

Simon   Right.

Julia   I told him it was good. That I liked it. That he should feel free to express himself in any way he wanted.

Simon   Yes.

Julia   His face softened. I saw it. He softened. With flattery. It took me by surprise.
He was looking for approval. Like a child.

Simon   Julia.

Julia   He looked at my tits.
I let him. I caught his eye. He licked his lips.
I noticed he has quite a substantial amount of bristles on his chin.
And a broad back. His hands are unexpectedly large I thought. But he is six foot. So.
I looked at his crotch.

Simon   I don't know what you're trying to do.

Julia   Although he is only fifteen I thought how absurd it would be to imagine that he was an innocent. He possessed some sort of instinct I thought for this sort of sexual play and then I thought that it was quite delicious actually his instinctive raw unashamed hunger. He looked like he wanted to gobble me up.

Simon   Please, stop it.

Julia   I waited for a twinge. A feeling. Something. Excitement. But there was nothing. Actually not nothing. I felt shifty. Unsettled. I thought of his face softening. Of his searching approval. And even though he looked at me with a convincing level of sexual want. I saw that he is a child.

Simon   What do you want me to say?

Julia   At the time there was talk of a book. A diary. A diary. With details of a seemingly inappropriate relationship. The diary that was given to the Head.

Simon   A book of lies.

Julia   What happened to the diary?

Simon   I don't know.

Julia   It's that one thing. Because without it there's nothing, no case. But it's in here. *(head)*

Simon   He said. The head said it was nothing more than fantasy. A teenage fantasy.

Julia   Where is it?

Simon   Forget about the diary. The diary is gone.

A dim pool of light isolates a solitary Victorian sash window.

A shadow behind the glass. Hands pulling at the window. Struggling. Pulling. Heaving. Eventually it gives and opens.

Steph climbs through.

She stands lit by moonlight in front of the window. In a bedroom. She stands. A long time. She breathes in. Smells the air.

Julia   I saw her.
I. Saw. Her.

Simon   You've seen her?

Julia   I looked for her. I went to where she lives.
I had a feeling. A gut feeling when I saw her.

Simon   Then you've seen the sort of kid she is. Where she's from. The mother. Did you see the mother?

Julia   I saw truth. I felt it. I saw truth in her.

She moves. Towards a traditional large pine dressing table, centre stage. (The dressing table has a large oval mirror in the centre with the glass out so the effect is a see through mirror).

She touches things.

Simon   I think it's all got too much, I think you need to rest. To sleep. You'll feel better after a good night's sleep.

Julia   The diary was in your drawer.

Simon   No.

Julia   In the dresser.

Fingers designer scarves and necklaces that are draped around the mirror. Runs her hand over expensive pots and creams and polishes and sprays. She sprays the air. Sniffs. Rubs her nose. Throws the perfume. She opens the pots and creams, sniffs them.

Simon   There was no diary.

Julia   And now it's gone.

Simon   It wasn't there.

Julia   I saw a book.

Picks up lipsticks and brushes. Plays with them, applies them crudely, childlike.

Simon   You've been through my things.

Julia   My ring has gone.

Opens the drawers, takes out tampons, letters, bits and bobs. Opens another drawer, takes out expensive lingerie, pretty bras and lacy knickers. Examines them, fingers the pretty soft fabrics, smells them, closes her eyes, breathes them in.

Simon   Your wedding ring?

Julia   I thought it might have dropped into your drawer.

Simon   Your wedding ring?

Julia   My ring wasn't there.
I saw the book had gone.

Simon   You read it.

Julia   I thought – I need to believe you – I wanted to trust you.

Simon   You *wanted* to? You *wanted* to trust me?

Julia   I trust you.

Simon   But you went back.

Julia   I saw a book and now it's gone.

Simon   You looked for it?

Julia   Yes.

Steph opens her eyes and sees herself in the mirror. Looks at herself.

Simon *leaves.*

Julia stands.

Paces.

Confused.

Distressed.

Picks up her bag and leaves.

Steph picks up nail scissors and looks at the knickers – thinks about it.

Looks at herself.

Puts the scissors down. The lingerie away. Closes the drawers.

Looks at herself.

Rubs at her face. Pulling her face. Lifts her hair pulling it this way and that, drags it down. Flattens it with her sticky palms. Flatter and flatter. Finds a band and ties it back as flat as it will go. She finds wipes and cleans off her face. Rubbing it clean, rubbing it free.

Looks at herself.

Again picks up the scissors. Picks up her hair. Starts to cut off her hair. Timidly at first then builds to great chunks. So finally she is left with short cropped hair.

She looks at herself. Ignores the hair all around her.

*Her own reflection catches and holds her.

Unrecognisable.

Indifferent.

A long time.

As long as she can comfortably get away with as the light fades to darkness.

*****Melissa*** *is in the kitchen.*

Her hair's in velcro rollers.

She checks herself out in a hand-held mirror.

She's got a big bag of makeup on the table.

She's peeling veg into a bowl.

Steph *enters.*

Home from school.

She has a beanie on.

She is caked in mud. Her hands, her face.

Obviously had her hands in earth.

She holds poppies in her hands, with earth attached. Recently dug.

Melissa *carries on peeling veg doesn't look at* **Steph**.

Steph   What you doing?

Melissa   You're home early?

Steph   Finished early.

Steph *puts the poppies on the side.*

Melissa   Whatever, Steph.

Steph   What you doing?

Melissa   What?

Steph   This. What's this? There's a table cloth? And is that – mats?

Melissa   What? Yeah.

Steph   Yeah.
Is this for me? Cloths and mats?
Makes me nervous.

Melissa   Right.

Looks at **Steph** *for first time.*

Melissa   What's that? Mud? Is that mud. What have you … Have you been digging?

Steph   Saw some flowers.

Melissa   You're covered in mud?

Steph   I am, yes. I'll have a bath.

Melissa   I give up.

Steph   I feel like a bath.

Melissa   Right. You do that.

Steph   Is this for me?

Melissa   What?

Steph   This – candles?

(Beat)

Not for me.

Melissa   No.

Steph   Right. So you're having someone over. For tea? Janine?

(Beat)

No. Who then?

Melissa   That fella. The one from before.

Steph   The soldier? He came back?

Melissa   He did.

Steph   That's something then.

Takes off her hat, revealing her hair.

Melissa   Your hair?

Steph   What is he? Your boyfriend? Is that what he is?

Melissa   What have you done?

Steph   How many times do you fuck someone before they're your boyfriend?

Melissa   What have you done to your hair, Steph?

Steph   Or are you just 'seeing' him.
Is he just a 'friend'.
Too old for uncles! That's one thing.

Melissa   Stephanie.
What have you done to your hair?

Steph   Oh yeah, that. Fancied a change.
You know me, always messing with my hair.
Ever happy.

Melissa   Something's happened?

Steph   Nothing's happened.

Melissa   You changed your hair.

Steph   What of it.

Melissa   This hair's about something.

Stop.

Look at each other.

Steph   I'm getting in the way. Don't let me stop you. You carry on.

Melissa   You're gonna tell me about this hair.

Steph   I'm a teenager you know what we're like.

Melissa   No. This – this isn't you.

Steph   It's my hair. My hair. I cut it.

Melissa   *You. You* cut your hair. Where?

Steph   Where?

Melissa   Yes, where?

Steph   What does it matter, where?

Melissa   You go to school and you comes back with your hair like that?

Steph   I done it last night, actually. Not that you'd know.

Melissa   You're not wearing makeup.

Steph   That's a crime is it.

Melissa   You're dressing like a boy.

Steph   I don't believe you.

Melissa   Now the hair … It's not you.

Steph   This is me.

Melissa   I don't see you.

Steph   You don't look.

Steph *storms off.*

Melissa *carries on making up.*

*Fusses her hair.

After a while goes to the poppies.

Light fades to black.

A modern family kitchen.

Lunchtime. Weekday.

*Julia dressed and stressed. Coat on, bag on shoulder.

Simon unkempt.

Not dressed.

Simon   There was dust. It's started. That's what I thought.

Julia   Right.

Simon   I'd run the shower. I was going to dress. I could feel it.
'Today', I thought 'I'm going to dress'.

Julia   And then.

Simon   And then there was no soap. So I came down to the
kitchen to get some soap from under the sink.

Julia   Not the bathroom cabinet?

Simon There was none in the cabinet Julia. It made sense to try under the sink. And then it happened.

Julia Dust you said.

Simon Practically rubble.

Julia Practically.

Simon The next stage would have been rubble.

Julia It looks fine.

Simon Now. It looks fine now. There was shaking. I swear there was shaking.

Julia Right.

Simon We should never have got your father in. We should have got someone who can bend and see.

Julia He likes to help.

Simon The whole sodding house is going to fall down.

Julia No. It's not.

Simon The ceiling will cave in and it'll be just my sodding luck to be stood underneath it looking for soap in a place where the bloody soap shouldn't have been to start with.
Naked. I'll probably be naked.

Julia You called me at work.

Simon I'd be in the local papers. Seth Roberts would love that. He'd love it alright. It'd be all about dropping your soap, watching your cracks and all that locker room stuff.

Julia You called me at work. For this.

Simon He'd not let it drop.

Julia I have to go. To work.

Simon You have to? Is there any point? I don't know that there's any point?

Julia   I work. I should be at work and I'm here. With you.
Listening to you.

Simon   By the time you get there it will be time to come home.

Julia   I have poetry slam.

Simon   Cancel it.

Julia   No.

Simon   I'll cook. I'll make something nice. Something without carbs.

Julia   I won't want anything.

Steph *enters kitchen.*

Melissa *plays with the poppy on the table.*

Simon   Vegetables. Chicken.

Julia   For Christ sake.
I should get back. I need to work. Can't have both of us, sick.

Simon   I'm not sick.

Melissa   Peace offering?

Steph *says nothing.*

Melissa   You know why the poppy is a symbol of remembrance?

Nothing.

Melissa   Poppies were the first flowers to grow in the earth on the soldiers' graves in France.
Imagine that, Steph.
Poppies, in all that sad brown earth. There's a poem.

Steph   In Flanders fields.

Melissa   In Flanders fields. I remembers that from school. All them graves. Them soldiers.
The churned up earth with all them men, underneath.
The lives they could have had.

Steph   And then there's just a field, a churned up field. But in time out of the earth comes the most perfect piece of nature and life.

Melissa   That's some sight, I reckon.
A field of poppies.

Steph   Yeah. Reckon it is.

Steph   Them poppies aren't a symbol of remembrance, Mam. You know what I thinks of when I thinks of them poppies?

Melissa   What?

Steph   Resurrection.

Simon   It's just with the break in. Last night.

Julia   You should get dressed, at least.

Simon   He was very understanding I thought. When I phoned him earlier. The head. Said at least it wasn't shit. Said he'd heard of people having shit up the walls with a break in. Said head of Maths in his previous school had come home to 'cunt' spelt out in shit over the walls. I think that would be worse. So. It was just a shock. An invasion. Someone in your home.

Julia   A violation.

Drops her bag.

Steph and Melissa in kitchen.

Melissa is sat at the table, peeling potatoes into a washing up bowl.

Melissa   I'll phone him. Tell him not to come. We'll have a night in, shall we. A girls' night.
Just you and me.

Steph   If you want.

Melissa   I want.
You know, it used to be amazing yer.
Won awards theses flats did. When they was first built.

Used to be a good area.

Steph   People like you moved in.
Area goes downhill fast with people like you in it.

Melissa   Cheeky sod you are.

Look at each other and laugh.

Nice to have you smiling.

Pause.

What's that thing.
You know that thing when good goes to good and bad to bad and
all that.

Steph   Karma.
Eye for an eye.
Two wrongs make a right.

Melissa   Two wrongs don't make a right. That's the saying.

Steph   I know the saying.

Melissa   You said it wrong. It's a proverb. There, that's
something else I learned in school.
A proverb.

Steph   I knows that. I knows what I said.

Melissa   You said it wrong.

Steph   Two wrongs make a right. Like evens init.
So. You scratch my car with a key. I kick in your fence. Two
wrongs. Now it's fair. Everything's evens.

Melissa   Two wrongs makes a right it is.
Come on, get your hands dirty. I'm gonna do us the best cooked
dinner ever.

Passes her a veg knife.

Steph   Christ does the oven work, does it?

Melissa   You got a nerve you.

(beat)
I dunno. You better check. The hob works. I'll do a stew.
Bung it all in.

Steph   Sounds divine.

Simon   What's the matter?

Julia   What's the matter?
Somebody broke into our home.
Sat in our bedroom and cut off their hair. Not somebody.
Her.
It was her, wasn't it?

Simon   You don't know that. We don't know.

Julia   She broke into our home.
And I want to know why.

A look.

Hold the look as long as they can.

Simon *breaks the look.*

Paces.

Julia *leaves the kitchen.*

Simon *pacing.*

Paces.

Doesn't know what to do with himself.

Melissa flicks water at Steph. Steph flicks back.

Laughs.

Melissa   There you go. Two wrongs makes a right!
I flick you, you flicks me.
Now we're square.

Steph   You know them people, them in the big houses I was
telling you about. They'd say that one that you said. Two wrongs
don't make a right. They'd say that cos they thinks it makes them

look good. Like they're all forgiving an' that. They lives in a
world where they pretends to be something they're not.
There's no peace in their lives, Mam.
Cos they eats away at you lies. They eats away at you till you
can't see straight no more.
I believe that Mam.
I believe that one hundred per cent cos I seen it.

Simon *sweeps the contents of the table to the floor.*

Melissa   Are you gonna be any help to me? You can get started
on them carrots.

Steph   He'll get it worse living the lie.
I think he's a kind man. I do. I think he is kind. Sometimes.
Which sometimes makes me feel bad but there you go.
Am I pretty?

Melissa   What?

Steph   Me.
Am I pretty do you think?

Melissa   Are you pretty?
I suppose.

Steph   I am.
I am pretty.
I know that.

Melissa   Good. Good for you.

Steph   I have something.
That thing.
Something about me.

Melissa   I don't know.

Steph   I do. I see it.
I don't know what it is.
They sees it. Men.

Melissa   Stop it.

Steph   They sees it. He saw it.

Melissa   Stop it.

Steph   I thought he liked me.

Melissa   Yeah.

Steph   I trusted him. I thought he was kind.

Melissa   You know, I worked in the Lion after I had you.

Steph   No, I didn't know.

Melissa   Cos I was skint.

Steph   You're always skint.

Melissa   You was about one.
I didn't want to leave you. But.
Didn't have a choice.
My Dad died.
Didn't have no one else. No one to turn to.
There was this woman, Tanya, lived in the flat next door and she
took you in so I could go out an
earn a couple of bob. You was no bother.
You was gorgeous. Big brown eyes, only had eyes for me.
You never cried.
Then I got a couple of days work down the road in the post office.
I thought my shit was chocolate with that little job. I did. I thought
it was.
Cos it was a step up, you know, from the pub.
I hated that pub, stinking of booze and fags and all the men, pissed
up trying to cop a feel.
But them couple of days in the post office. I thought that was
proper, it was respectable. Like an office job sort of thing.
(beat)
After a while the boss, he said I'd been nicking from him.
Said he was gonna call it in. Tell the police.
I had though, that was the thing.
I was beside myself. Cos it was bad enough that I was on my
own but then I thought if I ends up banged up and they takes you

off me. I thought that would be it, like. That would be the end for me.
Then he says he can sort it out for me.
He knows a way I can pay him back.
I didn't know what else to do.
I didn't like it but I could blank it out, in my head, pretend it weren't happening.
But then he keeps coming at me.
Coming back for more.
So, I tells him 'no'.
One day, I just comes out with it. 'No'.
He knocked the shit outta me.

Pause.

Steph   Mam.

Julia *comes back to the kitchen.*

Julia   What's that?

Simon *looks to where* **Julia** *is pointing.*

Julia   Under your papers. What is it?

Simon   What?
I don't know.

Julia   What do you mean you don't know?

Simon   I don't know. I don't know what you're looking at.

Julia   I'm looking under your papers. There. Sticking out.

Simon   I don't know.

Julia   Under your papers, for Christ sake.

Simon   It's nothing. It's nothing Julia.

Julia   You don't know. You said you don't know.

Simon   No. I've never seen it before.

Julia   How do you know its nothing then?

Simon   I know.

Julia   It looks like a book.

Simon   Please, it's nothing.

Simon *covers it. Hides it.*

Julia   It's the diary. Is it the diary?

Simon   I don't know how it got there. I don't.

Julia   I want to see it.

Julia *moves to get it.* **Simon** *stops her.*

Simon   It will upset you.

Julia   Why will it upset me?

Simon   He gave it to me. The head. He said it was a work of
fiction. Didn't want it getting in the wrong hands. The cleaners,
you know, they go through everything and his secretary.
He said. He said to put it somewhere.

Julia   But it was evidence.

Simon   I had it. And I didn't know what to do.
Believe me, Julia. I didn't know what to do with it.

Julia   You shouldn't have taken it.

Simon   I kept it. And then I thought the house might be searched.
I don't know. I'm not a criminal. This is all new to me. I don't
know how these things work. I thought it could be used against
me in some way so I hid it.

Julia   I think if the police were going to search this house for
indecent material I think one of the first places they'd look is your
drawer in the dressing table.

Simon   I hid it under the floorboards. In the bathroom. But then
what with the leak and your father.
I moved it.

Julia   To your drawer.

Simon   And then it went.
It went missing. I didn't move it again. It just went.
I thought it was you.

Julia   Me?

Simon   And I haven't seen it since. Until now. Until there.

Julia   Give it to me.

Simon   No. It's just a diary.

Julia   Her diary.

Simon   I'll burn it. It'll be gone. By the time you come home.
It'll be gone.

Julia   You kept it. You kept it, Simon.

Simon   Yes.

Julia   Why did you keep it?
Jesus Christ, why did you keep it?
Because you'd destroy it. Normal people would destroy it.
I would have destroyed it.
But you kept it. Hid it. Protected it.
Why?

Simon   I don't know.

Julia   Give it to me.

Simon   A teenager's ramblings. A stupid teenager rambling.

Julia   Give me the fucking diary.

Simon   No. Please Julia.

Julia *launches at him, hits him. He takes hold of her hands to stop
her.*

Julia   Please. Please for fuck's sake, Simon.

Simon surrenders the fight.

Gives Julia the diary.

An exercise book with scribbling on the covers.

Simon   It's a situation. A situation and there are two sides. There are most definitely two sides to this. There are illusions. And impressions. It is a book of illusions and impressions.

Pacing. Anxious.

She sits and opens it.

Reads.

Simon   The newspapers. The hacking. The journalists you know. They thought it was okay. How within their profession it was an accepted practice. It was almost ridiculous that we would not have realised. Because that happens I think. The way your behaviour in the safety of your own world becomes common practice or simply perfectly acceptable.
It's only when you step out of this you realise it's not right at all.
But historically this happens Julia. The MP's expenses, corrupt police, soldiers and that water blasting and torture. That sort of thing.
Perfectly normal people in an abnormal world, even the holocaust.
We judge them but we have not stood in their shoes.
Don't tell me they all were evil. All of them.
Everyone who knew what was going on.
All the soldiers, their wives, families, cleaners, cooks.
Even people who lived nearby. It was a practice
that was acceptable in their world.
In their wartime.

He is still pacing and anxious.

Julia *looks up from the diary.*

Julia   There are letters.
It says here there are letters.

Simon   She says a lot of things that aren't true.

Julia   She wrote you letters.

Simon   Not true. Not me.

Julia   Where are the letters?

Simon   No letters.
No letters Julia.

Julia puts the book down.

Julia   You're lying. You are lying to me.

Gets up.

Gets herself a glass of water.

Simon   No.
There was no case. Nothing to answer to. Unsubstantiated.
For Christ sake.

Stands and looks out of the kitchen window into the garden.

Simon   Are you not happy. Will you not be happy until I'm
rocking in a straitjacket in a cell. Is that what you want? Do you
want me repeatedly banging my head and dribbling in some cell
somewhere.

Still looking out of the window.

Julia   The poppies are dead Simon.
They didn't come to anything. Which is a shame I think because
the promise of them was really quite splendid.
The weight and length of their stem has made them curl over.
They've unearthed. Their roots are exposed.
I can see the soil around them. There's something else.
Underneath the soil something just showing.
It looks like a case of some sort. I think it may well be the
briefcase you lost. The one I bought you when you were made
Head of department.

Are the letters in the briefcase Simon?

Simon   I was kind to her. I should have known better. It was
Seth. Seth Roberts. You know how he was. How he is. How he
made me feel. He bullied me Julia. Bullied me for years. And he
was saying all this stuff and I didn't stop it. I didn't stop him. I
watched. I watched him. And I said nothing. I did nothing.

Julia goes to the door, exits.

Steph   I was waiting for him, I wanted to show him this thing I'd seen cos he was helping me, talking about my future.

Talking about me having a career an all that. He thought if I worked hard I'd be able to go to college even get a degree if I wanted. And I waited for him but he didn't come and then so I went down to the staff room to look out for him and there's no one around. Even the cleaners have gone by now. I can see the back of him.
Then I heard him talking to this other teacher and they was taking the piss. This one, Mr Roberts.
Seth Roberts they calls him, I think you knows him, he likes the dark.
He's saying that I'm some sort of easy pussy. Saying that he needed to watch himself around me.
My sort.
Saying that not so long ago a girl of my age would've been fair game. Legal. Said it's since women got the vote and contraception. Said that was when we stopped knowing our place. That was when all the trouble started. And he was laughing. And I was thinking you wait Simon's gonna give it to you both barrels now mate. He won't have you getting away with that. But you know what. He stood there laughing with him. Laughing at me. At me, mum.
I couldn't breathe. I thought my throat was closing. And my eyes was watering. It weren't crying. It was like I'd steamed up. Boiled over. I went out into the lane behind the carpark and I thought I'd scratch all their cars you know so I could breathe again. And he's coming after me.

Melissa   Simon had seen you?

Steph   Not Simon. No. Not Simon, Mam. Seth. He came after me.
Seth is in the lane. And he's looking at me. Looking through me. Looking through my clothes at my
tits, looking down me. I try to run past him. But he's grabbed me before I can get anywhere and he's putting his hand up my skirt. I

can feel his cock pushing through them stupid trousers they wear.
And I know what's going to happen, Mam. I knows all about that
don't I.
But I can't do nothing.
He's grabbing at my tits and then I sees he's got his cock in his
hand.
And he's forcing my head down. Forcing it in my mouth.
And its making me gag but he's pushing it harder in. And then I
looks up and I sees him.
At the top of the lane. Simon.
I can see him. And he's just stood there. He's not doing nothing.
He's not helping me. He's watching. Just stood there watching.
And then he lets go of me. Puts himself away, does himself up like
he's just finished a piss or something normal like.
And he goes back to Simon and he laughs about something,
smacks Simon on the back and they walks off back to school.
He looked back.
Simon.

Simon *talks after her – carries on, when she is off stage.*

Simon   Truth?
You said you saw truth in her. The irony.
She has a foul mouth. Her mother's a whore. You didn't know that
did you? A prostitute. Has a regular patch down the viaduct. She's
been giving Seth blow jobs for the last four years. This is who
we're talking about Julia. These people.

Julia *re-enters with the briefcase covered in mud.*

Simon   And you'd believe them.
You'd believe her.
Over someone like me.

She throws the briefcase, hits him, screams at him, loses it.

Then composes herself and leaves the room.

Simon *is left on stage with the briefcase.*

Steph   I knew he wouldn't do nothing.
Wouldn't say what had happened.

Wouldn't stand up for me. I saw that in him.
At that moment. And that got to me more than the other stuff,
Mam. He let me down.
That made me feel like nothing.
That was a wrong.

Melissa   Yes. That was a wrong.

Steph   They would have come here, you know that don't you.
They would have looked at us. At you.
They wouldn't have done nothing.
Evil prevails when a good man does nothing.

Blackout.

End

Bruised

Matthew Trevannion

Bruised was first performed at Clwyd Theatr Cymru in May 2012, directed by Kate Wasserberg, and featured the following cast:

Wendy	Sara Harris Davies
Stephanie	Bethan Witcomb
Noah	Sion Pritchard
Shane	Simon Nehan
Adam	Rhys Wadley
Lugs	Kristian Phillips
Designer	Max Jones
Wardrobe Supervisor	Ruth Hall
Lighting Designer	Nick Beadle
Fight Director	Rachel Bown-Williams

Scene One

Adam *is seventeen years old. He wears no shoes, white socks,
jeans and a jumper that's too big for him, rolled up to the elbow
and loose around the neck. Across the stage stands* **Noah**. **Noah** *is
twenty-seven years old. He wears a heavy coat, jeans and sturdy
pair of shoes. On his back he carries a large rucksack. He has one
black eye, a split lip and his hair is wet.*

Adam   We didn't have any windows. We had one bulb to save
us changing in the dark. The sound of boot studs over concrete
got the nerves going and when we were ready we settled on the
bench, each boy staring at the ground between their boots. In the
week leading up to it you couldn't turn a corner without talk of
the game; every parent, teachers, I go down to fetch our Mam a
pack a' fags and shopkeeper John wants to talk about our chances.
The headmaster called an assembly. He wanted to assure us that
regardless of the result we had done our school proud. Fuck that.
For the boys involved it was everything, more than that. I'm
sitting there and I feel sick. Mr Edwards stands in the doorway,
whistle round his neck; 'ready boys?' he says, and I'm gonna pop.
'It's been a long time coming', he says. We run out and half of
Pontypool's huddled in the grandstand. They clap us onto the field
and right then and there I could have been running out against
the English. It hits me as I get on to the pitch, that this can't be
right, this feels too good. So I brace myself for something to ruin
it. I lift my head and there you are, stood on the other side of the
field, as he liked it, alone and in opposition to the world. Soaked
in the rain, you wave and I feel proud, he glares and I'm spoiling
for it. The whistle blows and I can feel him, in every tackle, every
kick, every pass. He screams as others cheer, they clap whilst he
curses. And I know it's either I get these boys now or he gets me
later. So with every tackle I give that little bit more. At the centre
of every maul I'm ragging the ball from boys, possessed. I'm
charging at rucks like my life depends on it. And I'm not thinking
now. I take this boy high round the neck, and I meant it. His butty
takes a swing and it all goes up, both teams fly at each other. And
you're looking for anyone in the other jersey, everyone swinging

at anyone. And me and this boy, we stumble but I'm held up by the crush, and I'm stamping, fuck him, you get carried away, and I'm thinking fucking have some of that, and I hear screaming, I'm stamping, stop, the whistle's going, someone's shouting, stop, stop, stop! *(Beat)* I open my eyes, everyone's stepped back and this boy is screaming and he's clutching his jaw, and it must've been me because everyone's staring at me, at me and him and there's blood. Blood all over him. I just turn and walk away from it. I just focus on the road and I run, straight past the grandstand, and above all of their outrage I can hear him whistling. That's when he started cheering. That's when encouragement came. That's when he let his love show. It was late when I came in the door that night, he smiled at me as I took off my boots. You looked me in the eye and I could barely stand it.

The lights come up on the front room of a council flat in Pontypool, South Wales. It's a room that is comprised of items that don't co-ordinate. A room full of hand-me-downs. It's out of date. A dark sofa sits downstage right. Next to the sofa is a small table with a telephone and a lamp on it. Upstage stage left of the sofa is a small dining table with four chairs. One is different from the rest. In the centre of the back wall is the front door. It has a sheet of dimpled glass in it. Along the wall stage right is a glass-fronted drinks cabinet with a missing pane of glass. Stage left of the front door a mirror hangs on the wall. A small bookcase leans against the wall stage right, a few feet downstage from the kitchen doorway, which is without a door. On the opposite wall is the doorway to the rest of the house, to the bedrooms, bathroom etc. Sat on the sofa is **Shane**. *He is a man in his late thirties. He has short hair that thins towards the forehead and five-day stubble. He is wearing a pair of shorts and a short-sleeved rugby jersey. He has thick hairy forearms that are covered in cheap tattoos. He sits reading the paper.*

Silence.

Shane   Wendy. Wendy? *(Beat)* You alright in there or what?

Wendy   *(Off stage)* Yeah. Okay. Just a minute.

Shane   Still in the land of the living then? Is breakfast still on the cards or/

Wendy   /Coming, now in a minute.

Shane   *(To himself)* Mind you don't rush yourself. *(To **Wendy**)* Cooking the bacon over a candle is it? Well, do us a favour love, and light another one will you? Tell you what, you can come in here and strike the match off my tongue. At the very least get a shift on with the tea. *(Reading, to himself)* Will you look at this bollocks. *(To **Wendy**)* Listen to this. Amazing paintings and sketches by local girl Tracy Evans who, as it happens, can't walk or talk, are to be exhibited at the Town Hall at the end of the month. I mean, what? I'm sorry but you can't call these chicken scratchings paintings. They're shit, they're just shit, and call me what you like but the fact that she's a vegetable don't change nothing. They're still shit. *(Reading, to himself)* Aye. *(To **Wendy**).* And wouldn't you know, more than half of Tracy's eighty piece collection of still life's and abstracts have already been sold. I fucking bet they have and all, to patronising bastards that need to prove they've got a heart. If she could walk it'd be put down that brush, love, and pick up this mop, no fucking bother.

(Beat) Oh and here's a turn up, Mother, proud father Mark, who has been inseparable from his daughter for nineteen years since she was diagnosed with cerebral palsy, has written a book to coincide with the exhibition. Simply titled 'Tracy'. Touching stuff ha? It all worked out in the end, look.

Wendy *enters, she is a woman in her late forties. She is slim and tired in tracksuit bottoms and a shirt. She doesn't wear any make up and her hair is scraped back from her face. She hands **Shane** a cup of tea. She smokes a cigarette.*

Probably knocked the paintings out himself, the prick. Who's she gonna tell? *(He sips his tea)* You haven't put any sugar in this.

Wendy   I put sugar in it. I did.

Shane   *(Sips again)* You haven't. There's no sugar in it.

Wendy   Really?

Shane   Why would I lie?

Wendy   No. Sorry.

She takes it back and exits to the kitchen, mumbling inaudibly as she exits.

I'm sure I did, maybe not. I need my head reading …

Shane   *(Reads more of the paper, silence, he laughs)* 'Ere. Devastating scenes unfold today as Barry Sturgis, lorry driver, has been taken into custody. Gwent police were shocked to find his articulated lorry full of Chinese asylum seekers. Thirty-six in total and all of them dead. *(Reading. Laughs)* Unbelievable, the daft prick, he's only stuck them in the back of his air tight freezer unit.

Wendy *enters with tea.*

Wendy   If it isn't good news Shane …

Shane   He should've watched Blue Peter. You always punch a few air holes in the top Wend, ah? Rule number one. *(Taking the tea)* Still, few less for the Benefits Office to worry about.

Wendy   That's awful.

Shane   Where's my sandwich? *(Beat)* Fucking hell man *(tapping his temple with his finger)*. Where are you today?

Wendy   I … Sorry what?

Shane   Sandwich!?

Wendy   Yes! Coming, coming.

She exits hurriedly.

Shane   God, give me strength. *She enters.*

Wendy   Here we are.

Shane   *(Closing the newspaper, takes the sandwich)* Ta. Crossword? *(Beat)* Do you want the crossword?

Wendy   Oh, Thank you love.

Shane   *(Takes a bite of his sandwich)* Fuck's sake, man.

Wendy   What?

Shane   Brown sauce?

Wendy   Sorry, I'm sorry. Give it here, I'll/

Shane   /No, no, don't trouble yourself, I'll do it. Or else we'll be here till next fucking week.

Shane *exits.*

Wendy *makes her way to the mirror. She fiddles with her hair. A little downhearted by what she sees, she sits at the table.*

Shane *enters.*

Shane   'Ere, when you do the shopping next, just get white bread will you? You know I can't stand brown bread.

Wendy   It's healthier.

Shane   Who gives a fuck? Really? Could do with a few tins of lager and all, alright? *(Beat)* Oh?

Wendy   Yes love?

Shane   You're not with it at all today are you?

Wendy   No. Sorry.

Shane   What's the matter with you?

Wendy   Nothing.

Shane   Then stop your flapping. Go splash some cold water on your face or something. What time's he getting in?

Wendy   His plane landed at nine, he should be here now any minute.

Shane   Right, well, you wanna shape up then. You gonna stick some slap on for him or what? Tidy yourself up a bit?

Wendy   I put my earrings in, look.

Shane   *(Noncommittal)* Oh yeah. They're lovely.

He finishes his sandwich in four bites. He puts his plate on the table in front of **Wendy** *and exits towards the bedroom. Silence.* **Shane** *enters again with a shirt in his hands.*

I'm gonna have a quick shower. Do us a favour and run an iron over this, will you?

Wendy   Give us it here.

Shane   And have a fucking whisky or something.

Shane *exits.*

Wendy *makes her way into the kitchen. She returns with an ironing board. She drapes the shirt over the ironing board then stands, one hand resting on the shirt the other holding the iron, frozen. Silence. The door knocks. A dog can be heard barking faintly. The door knocks again. She makes her way over to the door and she opens it.*

Noah *enters.*

Wendy   Bloody hell!

Beat.

Noah   Bloody hell?

Wendy   No, your face!

Noah   Oh, right. Yeah, um/

Wendy   /Come in, sorry, come in. What's happened to your face?

Noah *enters.*

Noah   It's not as bad as it looks.

Wendy   Let's have a look. It looks pretty bad to me. What on earth have you done?

Noah   It's fine.

Wendy   Son/

Noah   /Boys on a night out. Drunken nonsense.

Beat.

Wendy Raining out is it?

Noah Just started.

Wendy You're wet.

Noah Yeah, I'd say mostly sweat. Dragging a heavy bag up that hill do take some doing don't it?

Wendy Does it? I get up and down it a couple a times a week. *(Beat)* Well, you'd better set your bag down now there quick, before you fall over. *(Beat)* I suppose you want a drink then, do you? A glass of water? Orange squash? I can make you a cup of tea if you want.

Noah A glass of water would be fine.

Wendy Okay. You rest up there a minute now. Catch your breath.

She exits.

She returns with a glass of water.

Noah Thanks.

Wendy *stares at* **Noah***, taking him in as* **Noah** *finishes his water in one.*

Wendy Do you want another one?

Noah Not at the minute.

Wendy Do you want a sandwich, or something? Are you hungry? What do you want?

Noah I'm alright for now. I had a quick bite on the train so I'll be alright for a while I reckon.

Wendy Oh right. Well don't hesitate to ask. You just let me know and I'll sort it out.

Noah I will.

Beat.

Wendy You got the train alright then?

Noah   Yeah, no problems.

Silence.

Wendy   I should get on/

Noah   /A man on the train had a ... Sorry I/

Wendy   /No ... Go on ...

Noah   Oh no, it don't matter, I was just ... um ... *(Clears his throat)* Sorry, you were saying. What were you saying?

Wendy   No, nothing really I was, just, the ironing, no rush, please, go on. The man on the train?

Noah   Yeah ... Er ... He had a fit.

Beat.

Wendy   Oh right.

Noah   Yeah.

Wendy   Was he alright? Was he young or old?

Noah   He was a young guy yeah, he was younger than me.

Wendy   Oh, there's a pity.

Noah   Aye, it is yeah. *(Beat)* He banged his head.

Beat.

Wendy   Other than that, was it pleasant enough?

Noah   Long ... Really long, you know. Twenty hours all in all with changes.

Wendy   Bloody hell.

Noah   But coming into the train station though, I had to laugh.

Wendy   Why? Laugh at the station?

Noah   Well, aye.

Wendy   What's wrong with it?

Noah   You start your journey at Tokyo Narita, the largest airport in all Japan and wind up at Pontypool train station.

Wendy   A bus shelter on train tracks.

Noah   That's exactly what it looks like. A bus shelter on train tracks. That's spot on that is.

Wendy   Been that way since I was a girl. Nothing much changes round here, son.

Noah   I'd say you were right.

Beat.

Wendy   You sure now you don't want nothing to eat?

Noah   Positive.

Beat

Wendy   Well I'll just get on with this shirt a minute, I/

Noah   /I got you some presents, you don't have to have them now, they're in the bag. Just … Whenever you're/

Wendy   /You got me presents? Plural?

Noah   Of course I got you presents, plural. It's nothing massive or nothing, don't get too excited. Do you want them now?

Wendy   Go on then, aye. Yes please.

Noah *starts to rummage through his bag.*

Wendy *takes a seat at the table.*

You didn't go spending too much on me did you, son? I don't like the thought of you spending your money on me, young man should be off spending it on himself.

Noah   No, it's just a token really. *(Beat)* You ready then or what?

Wendy   Aye, come on, hit me with it.

Noah *produces a bag with Cardiff Airport emblazoned on it. He hands it to* **Wendy**. *She looks inside the bag.*

Duty free?

Noah   You still smoke don't you?

Wendy   Like a trooper, son. I'm not proud of it.

Noah   Well, it's a good job, coz I got you a ton of 'em.

Wendy   Loads?

Noah   *(Reaching back into his rucksack and producing another plastic bag.)* Eight hundred.

Wendy   Strike a light. That's a lot a fags innit? Well, son, call the hospital and book me a bed because emphysema, here I come. Thank you, Noah. That's very thoughtful of you.

Beat.

Noah   I didn't think to buy you jewellery or ...

Wendy   Oh no, what's the point when I never wear it? Mind you, saying that, I did put a pair of earrings in for your homecoming, see?

Noah   Very nice.

Wendy   Thought I'd spruce up a bit. *(Beat)* You want to take your coat off? You must be warm.

Noah   Aye.

Wendy   Just out in the hall.

Noah   I remember.

Wendy   Shoes off too, boyo.

Noah   Nothing changes.

Wendy   No. Not round here it don't.

Noah *exits.* **Wendy** *goes to the ironing board and starts ironing.* **Noah** *re-enters.*

Wendy   There's better. Alright?

Noah   Aye.

Wendy   Oh, there's a lovely shirt you got on there, my boy.

Noah   Thanks. Nothing special.

Wendy   No, it's beautiful. Where'd you get it?

Noah   Italy, I think.

Wendy   *(Making fun, with a funny voice)* Ooh! Did you, now? Very suave.

Noah   *(Taking her lead, with a funny air in his voice)* Well, you know, you're not the only one who can scrub up.

Noah *takes a seat at the table.* **Wendy** *irons the shirt. She watches* **Noah** *as he examines the room. A loud boom from next door shatters the peace. Something has been thrown against the wall. It's followed by a young woman shouting. It subsides.*

Noah   What the hell was that?

Wendy   Love's young dream, son. That's what that is.

Boom! This time it's louder.

Noah   Bloody hell.

Wendy   Sounded heavy, that one, didn't it?

The woman starts shouting again, they listen. It goes on for a little while.

Noah   Is it always like this?

A man starts shouting.

Wendy   Shhhhh. He's standing up for himself, listen.

The man murmurs a bit more.

Noah   Sounds like an apology to me.

Wendy   Well, that's usually the way.

Another bang. The woman shouts again. This time it's more intense.

Oh. Sorry don't cut it, son.

The woman shouts. We can hear the door slam and a figure passes by the dimpled glass in the front door, still shouting.

She's just popped out for a pint of milk.

Noah *laughs.*

You'll get used to it. You'd better had. They're at it night and day they are. I don't blame her though. He's never in, and when he is he's too out of it to take any notice of her or the kids. There's no work in the bugger neither. Horrible looking lump he is, and she'd be quite pretty if she had a wash.

Shane *enters. He wears nothing but a towel round his waist.*

Shane   Those two fucking at it again are they?

Noah *stands, he turns to* **Shane***.*

Wendy   Noah, this is Shane. **Shane** *takes* **Noah***'s hand.*

Shane   Whoa ho! Shine on shiner. Look at that. That is a peach. How'd you get that?

Noah   Few drunken boys on a night out.

Shane   And you were on your own I bet?

Noah *nods.*

Aye, always the fucking way. Well take it from me, you can console yourself in knowing that it'll come back round on them butt, always does. Let's have a look at you,

Shane *grips* **Noah** *by the chin.*

Ah, you'll live.

Noah   Sorry, Shane, was it?

Shane   Shane, aye. Your Mam said you were back today. To be fair, you're all she's gone on about these last few days, so I've heard plenty about you innit, Mother?

Wendy   I've been excited.

Shane Excited!? Excited don't begin to cover it, butt. Truth be told she's done my fucking head in talking 'bout you. *(Beat)* Ah! No, I'm only winding you up man. She's been really looking forward to it, fair play. You must be shattered though, all the flying and all. How long was it?

Noah Fifteen hours.

Shane Fuck a duck! I don't know how you can do that, see. I couldn't. Went to Tenerife last year. First and last time I step foot on an aeroplane, let me tell you. There was this Arab bloke sat across from us, big fuck off black beard he had, and I was convinced he had a bomb on him, wasn't I?

Wendy You weren't very good on it.

Shane That's what you think though innit? I thought he was gonna hijack the plane, do a nine eleven, you know. *(Beat)* He didn't. But you won't catch me flying again. If you have to do it you get used to it though, I bet.

Noah After a while.

Shane Aye, that's the hammer. *(Beat)* I tell you what, Wendy, he's got awful lot of you in him haven't he?

Wendy Do you think so?

Shane Oh aye. He's a good-looking boy, fair play.

Noah Thanks.

Wendy He's a bit too skinny for my liking. I'll soon get him fed though. Could do with standing a little bit closer to the razor and all, my boy.

Noah Sorry, Mam.

Wendy Saying that though, you ain't got much in the way of facial hair. Don't you fret, love, I'll put some double cream on that later, get the cat to lick it off.

Shane *(To* **Wendy***)* Aye, get him to do your top lip while he's at it.

Silence.

Fucking hell, you gotta learn to take a joke, Mother. *(Beat)* I wouldn't say it if it was true would I? Christ. So, what you up to tonight then, Noah?

Noah   I don't know.

Shane   You do now. Chuck your glad rags on sunshine, I'm taking you out.

Noah   Well I think I'm just gonna/

Shane   /No, no, no, I will not take no for an answer. Me and you got a date with destiny. I want you shaved, suited and booted in the next ten minutes. Go on, hop to it.

Noah   I've had a really long flight.

Shane   Then a couple of pints'll be just the ticket. Get you acclimatised an all.

Noah   No. I really do think the best thing for me would be to just rest up tonight.

Shane   Don't be like that.

Noah   Like what?

Shane   Like what you're being.

Noah   What am I being?

Shane   I'm extending you a fucking courtesy here butty, alright? The least a person can do is/

Wendy   /Now, now. He didn't mean it like that. Did you? Another time. Just tired he is. Once he's settled in you can both go out, get pissed as newts. Yeah?

Noah   Aye. Yeah. Of course.

Wendy   Take him, meet all the boys.

Beat.

Shane   Is that shirt finished? I gotta get going now, look.

Wendy   Just finishing it.

Shane   I haven't got long.

Wendy   Almost done.

Shane *exits.*

Wendy *gets back to ironing.*

Silence.

Wendy   Maybe you should go stick your bag in your room, son.

Noah   Aye.

Noah *exits. Silence.*

The front door opens. **Stephanie** *enters. She is twenty years of age and pretty in a loose tracksuit. She is pregnant and she carries two shopping bags.*

Stephanie   Alright Mam?

Wendy   Aye, Aye, don't alright Mam me. No, I'm not alright. Where've you been, you?

Stephanie   Down the market. Don't start.

Wendy   Don't start? I'll start up if I want to. I tell you what, girl, you think it's clever, going down town in your state, do you?

Stephanie   *(Putting the shopping down, exasperated, patient)* And what sort of state am I in then, Mam?

Wendy   You know exactly what I'm talking about. Don't play silly buggers with me, alright. Worrying me sick round here.

Stephanie   Well?

Wendy   How are you feeling today?

Stephanie   Same as yesterday, same as the day before, happy, fine, dandy, Mam. Piss off.

Wendy   Oi! You watch your mouth. You let me do the shopping from now on, alright. I won't tell you again. You rest yourself. You listening?

Stephanie   I can't just sit around the house all day.

Wendy   I know what you're saying but/

Stephanie   /I'll go mad, Mam.

Wendy   Listen to me now will you please? Will you listen to your Mam now? Now, I don't want to patronise you, okay.

Stephanie   Right.

Wendy   But I worry, I worry about you.

Stephanie   I know you do.

Wendy   So just for my sake, for my peace of mind if nothing else, will you rest up these next few weeks? For me?

Stephanie   Whatever you want, Mam.

Beat.

Wendy   *(Discreetly)* Have you been bleeding today?

Stephanie   Christ alive. Will you listen to yourself?

Wendy   Steph, please, grow up. You're not a little girl anymore. You can't just bury your head about this. Have you?

Stephanie   No I haven't.

Wendy   Stephanie?

Stephanie   Promise.

Wendy   Are you sure?

Stephanie   Mam!

Beat.

Wendy   Well that's good then.

Stephanie   Aye, it is. So just wind your bloody neck in.

Stephanie *sits on the sofa. She takes her shoes off.*

Oh my God, oh my God, oh my God, ahhhh! That is lush. Oooohhh. Will you look at the state of my feet? You know what?

I'm sure they've swollen again today. Fucking hell my ankles have disappeared.

Wendy   Language.

Stephanie   Sorry. Town was murder and all. Sodding Gypos everywhere down that market. They use their prams as battering rams. That one with the bottle blond hair, you know the one, face like she's been dead a month. She walloped into the back of me. And the look she gave me Mam! Her poor baby's ears are pierced, sat there playing with her mother's fags, and she gives me a dirty look? *(Rubbing her feet)* Ooooh, put the kettle on, will you?

Wendy   He's back.

Stephanie   Who's back?

Wendy   Don't wind me up. He's in the bedroom. He's looking really well, Steph. Really well. *(Beat)* He's already met Shane.

Stephanie   *(Seemingly uninterested)* Oh right. How'd that go?

Wendy   Alright I think, yeah. Not too bad I reckon. He's turned into a really nice looking man he has and all. He's got a lovely way about him. And he was talking about your birthday too. Looking forward to it, he is. He said there was no way he would've missed his little sister's twenty-first.

Stephanie   Wouldn't he?

Noah *enters.*

Noah   No, not for anything.

Beat.

Wendy   Here, come and say hello to your sister. Look how big she's getting.

Noah   Bloody hell, she is.

Beat.

Wendy   I was just about to put the kettle on, do you fancy a cup?

Noah   Aye, go on.

Wendy   Sugar?

Noah   One please, plenty of milk.

Wendy *exits to the kitchen.*

Noah   Well done. Congratulations. *(Beat)* How pregnant are you?

Stephanie   Six months.

Noah   Right. Excited?

Stephanie   I am.

Noah   You're looking really well.

Stephanie   I look like a hog.

Noah   No you don't, you look healthy, happy. Must be that new mother glow or something.

Stephanie   I'm not a mother yet.

Noah   Well no, technically. And the father?

Stephanie   What about him?

Noah   What's he like? Who is he?

Stephanie   Shane.

Beat.

Noah   Shane. Shane!?

Shane *enters full of party spirit, as he's just taken cocaine.*

Shane   Right then Mother, where's my shirt? Let's get this show on the road here! Oh hello, hello! There she is. There's my princess, light of my life, the jewel in my golden crown. Come here.

He leans over and kisses her on the lips.

That's all I need, that right there. God, you're gorgeous. Isn't she gorgeous?

Noah   She is.

Shane   Bloody beautiful she is.

Shane *takes his shirt up off the ironing board and puts it on.*

Even the back of her head is stunning. I am even in love with the back of her head. You can't tell me that's normal. *(Beat)* Where'd you go this morning then, sweet pea?

Stephanie   Just popped into town to pick up a few things.

Shane   Right. And why pray tell, didn't you just let your Mam do it?

Stephanie   Fancied a walk.

Shane   Oh! Fancied a little walk did we? There's nice. Fuck it, why don't you take up fire eating or sky diving whilst you're carrying my child? It's bedlam down that market. What is so important that you had to get?

Stephanie   Bits and bobs is all.

Shane   We'll if it's all the same to you I'd rather you didn't play Russian roulette with my baby boy for the sake of a few bits and bobs. Alright? *(Beat)* Sorted.

Beat.

Noah   You're having a boy?

Stephanie   Well/

Shane   /Course we're having a boy. Fuck's sake, look at me. As if I'd have anything but. As soon as she got pregnant she said you could just tell it was a boy. Didn't you?

Noah   You've had a scan?

Stephanie   No, we haven't. I didn't want/

Shane   /Look at the size on her. He's gonna be a big bastard and all. There's a future Welsh Number Eight in there Noah boy, believe it. If that boy don't captain a Wales side to a Six Nations Grand Slam then I'll eat my own manhood, fried. You can have that as fact.

Wendy *enters.*

Wendy   There's smart you do look.

Shane   Thank you Mother.

Wendy   Do you want a cup of tea now before you go?

Shane   No. I'm out the door. Do us a favour, will you, keep an eye on her tonight.

Wendy   She'll be fine.

Shane   It's not her I do worry about. Right then, *(Checking himself)* Keys, wallet, phone, sorted. Here we are, give us a kiss. *(He kisses **Wendy** on the cheek.)* Princess. *(He kisses **Stephanie** on the lips)* Noah. *(He leans in to kiss **Noah**, **Noah** backs away) (Laughs)* Ha. Look on his face. Fucking shit himself. Priceless. See you later. *(To **Stephanie**)* Oi, you behave yourself.

Wendy   Tarah.

Shane exits.

Silence.

What was I just thinking about, now? *(Beat)* That's it! Right, you gonna be alright here for half now while I pop down the market? I'm gonna go get you a steak.

Noah   That's ok. You don't need to do that.

Wendy   I'll pop down now and grab you one before the market closes.

Noah   No, I'm fine, honestly.

Wendy   I want to.

Noah   Mam.

Wendy   I want to. My boy comes back home and I want to cook him a steak if it's all the same to you. Ok? Alright?

Noah   Ok.

Wendy   Right then. Enough said, you rest up here, recover yourself after the hill.

Wendy *exits into the hallway.*

Silence.

Noah   Do you want to stick the telly on? Or watch a film or something?

Stephanie   I'm gonna have a lie down.

Noah   Oh right. Fair enough.

Wendy *enters.*

Wendy   Where you going?

Stephanie   Lie down. **Stephanie** *exits.*

Wendy   Right I won't be long, you sure gonna be alright here now?

Noah *nods.*

Alright then. See you in a bit.

Wendy *exits.* **Noah** *is alone for the first time in the house. Silence. He hasn't been in this space for a long time.* **Adam** *enters through the front door. They stand and look at each other for a little while.*

Adam   Alright? *(Beat)* What are you staring at?

Noah   What?

Adam   You're staring.

Noah   Sorry. It's good to see you.

Adam   Well, just see me then.

Noah   Right, Okay, sorry.

Adam   Looking at me, like, with intensity. It's odd. Looking at me like you want to do things to me. Unnatural things.

Noah *smiles.*

Probably how you ended up with that black eye I expect. Glaring across the bar at someone else's girlfriend, was it? Giving her the old Psycho stare out.

Noah   No, I save that special for you lot.

Adam   Yea? How's our Mam get on with it?

Noah   She loves it.

Adam   Reminds her of our Dad I expect.

Noah   *(Laughing, shocked)* Oh my God! You are sick in the head butt.

Adam *shrugs his shoulders and exits to the kitchen. He returns with an apple.*

Adam   So, you back for good?

Noah   Back for the foreseeable, aye.

Adam   Why?

Noah   What?

Adam   Why've you come back at all?

Silence, he waits for a response.

Fair enough. Where's our Mam?

Noah   Down the Market.

Adam   Already got her running round after you?

Noah   No.

Adam   She will though, you let her.

Noah   I wouldn't ask her too.

Adam   No. You don't want for nothing, do you?

Noah   I don't.

Adam   She does. She won't ask for it. You've got a lot of ground to cover.

(Beat)

Noah   You off?

Adam   Aye. I got what I came for. Places to go, people to avoid, son. See you later.

Noah   Tarah.

Adam *exits.*

Beat.

Lights down.

End of scene.

Scene Two

The front room. Night time. **Adam** *sits at the kitchen table.* **Noah** *enters from the kitchen. He opens a can of Macerson's stout.*

Noah   Go on then.

Adam   You won't get it. You're thick as fuck.

Noah   Just shut your face and get on with it will you.

Adam   You are thick.

Noah   Aye.

Adam   You know that?

Noah   Yep.

Adam   *(Rapping his knuckles on the table top)* Like, that.

Noah   Just like that. Sod it, I'm bored, I don't care.

Noah *makes for the sofa.*

Adam   Alright, alright, sorry, sorry, come back. I love this. *(Beat)* What is the longest a chicken has ever survived without its head?

Noah   After it's had its head cut off?

Adam   Yeah. What's the world record for survival of a chicken, once you've cut the head off?

Noah   It's gonna be something stupid, innit? Something like fifteen minutes or something.

Adam   Higher.

Noah   Twenty minutes.

Adam   More than that.

Noah   Come off it. Hour?

Adam   More.

Noah   Seriously?

Adam   Seriously.

Noah   A day then. Twenty-four hours.

Adam   Much, much higher. You're cold, you're not even close.

Noah   You're winding me up.

Adam   I'm not. Guess?

Noah   A decade.

Adam   Don't be a knob, play properly.

Noah   A week then. What?

Adam   Eighteen months.

Noah   Shut up.

Adam   A year and a half.

Noah   No way! A year and a half without a fucking head?

Adam   In 1945 an American farmer named Lloyd Olsen cut the head of his rooster and it survived. The local university, they couldn't explain it, and when it went on living he has this brainstorm, right? He takes him all over America charging people to look at him. He makes a mint. And the only reason he eventually dies is Olsen, the farmer, right, Olsen fed him corn and water with a syringe, in the hole in his neck, and one night the rooster chokes in a hotel room. He choked! He didn't even die of natural causes. Can you believe that?

Noah No.

Adam Look it up.

Noah How did it survive all that time without a brain though?

Adam You've managed well enough.

Noah *(Claps)* Ah, very good. Very well done.

Adam Seriously though, you're properly thick …

Wendy *enters.*

Wendy Alright?

Adam Yeah/

Noah /Aye.

Wendy Having a quiet beer is it my boy?

Noah Yeah. I'll buy them back.

Wendy No, it's no problem. *(Beat)* Do you mind if I join you for one?

Noah Course. No.

Wendy *exits.*

Adam They say that eating fish helps with brain development. Just a thought. Get our Mam to fetch you a couple of tonne from down the market.

Noah I'll do that.

Adam No harm in trying is there?

Noah You're a good brother.

Adam Anything for you butt.

Wendy *enters. She opens her can, she takes a sip.*

Silence.

Wendy   It's good stuff, innit?

Noah   It does the trick.

Wendy   Well aye. *(She takes another sip. Beat)* You know, I started drinking this when I was pregnant with you lot.

Adam   Never stood a chance, did you?

Wendy   The doctors would recommend it to pregnant women years ago. Good for the child, full of iron see. Can't get Stephanie to touch the stuff, mind you. But that's the culture these days innit. Give birth in a pool, hand the brat to a nanny, and down the gym to get your arse back nice and tight.

Pause. They sip their cans.

Noah   Mam?

Wendy   Yes?

Noah   Why didn't you tell me about Steph?

Adam   You didn't know?

Wendy   I didn't think.

Adam   Shit …

Beat.

Wendy   It wasn't until you were both in the same room that it even occurred to me.

Noah   Right.

Wendy   That might sound daft, but it's been so long since I've thought of you both in the same … *(Beat)* I dunno, the same/

Adam   /And I missed your face. Gutted.

Wendy   I didn't think.

Beat.

Noah   Shane's a bit of a character in he?

Adam   He's got plenty of that.

Wendy   He's a bit rough round the edges.

Noah   Rough? He's ragged.

Beat.

Wendy   Very loyal mind.

Noah's *eyes roam the room, he starts to smile.* **Wendy** *picks up on it.*

What? What you smiling at?

Noah   Nothing.

Wendy   No, come on. Out with it.

Noah   Mam. This place.

Adam   Bad move.

Wendy   What's wrong with it? *(Beat)* Oi you, what's wrong with it?

Noah   Nothing's wrong with it. It's nothing. Stop looking at me like that will you.

Wendy   Tell me what's so funny then?

Noah   I'm not laughing, it's just … all exactly as I left it.

Wendy   And?

Noah   I mean, exactly.

Adam   Circa 1981.

Wendy   Well that's how I wanted it. I didn't want you coming back and thinking that we'd forgotten about you.

Noah   People accumulate things over time though, don't they?

Wendy   Aye, just for the bloody sake of it.

Noah   Table, chairs, sofa. *(Beat)* carpet! Mam! I'd be surprised if you'd changed the bloody light bulbs round here.

Wendy   *(Hurt)* Alright then, sod it. Tomorrow morning we'll get a skip round here shall we? Gut the place. Sod the memories, and the years our family's lived here. My parents before me mind, but what's that matter? Oh no! Let's just replace it all with plywood tat from down B&Q.

Noah   Come on now, I didn't mean it like that.

Wendy   No, well sod it Noah.

Adam   Mam, don't wind yourself up.

Wendy   I didn't want to wipe away a single memory. Any one of my children's. I didn't want to look around the place and not be able to remember you running in and out, and see you crawling. I didn't want to replace them. The bad ones and all, they're just as important.

Noah   No. They are. You're right.

Beat.

Noah *notices the drinks cabinet. He stands and walks over to it. He refers to the missing pane of glass.*

Do you remember how this happened?

Wendy   Look on the floor below.

Noah   Shit the bed. I don't remember there being that much blood.

Wendy   That'll teach you for fighting with your brother.

Adam   Shouldn't have messed with the champ, should he?

Noah   Twelve stitches mind.

Wendy   I know.

Noah   Left me with a tasty old scar and all. I can't feel nothing down to there.

Wendy   You won't get no sympathy from me. I've never been able to get that stain out.

Noah *makes his way over to the bookcase. He sifts through the books.*

Noah   Loads of quality literature to be had here, Mam.

Wendy   More of a TV household son, always were, so don't be a snob. Come away from there now.

Noah   Still into your Mills and Boone then.

Wendy   My granny porn? Well aye.

Noah   There's loads of the stuff.

Wendy   Yeah, well, there comes a time in every woman's life when she realises she's better off with a book. Now come away from there will you, sit down.

Noah *spots scrap folders on the bookshelf. They take up an entire shelf.*

Noah   What are these?

Wendy   *(On edge)* Nothing. Stop your bloody nosing. Will you come away from there and sit down Adam?

Noah   Noah

Adam   Adam

Noah puts the folder back.

Wendy   Yes well … what do you expact when you're making me nervous walking round the place. Poking round in things when I'm telling you not to.

Noah *breaks from the bookshelf.*

Noah   Sorry.

Wendy   You can't just come back in here and start riffling through the house, scouring the house, searching.

Adam   Mam, come on now.

Wendy   It's not on. I won't have it. It's not fair!

Noah   I didn't mean/

Wendy   /No … *(Beat)* Course you didn't.

Silence.

Did you remember to get your sister a present for tomorrow?

Noah   Yes.

Wendy   Did you remember to get her a card?

Noah   No.

Wendy   Right, well I thought as much. I got one for you, so just remind me in the morning, alright?

Noah   Thanks.

Wendy   And don't forget you've got that steak there in the fridge. *(Beat)* Do you want me to do it for you now before I go to bed?

Noah   No thank you. Bit late.

Wendy   Alright, well I'll do it for you tomorrow then.

Noah   Okay.

Wendy *hands* **Noah** *her can of Macerson's.*

Wendy   Here, you can finish this off. I'm off to bed. Don't be up too late now, try and get a good night's sleep.

Noah   Alright.

Wendy   Goodnight.

Noah   Goodnight.

Adam   Night.

Wendy *exits. Silence. The sound of a toilet flushing, a door closing.* **Noah** *makes his way over to the bookshelf.*

Adam   What are you doing? Noah?

Noah *pulls out one of the folders.*

Noah, leave it. Honestly …

Noah *opens it. He reads.*

Take it from me, best thing you can do is steer well clear. It's/

Noah   /Shut up a sec.

He reads some more.

Adam   Don't even try and rationalise/

Noah   /She just leaves this lying about?

Adam   No. She tucks them in the bookshelf where they're left alone.

Noah   Fucking hell/

Adam   /Because people should know better than to pull at the stitching. Shouldn't they?

Noah   Fuck off. You can't ignore this/

Adam   /You better try.

Noah   Have you seen?/

Adam   /Trust me, front to back. It's not ideal/

Noah   /No! No, you're bang on the money there butt. Fuck me, it's/

Adam   /It is what it is. And I'm sorry Noah but you haven't got the right. *(Beat)* So put it back.

Beat. Talking can be heard as we see two figures emerge in the dimpled glass of the front door. **Noah** *quickly puts the folder back in the bookshelf.* **Shane** *enters. He is eating a kebab and chips. He is followed by* **Lugs**. **Lugs** *is twenty-eight years old, dressed in a hooded jumper and tracksuit bottoms.*

Shane   Well as I live and breathe, it's Noah Williams. The prodigal son, he has returned. How's it hanging boss man? What are you doing with your fine and precious time?

Noah   Having a can.

Shane   Well why didn't you say so? Let's get it fucking going here is it? Wanna chip or what?

Noah   Oh, thanks.

Noah *takes a chip.*

Shane   Watch that chilli sauce on there mind, it'll take your fucking head off. Here, you ever met Lugs? Lugs, this is Noah.

Noah   No. How's it going mate, alright?

Lugs   Noah mate … it's me Nathan.

Adam   You know Nathan.

Noah   Nathan?

Lugs   Nathan Reed. *Beat.*

Noah   Fucking hell, it is and all! Sorry butt! How you doing Nath? You alright or what?

Lugs   I'm cracking yeah.

Shane   You know each other then?

Noah   Well aye. Since I can't remember. We grew up together, didn't we?

Lugs   More or less.

Noah   He was round here every day.

Shane   Still is the scrounging little shithouse.

Noah   Sorry Nath. I didn't recognise you at all. To be fair though, last time I saw you, you was two foot shorter, and about three foot wider.

Shane   Right little pudding was we?

Lugs   Just puppy fat.

Noah   You've lost a lot of weight.

Shane   You would and all if you here living off two grams of charlie and a handful of nuts a night.

Noah   Nathan Reed?

Shane   He goes by the name of Lugs these days. Don't you?

Lugs   Because of my ears.

Shane   Fucking right. Did you ever see anything the size of 'em?

Shane *puts his kebab on the table. He steps behind* **Lugs** *and pulls his ears out and sings.*

I seen a horse fly! I seen a dragon fly! I seen a needle with a great big eye! Well I think I seen about everything till I seen an idiot fly! *(Stops singing)* Lugso! Lugso! Go on son, grab us a can and let's get the party started round here, shall we?!

Lugs *exits to the kitchen.*

Let me tell you, he's the best pet I've ever had.

Beat.

Lugs *enters with two cans of Maccerson's.*

Ain't you butty? Ah? Man's best friend?

Shane *takes the can of Maccerson's.*

What the fuck is this?

Lugs   It's all there was in the fridge.

Shane   Like fuck am I drinking that. I'd sooner drink your cheesy piss. Here, there's some whisky in the cabinet, fetch that. Here you go, Noah boy. *(Throwing* **Noah** *the can.)* Get that down your neck.

Noah   I was just off to bed.

Shane   Oh, I don't think you were. No, no you've dodged the bullet with me once already today. It's not happening twice. Me and you are gonna kick back and bond like we mean it sunshine. Sit down, relax.

Noah *sits.*

You missed a hell of a night tonight, let me tell you. One of my best mates in the whole world was back tonight. Just finished a tour of Basra he has. We got him fucking melted. Good craic. Do you know the Scrum Half?

Noah   I don't.

Shane   It used be the Greyhound.

Noah *shakes his head.*

I know the landlord, so we get drinks cheap. Pool table, bit of chokey. Got him up on it. You've never seen a shape like it. Do you do karaoke Noah?

Noah   I can't really sing.

Shane   What do you mean you can't sing? You're fucking Welsh, course you can fucking sing. *(Beat)* Besides, pretty boy like you, don't really matter what you sound like. If you look like me then you better be able to bang a tune out.

Noah   So you can sing?

Shane   You agree with me then?

Noah   Ah?

Shane   That I'm an ugly cunt. *(Beat)* Oh Dumbo! What's going on with the whiskey, butt? I'm sobering up here!

Lugs *brings him the bottle of whisky.*

Are you a whisky drinker?

Noah   From time to time.

Shane   Good man. Good man. You know what, I've had a guts full of this, do you want it?

Shane *offers* **Noah** *the kebab.*

Noah   No, I'm alright, thanks.

Lugs   I'll have it.

Shane   I know you'll take it butt. You'd chew a dog's arsehole if it was covered in ketchup. Go on, take it from me, I can't even look at it. *(Beat)* We got my butty proper fucked tonight, didn't we?

Lugs   He pissed himself.

Shane   Aye. People go on about Newport, Cardiff, Swansea look and I can't see the fuss. If you ask me, don't matter who you are, you can find a place to suit you round here.

Shane *takes out his wallet, and from it, a wrap of cocaine.*

Here, grab us that mirror down of the wall will you, butty?

Adam   Night Noah.

Adam *exits.* **Lugs** *takes the mirror from the wall and hands it to* **Shane***, who puts it on his lap.* **Shane** *opens and tips the wrap of cocaine onto the mirror and proceeds to chop it up with a bank card, talking all the while.*

You're an old bloke, you like a pint and a bet on a Sunday afternoon; go the Legion. If you wanna take your missus out and you don't wanna spend a fortune, Workingman's Club, pint costs one pound sixteen. You want food then you got the Scrum Half. And if you're looking for something a bit more lively you get yourself down Wetherspoon's. What more do you need in life? Oh! And if you like the gay scene, take it elsewhere, coz if I see it I'll kick your fucking guts out. Ha? *(Laughs)*

Lugs   Ha! *(Laughs)*

Shane   *(To himself, mumbles)* Fucking hell.

Beat.

Noah   So, how you keeping Nath?

Lugs   Can't complain like, you know.

Noah   Still living up the top?

Lugs   Aye. Can't leave our Mam up there on her own.

Noah   She alright or what?

Lugs   She's alright up there, yeah. She got the old Alzheimer's at the minute.

Noah   God.

Lugs   She's getting on now like. Had me late didn't she?

Noah   I'm really sorry to hear that.

Lugs   No, don't worry about it. She don't. To be honest with you, most the time it's funny as fuck. Like, the other day we're sat watching the telly and she farts right, and it's rotten. Well she forgets she's done it don't she, few seconds later she smells it and starts cursing me, like.

Noah *laughs.*

Proper livid she was. Going 'You dirty little bastard,' she's going. *(Beat)* So how long you back for?

Shane *snorts a line of coke. Beat.*

Noah   I'm not sure. We'll just have to see how it goes.

Shane   You can stay here as long as you want, butt. It's nice having you.

Noah   Thanks. But I wanna see how they adjust to having me back first. I don't want to step on anyone's toes.

Shane   Fuck that. I pay the rent round here and I'm telling you now, you can stay as long as you want.

Noah   That's very kind.

Shane   Don't mention it.

Beat.

Lugs   So where the fuck've you been then?

Noah   Good question. All over.

Lugs   Yeah?

Noah   Well aye. Got to do it, don't you?

Lugs   I bet you've had a belter haven't you? *(Beat)* Women?

Noah   We all get lonely from time to time.

Lugs   Awesome.

Shane   What do you do for money?

Noah   I've been teaching English in Japan, actually.

Shane   Fuck off! They let you teach English?

Noah   It's no big thing. If you speak the language, they'll let you teach it.

Lugs   What's Japan like?

Noah   Absolutely bonkers.

Lugs   Why?

Noah   Just is. Everything about it, the food, culture, the people are off the wall. Sex is proper mixed up. Business men read Hentai, cartoon porn, on the train on the way to work. School uniforms they love. And this is true, they got vending machines on street corners where you can buy used knickers.

Beat.

Lugs   What for?

Shane *snorts a line of cocaine.*

Shane   So you can have a good old fucking sniff of 'em. What do you think?

Beat.

Noah   It's true.

Lugs   Here, you wanna get yourself down Wetherspoon's on a Saturday. Pinch a few pairs off the girls down there Noah. Go back and sell them on as extra strength. *(Laughs)*

Beat.

Noah   So what do you do for work then Nath?

Lugs   I've been roofing on and off for the last two years like.
But it's been really slow at the minute. When I'm stuck for work
though, Shane sorts me out.

Noah   Yeah?

Lugs   Yeah. Odds and ends like.

Noah   Nice one. Sorry, Shane mate, I don't even know what it is
you do.

Shane   I, Noah, am a purveyor of exotic substances. A modern
day apothecary to Pontypool's lost and disenchanted youth.

Beat.

Lugs   He sells drugs.

Beat.

Shane   I sell drugs.

Noah   Out the flat?

Shane   No, no I got a nice little shop down the market. You
know the one, big shop window with 'drugs' written across it,
opposite the police station. Of course out the flat. *(Beat)* Have you
got a problem with that?

Noah   Well …

Beat.

Shane   Well what? *(Beat).* It's been keeping your mother fed and
watered the last couple of years.

Beat.

Noah   You can't say fairer than that.

Shane   No you can't. *(Beat)* You want a line?

Noah   No thanks.

Shane   Suit yourself.

Lugs   Can I have one?

Shane Course you can, why you asking me? Where's your gear?

Beat.

Lugs I finished it.

Shane So how do you plan on sniffing then?

Lugs I was thinking/

Shane /What? What was you thinking? *(Mock realisation)* Oh! I'm sorry, I was being thick there for a second, wasn't I? My apologies. So what's happened is, you've done all yours whilst we were out, and you fancy a buzz on my gear now we're back in the house. Is that about the size of it?

Silence.

Speak up. *(Beat. Aggression rising)* Is that about the size of it? Speak up!

Lugs Don't worry about it.

Shane But I do worry. See I worry that you're taking the piss out of me.

Lugs No.

Shane That the only reason you even bother with me is because of the fucking chalk.

Lugs That's not true.

Shane Do you want a go?

Lugs What?

Shane Do you want a fucking pop, Lugs?!

Lugs Sorry Shane, I just don't … I was … no.

Beat.

Shane Aaaaah! Look at your face. You might wanna check your pants butt.

Lugs Fucking hell.

Shane *passes* **Lugs** *the mirror.*

Shane   Here, get it down you. Take your fucking time.

Lugs   Cheers.

Shane   Aye. It's on tick though, alright?

Lugs   Yeah, course.

Shane   See that's why it's making me money. The pond life round here; *(referring to* **Lugs***)* Exhibit A, can't get enough. Honestly, selling that stuff I wouldn't wanna live any other place on earth. That powder there makes you feel sexy, confident, the most interesting person in the room. And who do I sell it to? Pumped up, steroid addled valley commando's who wanna feel like the biggest bloke in the pub, and stupid, munting slags that want to feel desirable come the weekend. And all for forty quid a pop.

Noah   So you're doing alright for yourself?

Shane   This family will never have to worry.

Noah   Fair enough. With all that money though, why live here?

Shane   What's wrong with this? The police can't be bothered with the estate so they leave me alone. It's five minutes' walk into town. Sorted.

Noah   Don't you want a place of your own?

Shane   I've been paying the rent on this flat solidly since the day I moved in, butt. As far as I'm concerned this is my place.

Silence.

Lugs *sniffs his line.*

You're a piss taking cunt, Lugs, you really are.

Lugs   What? What?

Shane   That line you had there was the width of my fucking wrist. Pass it back man.

Stephanie *enters.*

Stephanie   Shane.

Shane   There she is look, my gorgeous girl. Alright or what?

Stephanie   Shhh, keep it down babe. It's late.

Shane   What time is it? Here, it's gone midnight! It's your birthday!

Stephanie   Shhh, be quiet, our Mam's asleep. Can I have the keys please?

Shane   Don't go to bed, stay up and have a bit of craic with us for a bit.

Stephanie   Babe. Keys.

Shane   Your brother's back.

Stephanie   I'm shattered babe. Our Mam's snoring like a drain in there. Can I just have the keys please? I need to sleep.

Shane   Come on, sweetheart.

Stephanie   No.

Shane   Don't be like that.

Stephanie   No.

Shane   It's your birthday!

Stephanie   Shane! For fuck's sake, just give me the fucking keys!

Beat.

Shane *throws the keys across the room at* **Stephanie***. She fumbles them. They fall to the floor.* **Stephanie** *crouches down to pick them up.*

Stephanie   Night.

Noah   Goodnight.

Lugs   Goodnight Steph.

Stephanie *exits.*

Noah   You've put a lock on her bedroom door?

Shane   Listen, I think there's been a few too many questions tonight. Best leave em until I'm in a better mood. *(Beat)* You sure you don't want one of these now?

Noah   No, I'm off to bed. Goodnight.

Lugs   Goodnight. Great to see you.

Noah   Yeah. Good to be back. Noah exits.

Shane *snorts a line of coke, the lights fade.*

End of scene.

Scene Three

Adam *stands on stage.* **Noah** *once again stands across the stage with his jacket on and his bag slung over his shoulder.*

Adam   We sat on tin trays at the top of the park in darkness, arses wet and cold and Pontypool looked like any other town. Sort of anonymous orange lights, like we could walk back down into any town or place. I spent hours thinking about the different places, I had a list. In the middle of the glow was our estate. He'd be home by now so I look away and try to think of something else. I knew guilt better than most boys I reckon. In the end the cold got too hard to ignore, and we were too late anyway, the snow had turned to soup days ago. Quietly you stand and walk away and quietly I follow you into the woods. We fumble our way from tree to tree, neither of us talk so I get back to my list. Newcastle, Melbourne, Stoke, Cardiff, Edinburgh, Colwyn Bay. I turn to involve you and you're not there. I call out your name but you don't answer back. I call again, nothing, again, silence, nothing. You left me alone in the woods or something worse. Lamps light up a footpath, and I run towards it, the darkness reaching out to pull me back. I run out into the light, on to the frozen path and I slip and fall and cut my hand. All I can hear is my breathing, and all I can think of is our Mam crying and policemen taking notes. Policemen looking at him as he watches TV thinking what sort of father shows nothing at all! I call again, and then I hear you, screaming, shouting, laughing!? Laughing as you come flying round the bend and crash straight into me. Your tin tray keeps going as we lie on the ground, while you keep laughing. And fuck my list I don't want to be anywhere else but in a bundle in the woods with you.

The front room. Morning. **Adam** *sits at the table.* **Wendy** *enters from the kitchen with breakfast things. She exits back into the kitchen.* **Noah** *enters through the front door. He carries a shopping bag. We hear the dog barking.* **Wendy** *enters with knives and forks.*

Adam   Alright?

Wendy   Good morning, darling boy.

Noah   Morning.

Wendy   Is it raining?

Noah   Just started when I was coming up.

Wendy   That's alright then. What's this?

Noah   They didn't have any Maccerson's.

Wendy   You're a soft bugger, I told you you didn't have to buy them back.

Noah   Oh, I got a taste for them now Mam. Go on, bang 'em in the fridge and we'll crack on in a bit.

Wendy   Thank you son, that's very thoughtful. I heard you this morning, out the door. You were up and at it.

Noah   Fancied a walk.

Wendy   Where to'd you go?

Noah   Everywhere, really. Started on the canal and just kept going.

Wendy   Did you see the new Tesco's down town?

Noah   No.

Wendy   I'll take you to have a look. It's the biggest one around.

Beat.

Noah   I went up the top of the park. Up through the woods.

Wendy   Aye?

Noah   Yeah. What's happened? It's absolutely disgusting up there. All that rubbish.

Wendy   Aye. Poxy teenagers it is. Got no bloody values.

Noah   Aye.

Wendy   Up to all sorts up there the dirty little beggers. You can't walk in that park for condoms and shopping trolleys. They wanna learn to keep their hands to themselves till they got a place of their own to … Muck about in.

Noah   Hang on a minute now Mam.

Wendy   What?

Noah   You had me at seventeen.

Wendy   No, no. That's totally different.

Noah   How?

Wendy   Well, we didn't have the education.

Noah *and* **Adam** *laugh.*

Noah   Come off it.

Wendy   We didn't.

Wendy *exits to the kitchen.*

Adam   You should've woke me. *Beat.*

Noah   *(To* **Wendy***)* I popped in shopkeeper John's, on the way up.

Wendy   *(From the kitchen).* Oh aye?

Noah   Yea. On his last legs now in he?

Wendy   He's been bad for a while. Did he recognise you?

Noah   He didn't even look at me. He couldn't get off his stool to serve me.

Wendy *steps back into the room, she has an unlit cigarette in one hand and a lighter in the other.*

Wendy   Poor sod. That shop's gone right downhill since Elsie died.

Noah   Fucking right!

Wendy   Language.

Noah   Sorry, but he had a can of tenants super sitting next to the bloody till!

Adam   He stinks don't he? Teeth on him like raisins.

Beat.

Noah   Where's the birthday girl then? Still in the pit?

Wendy   Yeah. Leave her be for a bit.

Noah   You sure she ain't shut in there? Do we need to call the locksmith out? *(Beat).*

Where's Shane?

Wendy   *(Short with him)* Ok. Point taken, move on.

Silence. A commotion outside. The dog barks and growls. We hear **Nathan** *in distress and the neighbour shouting. The dog yelps. A door slams.* **Wendy** *makes her way to the door, she opens it and steps out.*

Wendy   What's going on out here? *(Beat)* Are you alright?

Lugs   *(Stepping into the door way. Shaken)* Yeah, yeah, yeah, fine yeah. Alright?

Wendy   Get in here.

Lugs *enters.*

Noah   Alright Nath?

Lugs   Aye, yeah, yeah, good yeah.

Wendy   Oi! Stop there. Are you limping? Bloody hell, look what he's done to your trousers!

Lugs   Oh no, it's nothing.

Wendy   Nathan. Stand still.

Lugs   Never mind.

Wendy   Never mind never mind. Look at the state of you. I'll be round there. He'll be giving you the money for them.

Lugs   Leave it.

Noah   Nath mate, you're bleeding.

Wendy   You are as well. Sit yourself down there now and shut up.

Lugs   Wendy/

Wendy   /Shut up.

Wendy *exits.*

Adam   Dickhead.

Noah   Does it hurt?

Lugs   Not too bad.

Noah   Shouldn't we phone an ambulance or something?

Wendy *enters with a damp cloth.*

Wendy   Ere, *(taking his leg)* let's have a look at you. *(She rolls up his trouser leg and mops the wound)* There. *(Beat)* No, it doesn't look too serious. You shouldn't need stitches I don't think. You'll live.

Noah   We should phone the police though.

Lugs   Why?

Noah   Mate, you just got mauled.

Lugs   I'm fine.

Wendy   He won't listen.

Noah   This has happened before?

Adam   All the time.

Wendy   I've lost count, son.

Noah   Well then you've gotta ring the police. Next time it could be some poor nipper's throat.

Lugs   No, he only does it to me. Since he was a pup, innit? He don't even go for the postman. And the kids round the estate love him, you always see him running round with em.

Noah   Nath/

Lugs   /The kids love him.

Wendy   There's no talking to him.

Noah   Fucking hell man.

Wendy   Language!

Noah   Sorry.

Beat.

Lugs   Steph still in bed is she?

Wendy   Aye love. I was just gonna wake her with a cup of tea. Do you want one?

Lugs   Course.

Wendy   Ask a stupid question. Noah?

Noah   Aye.

Wendy   And do us a favour and put your jacket away in the cupboard, please. Since when did we leave them on the back of the chairs? Your shoes too, Nathan, or it'll be me biting you next. And you'll need more than a wipe down with a damp rag, Sunny Jim. Aye, you can smile and all.

Noah *takes his jacket off the back of the seat. He stands and waits as* **Lugs** *slips off his shoes. He offers to take them.*

Noah   You are.

Lugs   Oh, cheers.

Noah *exits. He returns.*

Noah   You sure you're alright?

Lugs   Aye.

Beat.

Noah   What time did you finish up last night, after?

Lugs   God, I don't know. It was still dark walking home so it can't have been that late, like. Feeling a bit ropey today, to be fair.

Noah   I bet.

Lugs   Haven't been to bed yet. I was just drifting off this morning and the door goes. It was the home help for our Mam so you can't get too pissed off, like.

Noah   No. *(Beat)* Shane was on form last night.

Lugs   Yeah.

Noah   Life and soul once he gets going, in he?

Lugs   He likes a laugh and a joke.

Noah   Oh aye, loves it. Bit of a dab hand round the house and all by the looks. Locks on the doors, so my sister can't go to bed.

Lugs   He's just being careful.

Noah   Right. Well are there any other home improvements I should know about? Barbed wire in the letter box? Bear traps in the fucking bread bin, or what?

Lugs   *(Laughs)* He is a bit paranoid.

Noah   Is he? Good. Because I was worried it might be me. I was starting to think maybe my sister's shacked up with a total lunatic.

Lugs   I'm still bleeding.

Noah   So clear it up for me Nath.

Lugs   It's none of my business.

Noah   I'm not trying to drop you in it. For my peace of mind.

Beat.

Lugs   Why don't you talk to Steph?

Noah   Why would she speak to me?

Adam   Our Steph's no victim, Noah.

Noah   She likes a good time then? Bit of a party girl is she?

Adam   What do you think?

Lugs   She don't touch it now she's pregnant.

Noah   Good for her.

Lugs   It wasn't me that started her on it.

Beat.

Noah   Is he violent?

Wendy *enters with the teas.*

Wendy   Here we go my boys. Now I got rich tea, custard creams or hobnobs, what's it gonna be?

Lugs   Well you can't go far wrong with a custard cream Wendy.

Wendy   Custard creams it is then. Here, sign this now for Lady Muck.

Wendy *hands* **Noah** *a birthday card.*

Beat.

Noah   I don't know about this, Mam.

Wendy   Don't know about what?

Noah   This card.

Wendy   What's wrong with the bloody card?

Noah   Bit childish, innit?

Wendy   No.

Noah   It's got bunny rabbits all over it.

Wendy   Listen, your sister loves bunny rabbits, she's always has, so don't try and teach your granny how to suck eggs, alright. Besides, what choice you got? Just sign the bleeding thing.

Noah *reluctantly signs the card.*

Your handwriting's bloody awful.

She takes it off him, she puts it in the envelope, she licks it and sticks it. She passes it back.

And the front.

Noah *signs the front.*

You gonna be round here for the afternoon now, Nathan?

Lugs   Is there a bit of cake going?

Wendy   He's a cheeky little sod in he? Course there's cake.

Lugs   Did you make it?

Wendy   No, I bought it.

Lugs   I'll be sticking round then.

Wendy *clips* **Lugs** *lightly round the back of the head.*

Wendy   You keep talking like that boyo! Keep on till you see the back of my hand.

Stephanie *enters. She carries a bundle of bed sheets.*

Noah   Morning, birthday girl!

Wendy   Oh! Good morning, my girl!

She starts to sing happy birthday and is quickly joined by the three others. Once they've finished.

Hip, hip!

All   Hooray!

Wendy   Hip, hip!

All   Hooray!

Wendy   Hip, hip!

All   Hooray.

Wendy   Oh, happy birthday, love. Here, that's your washing is it? Give us it here and I'll put it on for you now.

Stephanie   It's all right, I'll do it.

Wendy   Give us it here, will you?

Stephanie   No, I'll do it.

Wendy   I'll do it. Give us it here, man.

Stephanie   Mam. I'll bloody do it, alright. God, somebody check her blood pressure.

Stephanie *exits to the kitchen.*

Wendy   *(Out after her, overly nice)* There's a tea there on the surface for you sweetheart. I haven't put any sugar in it yet. *(Beat)* You sure you don't need a hand in there now?

Stephanie   *(off stage)* I can put sheets in a washing machine Mam. I'm not a bloody invalid.

Wendy   *(To the boys, quietly)* No, but she will be if she keeps talking to me like that.

Stephanie *enters.*

(Nice again) Aww, there she is look, my little girl all grown up. Twenty-one today?! God, that makes me feel ancient.

Lugs   You don't look a day over forty.

Wendy   Careful you! *(To* **Stephanie***)* Come on sweetheart. Sit down. Oi! Move your hairy arse, you.

Noah   Sorry.

Lugs   Got any plans for the day Ste-far-nee?

Stephanie   Today I think I'll be mostly sitting on my fat arse Nathan, feeling sorry for myself. Wondering how much longer till I can see my feet again. Or smoke a fucking cigarette. Or look at myself in the mirror and not feel like I want to cry. That's what I'll be doing today.

Lugs   Sounds lovely.

Stephanie   What was all that going on out there earlier? Woke me up, barking and shouting?

Wendy   This one wasn't it.

Stephanie   Got you again, did he?

Wendy   He bit hole in his trousers and all, mind.

Stephanie   Never. Let's have a look. *(Beat)* He should buy you a new pair.

Wendy   Oh, I'll be going round there later to get the money off him, don't you worry.

Lugs   No.

Wendy   Nathan, it's the principle of the thing. He still owes me a couple of quid for the microwave they had off us and all. We'll sort it.

Noah   Aye, now we're getting to the bottom of it.

Wendy   I don't know what it is you're insinuating, but you can stop right there. Now then birthday girl, what do you want for your special birthday breakfast? We got eggs, bacon, sausages, we got mushrooms …

Stephanie   I'm alright with tea for the minute.

Wendy   Cereals? I bought crumpets. You don't want crumpets with marmalade?

Stephanie   Not at the minute.

Wendy   It's got bits in it?

Stephanie   I can't.

Wendy   You gotta eat something love. How about some toast? Have a piece of toast, will you.

Stephanie   Is there any cake?

Wendy   Of course there's cake. You can't have a birthday without a birthday cake.

Stephanie   Did you make it?

Wendy   I bought it down Tesco's.

Stephanie   Well I'll have some cake later on. I just feel really iffy at the minute.

Wendy   You alright?

Stephanie   Fine. *(Beat)* I'm fine Mam. *(Beat)* Birthday cards?

Wendy   There's one off me there, and that one's off your big brother.

Lugs   I got you one too.

Lugs *produces a card from his pocket.*

Stephanie   Thank you Nathan. *(She opens* **Lugs'** *card. She laughs)* Aw, that's really good, I like that.

Wendy   Let's have a look.

Lugs   It's off me and our Mam, she couldn't really sign it for you, but I know she wants to say happy birthday, you can tell, she was getting all frustrated.

Wendy   *(Referring to* **Lugs'** *card)* That is good.

Stephanie   I'll pop up and see her to say thanks.

Lugs   She'd love that, aye.

Wendy   That one's off your big brother.

Stephanie *opens the card. Beat.*

Bunny rabbits.

Stephanie   I can see that.

Wendy   You like bunny rabbits, don't you?

Stephanie   Hmm. Hm. Thank you, Noah.

Noah   You're welcome.

Stephanie *opens the other card. Beat.*

Stephanie   Bunny rabbits. Thanks Mam.

Silence.

Wendy   Presents!

Noah   Aye. Let me just go grab 'em.

Wendy   Give us a second, sweetheart. **Wendy** *and* **Noah** *exit.*

Beat.

Lugs   I got you a present. Do you want it now, or …? Maybe save it until you've opened your brother's/

Stephanie   /I'll have it now.

Lugs *produces a small box from his pocket.*

Lugs   It was really fiddly trying to wrap it. Most of it's sellotape really. Do you want me to?/

Stephanie   /No, it's alright. Give us a sec.

Stephanie *struggles with the wrapping paper, finally she gets it off, she holds the small box.*

Ooh, bit of jewellery is it? What have I done to deserve jewellery?

She opens the box. Beat.

Lugs   If you open the locket, look, you can put a photo in either side. I thought you could put one of yourself and one of the baby in it, or Shane or …

Stephanie   I'll do that.

Lugs   It's off me and our Mam. *(Beat)* And if Shane asks, you didn't …

Stephanie   I know. Thank you.

She kisses **Lugs** *on the cheek.*

Lugs   *(A little surprised and embarrassed)* Oh! Okay, all right, yeah.

Stephanie *puts it in her pocket.* **Wendy** *enters with a large rectangular box wrapped in paper.*

Wendy   Now, this is something I saw you looking at so you better bloody like it. But I've kept the receipt just in case, so, there, okay, there you go. Happy birthday.

Stephanie   It's not a rabbit is it?

Wendy   No, it's not a bleeding rabbit. Open it, come on.

Stephanie *opens the box. She lifts out a dress and holds it out arm's length.*

I saw you fawning over it when we were down in Cwmbran last. You won't be able to wear it now obviously, but when the baby's here and you're settled and you're up and about, you can put your nice dress on and you can go and have a night out.

Stephanie   Okay.

Wendy   Because life don't stop for you now, girl. You're a young woman, and remember that. I know it might not feel like it, but once the baby's here and … Well you know. You'll still do all the things you want to with your life. And I'm always gonna be here to take the pressure off. Okay? Alright?

Stephanie   Aye.

Wendy   Come here. She kisses Stephanie.

Noah *enters, he holds a plastic bag.*

Wendy   Oh, here we go, few more prezzies off your big bro here now, look.

Noah   Right then, close your eyes.

Stephanie   Why? You better of wrapped these bloody presents, Noah. It's bad enough you had our Mam buy your card.

Noah   What're you on about?

Stephanie   I didn't come up the canal on a biscuit, alright?

Noah   Just close your eyes will you.

Stephanie Noah.

Noah Just close 'em.

Stephanie *closes her eyes.*

Keep 'em shut now. Hands out.

He places a small jewellery box in her hands.

Right, go on then.

Stephanie *opens her eyes.*

Stephanie What is it?

Wendy Open it.

Stephanie *opens the box.*

Stephanie Fucking hell!

Wendy Oi! Language you!

Wendy *comes round to look at it.*

Oh, my Christ in heaven!

Stephanie How the hell can you afford something like this?

Wendy What sort of question is that to ask?

Stephanie Is it real?

Wendy Stephanie Williams!

Noah Of course it is. I take it you like it then?

Lugs That's lovely that is Noah.

Stephanie Look at the detail in there. Look Mam. That bit. Is it silver?

Adam Fair play.

Noah White gold.

Stephanie One, two, three, four, five diamonds!

Wendy That one in the middle's the size of a bleeding light bulb.

Noah   So I did good then? Do you love me now?

Wendy   She's always loved you.

Stephanie   It's the most stunning piece of jewellery I've ever seen. Only jewellery I ever get is from Argos. *(Beat)* It's not from Argos is it?

Noah   No, it's not from Argos. *(Beat)* Does it fit?

Stephanie   Perfect.

Wendy   What do you say to your brother then?

Stephanie   Thank you Noah.

Noah   You're welcome. *(Beat)* I got something here for the baby and all. Do you want it now?

Beat.

Wendy   Steph? Stephanie?

Stephanie   What?

Noah   No, it's all right, I'll give it to her later.

Stephanie   What? Give me what? You got me another present?

Noah   For the baby.

Stephanie   Let's see it.

Noah *reaches into the bag and produces an old tattered toy bear.*

Adam   That's mine.

Noah   Do you remember him?

Adam   I bloody do, it's mine.

Stephanie   No.

Noah   Mam? Do you remember him?

Wendy *stands stunned.*

Beat.

Stephanie   Mam? You alright?

Wendy *starts for the kitchen. She stalls.*

Wendy   Um, No, um it's okay … Right now … I … So.

Stephanie   Mam?

Wendy   Tea! Who wants another tea then? Everyone alright for a tea?

Stephanie   We're fine for tea.

Wendy   I'll just put, um … I'll tell you what I'll do… I'll… put a pot on for Shane.

Stephanie   Mam, calm down.

Wendy   He'll want a cup when he's in the door Steph! Okay … Right. Um. Yes. Okay. Tea.

Wendy *exits. Silence.*

Stephanie   She'll be right now, give her a minute. Give us a look. See, I don't remember him at all. What did you call him?

Adam   Bruce.

Beat.

Noah   Maybe I should get rid of him.

Stephanie   No, don't do that. It's not your fault. She gets like this.

Adam   Look at the state of him.

Noah   Have I been an asshole?

Stephanie   With you coming home … If it wasn't this then it would have been something else.

Adam   Give me a look.

Stephanie   Probably best to put him away though, for the time being.

Noah   Okay.

Stephanie   And don't worry about it.

Noah   Right.

Noah *exits.* **Adam** *follows.*

Adam   'Ere, give us a look at him!

Lugs'*phone rings. He answers.*

Lugs   Alright? *(Beat)* Yeah, I'm at the flat *(Beat)* Alright then, Yeah, yeah I'll be down now. Okay. See you in a sec. *(Putting the phone back in his pocket)* Shane. Got to pop down and help him a sec, I'll be back now.

Lugs *exits.*

Wendy *enters.*

Wendy   Who just went out the door? Noah? That wasn't Noah?

Stephanie   Nathan.

Wendy   Right, okay.

(Beat)

Stephanie   Mam? *(Beat)* Mam. Mam!

Wendy   What's that? Sorry. What was you saying, love?

Stephanie   I think we oughta go to the doctor's.

Wendy   Do you?

Stephanie   I started … Again … Last night. It's worse.

Wendy   Come on then. Let's get you dressed.

Stephanie   Not yet Mam, we need to wait.

Wendy   Stephanie/

Stephanie   /Mam, Shane's just parking the van now. I can't be straight out the door when he comes in. I haven't got it in me to be interrogated today, so let him make a fuss for half hour, then drag me off to some ante-natal or something.

Wendy   That's ridiculous. I tell you girl if it were me/

Stephanie   /But it isn't you is it? So just do as you're told. Okay? *(Beat)* Mam?

Wendy   You can't take chances with your health. We should be straight out the door. **Wendy** *picks up the telephone, she dials.*

Stephanie   What're you doing?

Wendy   Booking you an appointment. What's it look like?

Stephanie   Mam, he's just parking up!

Wendy   Hello? Hello, I'd like to book an appointment please … with Doctor Brooks … Yes, it's for Stephanie Williams … *(Beat)* I was hoping for today … Well it's a bit of an emergency … We can't get her down the hospital, and Doctor Brooks knows her history so we would prefer … yes, she is heavily pregnant … Who am I speaking to? *(Beat)*

Noah *stands in the doorway.*

I know it is … I know, and I don't like to do this but … As soon as possible please … Yeah … Five o'clock? Well I suppose we don't have much of a choice do we? Okay, thank you … thank you, b … Charming.

She puts the phone down.

Noah   You off down the hospital?

Wendy   Just the clinic, love.

Noah   What for?

Stephanie   Routine pregnancy stuff.

Noah   You said it was an emergency.

Stephanie   You know what she's like.

Wendy   Won't get seen till next summer if it ain't, son, awful slow they are down there. So, five o'clock alright?

Noah   Do you want me to come?

Stephanie   No need.

Wendy   What do you know about pregnant women? Say? You'd be 'bout as useful as you are with a can of polish. You can come down to town with us though, pop in the Job Centre, get yourself registered.

Noah   I can sort that out in the week.

Wendy   It's better sooner rather than later son.

Noah   I'll pay my way.

Wendy   I didn't mean it like that. I don't want a penny from you. It's just, I dunno, work gives you purpose don't it? I don't want you sitting round the house brooding, is all.

Noah   I wouldn't. What makes you think I even would?

Wendy   Nothing, just/

Noah   /Like father like son ain't no sure guide to me, alright?

Stephanie   She wasn't saying it like that.

Noah   Better not be. I'll sort myself a job out, don't worry. I'm not afraid of a bit of work.

Wendy   Nobody's saying you are.

Noah   And I'll get something tidy and all. I won't be peddling powder out the house for a couple of quid.

Silence.

Shane *and* **Lugs** *enter. The door is left ajar.*

Shane   Happy birthday princess! There she is look. Fucking hell, she's getting on now ah? I'm sure I can see a few extra wrinkles round the eyes. Might have to trade you in love, ah!? Pop down the sixth form and pick up something fresh.

Wendy   Don't wind her up today.

Shane   I'm only having a laugh. You had a lovely day so far? Did you have a nice birthday breakfast?

Stephanie Our Mam's bought plenty of food.

Shane I trust you've put some aside for me, Mother.

Wendy There's plenty left.

Shane Proper job. So, what'd you get for your birthday? Anything nice?

Stephanie Mam got me a dress.

Shane Well done Mother. And what about Noah? Ah? What did Noah bring you from his travels? Jewel of the Nile? The finest spices from Arabia? Ah? Gold, frankincense and fucking myrrh, or what?

Stephanie This ring?

Shane *(Taking her hand)* Give us a look at that. Fucking hell, that can't be real.

Wendy Shane.

Shane Is this real?

Noah What do you take me for?

Shane Well, fair play butty, it's hell of a ring. *(Beat)* How much?

Silence.

What? What? I'm interested. Come on, how much did it cost you? *(Beat)* Alright, fair play. Discreet, I like it. And I have to say Noah, it's a beautiful ring.

Stephanie I think so.

Shane I'd have said we were a bit far down the valley to be buying our sisters' engagement rings, but to each their own. Right then, anyway, are you ready for the main event or what?

Stephanie Ok.

Shane You gotta look the other way now whilst I get it, mind. You stay looking that way, alright?

Stephanie   I will.

Shane   Don't be sneaking a fucking peek.

Stephanie   Alright.

Shane *exits with* **Lugs***, briefly. Silence. They return carrying a baby's cot.*

Shane   Don't look. Don't look.

Stephanie   I'm not.

Beat.

Shane   Okay. You can look.

Silence.

Fucking beauty ain't she?

Wendy   Oh, it's gorgeous Shane. Innit Steph?

Shane   What do you reckon of the old baby boudoir, Noah?

Noah   It looks the business.

Shane   Most expensive one in the shop. Me and him went and got it last week. Went in there, and the girl in there said herself that this cot will guarantee the baby will never be up crying, it is that comfortable. Didn't she?

Lugs   She did yeah.

Shane   I can't see where the money goes in it myself. Only the best for my boy though. Got him a … *(Clicks his fingers)* a … Whatsaname too. Spinning thing.

Lugs   A mobile.

Shane   Aye. Down in the van. You should see that fucking thing. Got all the planets on it, they all light up and all they do, plays music, the lot. *(Beat)* So, what do you think?

Stephanie   It's lovely.

Shane   To say the least. Just lovely is it?

Stephanie   No, It looks like a really good one.

Shane   It's the most expensive one going, of course it's a really fucking good one. He won't need another bed till he's got hairs on his bollocks, the size of the thing. *(Beat)* I'll be honest, I was expecting a bit more enthusiasm from you, love. I spent an age shopping for this, mind.

Stephanie   Sorry.

Shane   Half the kids round here sleep in the fucking dog basket. I bring you back the best you can get and all I get's a shrug of the fucking shoulders.

Stephanie   No, no you're right, I'm sorry. It's a beautiful cot, Shane. I think our boy'll be really happy in it.

Shane   Fucking right he will.

Stephanie   Thank you.

She stands and kisses him.

Shane   That's a bit more like it. Right then mother, cup of tea on the cards or what?

Wendy   I just put a pot on.

Shane   Well get a move on, I'm fucking parched.

Wendy *exits to the kitchen. Shane's phone rings.*

Shane   Coco boy! What's happening!? Alright shag or what? *(Beat)* Yeah, aye, it was a great night. Awesome to have you back in one piece, butty. Saying that I'd have said the Taliban've blown the bollocks off you the way you was drinking, you fucking pussy. Ah?! *(Laughs) (Beat)* Tonight? Oh aye, I'll be down there for a few, no danger… yeah, yeah. *(Beat)* So listen, what can I do you for? … Just the three is it? *(Laughs)* Aye, taking it easy. Right well I'll send Igor round and he'll be with you in about fifteen, twenty, alright? *(Beat)* Alright, well look after yourself and I'll see you later, butt. Tarah now.

He puts his phone in his pocket.

Right then Lugso, three down to Coco.

Lugs   Okay.

Shane   They're back in the place they were two weeks ago. I switched them around from last week. Do you know where I'm talking about?

Lugs   Yeah, I think so.

Shane   Here? Where's the keys I left you.

Stephanie *hands* **Shane** *keys.*

Good girl. Is it locked?

Stephanie   Yeah. Of course.

Shane   Here.

He throws the keys to **Lugs**.

And I know how much is there, to the molecule, so you keep your hands to yourself.

Lugs   I would never mess about.

Shane   Not if you know what's good for you.

Lugs *exits.*

What you doing tonight then? Fancy coming down town?

Stephanie   I'm knackered.

Shane   Suit yourself. What about you Noah? Fancy it? Meet my butty. Just back from Afghanistan.

Noah   You said, aye.

Shane   You up for it?

Noah   No, I'm gonna stay in with our Steph.

Stephanie   You don't have to.

Noah   I want to.

Shane   What you want to sit round painting each other's toenails for? Get yourself down town with us and get down to some proper drinking, with proper men, hearing some proper stories. You ever visit Afghanistan on your travels, Noah?

Noah   Never been to Afghanistan, no.

Shane   No, I wouldn't have thought you had. See that's what I'm talking about when I say travelling. Rifle in your hand dodging roadside bombs, butt.

Wendy *enters.*

Wendy   Here you are.

She gives **Shane** *a tea.*

Shane   Ta. *(Back to* **Noah***)* No, if you're gonna leave the country, go round the world, then do it proper, with purpose. Don't just lounge about by the water with some pool boy rubbing sun-cream between your shoulders.

Stephanie   You don't know what Noah's done with his life.

Shane   Nobody does. That's the mystery of the man, innit Noah?

Wendy   Been all over the world, haven't you?

Noah   I've seen a fair old chunk of it, aye.

Shane   But how much has he experienced? I mean it's all fine and well sitting on top of a mountain, but if you're only up there looking for a few bars of signal then it's a waste of fucking time. You catch my drift?

Noah   Aye, sophisticated as it is.

Shane   Good.

Beat.

Wendy   You've done it all haven't you my boy?

Noah   I've had a good go.

Shane   Tell us a story then.

Noah   I haven't got no stories.

Shane   Make one up.

Wendy   Oh go on, please. Go on. Tell us anything.

Noah   Mam.

Wendy   It's your sister's birthday. She'd love to hear you tell a story.

Noah   Really?

Stephanie   Don't ask me. You know you want too, so just get on with it. We're not gonna beg.

Beat.

Noah   Fair enough. I met this girl in Bangkok/

Shane   /Here we go Mother. Got himself a chick with a dick.

Beat.

Noah   I was due to leave but the sun's shining … I don't know how to put it but she's a good looking girl and well …

Wendy   Enough said.

Noah   I decided to extend my stay. I was supposed to fly back out to Japan for work.

Wendy   What work was that?

Noah   I'd been working as a teacher.

Wendy   Really? Teaching what?

Noah   English, to children.

Wendy   You were teaching the little kiddies?

Shane   I wouldn't get too excited mother, they'd let a monkey teach it, so long as he's got a passport.

Wendy   I don't care. My boy, teaching English. Oh my God, they'd call you Mr Williams, wouldn't they?

Stephanie   Let him tell his bloody story, will you?

Wendy   I'm sorry, but I think it's wonderful, my son teaching the world leaders of tomorrow, coz that's where we're heading. I read it.

Stephanie   Mam!

Wendy   Alright. I'll shut up.

Beat.

Noah   I was only supposed to be out there three weeks, I ended up staying months. I met the family. They let me live in their house.

Stephanie   Did they live in a hut?

Noah   No. Not far off, though. They weren't starving poor but, you know. What we ended up doing was, in the day whilst the girl was at work I did this thing with her dad. He was a taxi driver. And out there they get money for every westerner they drop off to local businesses, right. So we just made our way round the whole place. I didn't have to buy nothing just have a look, and he got his money.

Shane   He was on the scam.

Noah   Not really.

Shane   Course he is.

Noah   Well it was a great way to see the island, regardless. And he'd still be picking up punters so I was meeting all sorts in the taxi, like. I loved it. This one day he picks up this Japanese business man. Course I'd been living in Japan and my Japanese was half about so I was showing off to the old man a bit. Anyway, turns out he's this big importer of jewels, and he was banging on about these special blue sapphires, and all the tax being lowered on some government initiative, for export. He buys them in Thailand and sells them on for a big mark up back in Japan. Now my ears prick up a bit here look, because at that point I'd been seriously thinking about asking the girl to come to Japan with me.

Wendy   What did she say? Did she go with you?

Noah   Well this is it. I had a feeling she'd say yes but she was an only daughter. The family were skint and they'd struggle without the money she brought in. *(Beat)* My plan was to buy a load of these blue sapphires the business man was on about, take them over to Japan, sell them there and send back the profit to her parents.

Shane   You're buying her basically.

Wendy   No, no it's a wonderful, wonderful thing to do. I'm proud of you son.

Shane   Ease up on the praise, he hasn't finished his fucking story yet.

Noah   Just give us a minute and I'll finish my fucking story. *(Beat)* I already had my plane ticket so I spent everything else I had.

Shane   How much was that?

Noah   Just under five grand. *(Beat)* I flew out and she stayed behind to say goodbye to her family. When I landed in Japan I went straight to the jewellers. *(Beat; to* **Shane***)* And you'll like this. I remember walking in there like I was the main man. I poured them out on the counter and the bloke looks at me like I'm stupid.

Wendy   Why?

Noah   They were absolutely worthless.

Wendy   No.

Shane   Of course they fucking were.

Wendy   No. What about the girl? She still went to Japan with you?

Shane   Oh yeah! And they lived happily ever after in a house made of hopes and dreams. Get a grip will you, she was part of the scam.

Wendy No?!

Noah Her, her dad, the businessman. The jeweller, obviously.

Shane Five grand for a fucking rub.

Wendy But he loved her.

Shane Aye and I love a curry, but if I spent five grand on one it would be fair comment to call me a cunt. Couldn't you see that coming a mile off? The girl, she was a stunner, wasn't she?

Noah Absolutely.

Shane Course she fucking was. Probably fleeces half a dozen pillocks a year.

Wendy Did she break your heart?

Shane Fuck his heart, my heart's breaking just listening to you. You want your head reading, because if I was you my piss would be boiling right now.

Stephanie Alright now, Shane.

Shane No, no, coming back here, swanning back in after all this time. First fucking phone call you get in years is 'Alright Mam? How's it going? Listen I'll be back in two days so knock the kettle on will you!'

Wendy He's back and that's what matters.

Shane Aye, but what good's he to us? Skint and with the clap? It's a bit late in the day. And I'm being serious here, mind. He should've been here. And you'll sit there and swoon when he tells you a story of him burning his money, whilst you two were in all sorts of trouble back here.

Beat.

Noah What's he talking about?

Beat.

Shane He don't know nothing does he?

Wendy   Not on her birthday, love.

Shane   Because if he had any idea he wouldn't be taking the piss with stories like that.

Stephanie   Shane.

Shane   Why protect him though? He rings you two days ago for the first time in what?

Wendy   I'm going out for a walk.

Stephanie   Mam.

Shane   Don't you dare walk away from me! I asked you a question, how long?

Beat.

Wendy!

Stephanie   Shane.

Noah   Six years.

Shane   Six fucking years! Hasn't been home in ten, and now he's back I gotta wear dark glasses round the house to protect my eyes from the sun shining out his arse!

Stephanie   Will you just leave him alone!

Shane   *(With calm menace)* Back in your box. *(Beat)* I would have killed to have had a mother like yours growing up, and you couldn't give a fuck. Flying round the world without a second's thought, and hey, they can make their peace with that coz what choice they got? But for you to carry on unburdened in this house? To have the gall to tell stories of you pissing your money up the wall whilst your poor old mum was locked up in the fucking nut house? No.

Stephanie   Don't call it a nut house!

Shane   What would you call it? *(Beat)* There isn't a single photograph of you in this place, they never mentioned you. It wasn't until two days ago I even knew you existed.

Stephanie   Who the hell do you think you are/

Wendy   /Steph/

Stephanie   /Just throwing our business about?

Shane   I love this family.

Stephanie   No, you love minimum back-chat and three square meals a day.

Shane   No, I love this family.

Stephanie   Why? When it don't love you?

Wendy   Stephanie.

Shane   What?

Wendy   She's all hormonal. She's been like it all day. Take no notice.

Shane *grabs* **Stephanie** *by the arm.*

Shane   Say it again. Go on.

Wendy   She didn't mean it.

Shane   Feeling brave now your brother's back is it? Don't you think for a second he'll save you.

Stephanie   With you, love, (hand on her belly) with this! I'm beyond saving, so you can do whatever you please.

Shane *slaps her across the face.* **Wendy** *lunges at him.*

Wendy   Don't you dare!

Shane *pushes her off, she lands in a heap by the front door.*

Noah   Oi!

Shane   What?! What are you gonna do?! Ah!?

Noah stands rooted to the ground. Beat. (Back to **Stephanie***) Take it back.* **Stephanie** *shakes her head.*

Wendy   No, no, please, no.

Shane   Shut up, shut up! Take it back Steph. Coz I swear to god, you'll find no hero in him. Take it back.

Stephanie   No.

He slaps her.

Shane   Where is he? Say? Where's your hero now?! Stood across the room with his hands in his fucking pockets. *(Beat)* He's nowhere love. It's just you and me.

Beat.

Lugs *enters.*

Come on butt. Let's go.

Shane *and* **Lugs** *exit.*

Silence.

Lights down. End of scene.

Scene Four

Adam *stands on stage.* **Noah** *stands across from him. Again, dressed in his coat with his bag slung over his shoulder.*

Adam   We were those boys. Those poor boys from down the way, you know, the Williams boys. Always the last to go home. Home!? Our childhood is thick jackets and street lamps. I hated the other boys when their Mothers called them in, I'd hate them more when they'd sulk. In the end and every night it was just us, those poor boys. We had mothers everywhere mind. Mothers who knew our situation, who'd find us a little something so long as we didn't call too often, or stay too long, or sit on the furniture. A sandwich on Osborne road, pair of gloves from number fifty-two, and a warm inside the kitchen door from Mrs Powell. Our childhood is one long walk in the dark waiting for the old man to finish. Every night she stood by the window to watch us up the hill, to quietly open the door, to smile despite him. But on that night she wasn't there, he was stood in her place, so we turned around. We huddled in a car park. And that's where they found us and that's when I realised you'd be ok. When those boys turned the corner, as they stood over us, when you let your head bow to give them permission and your voice trembled as you spoke. As they laughed. As you ran. As I lay on the ground, as they kicked me. As I watched you run away I knew that you'd be fine.

Adam *sits at the table.* **Noah** *enters. He has his bag slung over his back and he wears his jacket.* **Wendy** *enters, she carries a plate with a steak on it, and chips, a steak knife and a fork. She places it on the table.*

Wendy   Sit. *(Beat)* Sit down. There. Let me feed you. I want to feed my boy.

Beat.

Noah *sits at the table. He starts to eat.* **Wendy** *sits the other end of the table. An argument flares next door. It gets worse and worse. The woman and man scream and shout. Something hits the wall. We hear a door slam and someone walks past the dimpled glass in the front door.*

Silence.

Wendy   How is it?

Noah *nods.*

Three pounds for that. Can you believe that? Three pounds.

Noah   It's a big steak.

Silence.

Wendy   It's a good stall down the market. There's a really nice man. He always sorts me out with the best cuts.

Adam   Where are you going?

Beat.

Wendy   I used to go to school with him. We weren't friends or nothing, but he always puts the best ones aside for me. We have a joke like I'm a spy picking up some important thing or something. I say to him, I say, do you have the package? *(Beat)* It's only a bit of fun.

Adam   Back for the foreseeable? What did you foresee then, Noah?

Wendy   There ain't many chips, sorry, I only had one potato. Got you some sweet corn though so two of your five a day. *(Beat)* I do wonder who came up with five a day. Somebody with plenty of bloody time on their hands.

Adam   Don't humour him.

Wendy   When I was a kid, you'd have your meat and two veg. When you were young it was no different so you gotta wonder where all this comes from. I'm not saying there's nothing to it, mind you. Some of the kids round here could definitely stand to cut down on the chocolate. Their little 'un next door, he's out of breath at the top of the steps. And that playground out front is always empty. When you were young you wouldn't spend no time round the house. You'd be out until it was pitch black.

Adam   And why was that?

Beat.

Wendy   You don't want no more?

Noah   I'm not hungry.

Beat.

Adam   Where're you going then?

Noah   I spoke to a mate of mine, he's gonna let me stay on his couch for a bit. He's running a bar so I can work there for a while.

Wendy   Where's that?

Noah   Spain. He's doing a season out on some resort so he can sort me out. Cheap flights.

Adam   Bit of sunshine. Happy days.

Noah   I think it's probably for the best.

Beat.

Wendy   We could come out and visit you.

Noah   Yeah. I don't know how long I'll be out there mind, just need to make a bit of money. Pay for a ticket.

Wendy   Where?

Noah   I haven't even thought about it.

Wendy   I could give you some money.

Noah   No, I don't want anything off you.

Adam   What if she needs something from you?

Silence.

Noah   I should probably get on …

Wendy   Why'd you come back?

Adam   He had to.

Noah   Stephanie's twenty-first.

Beat.

Wendy   No, tell me the truth son. I don't care what it is. Really I don't. I know it was because of the girl, I do, so just say it for your Mam. *(Beat)* Did you love her?

Beat.

Noah   As close as I've come.

Wendy   And the ring you gave to Stephanie?

Noah   I was gonna propose.

Wendy   Right. *(Beat)* You had nowhere else to go.

Noah   No.

Wendy   Son, I don't think you even realise it but you had nowhere else to go.

Beat.

Noah   Am I a bad man?

Wendy   No son.

Noah   Am I like him?

Wendy   Not even a little bit. *Beat.*

Noah   *(Almost laughing)* I would have married her, had kids with her.

Wendy   You'd make a wonderful father.

Noah   For the first time in my life I was looking that way *(Pointing forward)* Not over my shoulder. Probably why I didn't see it coming.

Wendy   You've got a good heart.

Noah   I really don't.

Wendy   Of course you do.

Noah   When that jeweller told me they were fake I didn't even argue.

Wendy   It's not fair.

Noah   But I didn't even put up a fight. I didn't shout or curse or anything I just walked out the shop.

Wendy   Coz you're a good man Noah.

Noah   Because of course it was too good to be true. Of course it was.

Wendy   You've got your whole life/

Noah   /And this couple come walking towards me, laughing.

Wendy   Not laughing at you, were they?

Noah   They looked straight through me.

Wendy   Right?

Noah   Like I wasn't even there.

Wendy   I think you need to remember/

Noah   So I made sure they saw me. I made certain.

Beat.

Wendy   What did you do?

Noah   He's in there somewhere Mam.

Silence. **Stephanie** *enters.*

Stephanie   Going then are you? *(Beat)* Go on then, fuck off. Go on, don't stand there gawping, fuck off!

Wendy   Stephanie.

Stephanie   Get from here. I'm surprised you lasted a day you … gutless … fuck you. Go on, and don't you dare think of coming back. I mean it. With all of me. I will harm you.

Adam   Don't go.

Noah   I'm sorry Steph.

Stephanie You're not sorry so don't say it! Don't even say it. You're worse than him. At least he's got the guts to follow his convictions. You're pathetic. Run away. And I hope one day it dawns on you. God I hope you realise what a coward you are and I hope it crushes you. I really, really do.

Noah I know I'm a coward.

Stephanie Oh, very noble. I suppose admitting it absolves you of the guilt does it? This ain't the catholic church.

Wendy He needs to go.

Stephanie Well whatever he fucking needs Mam!

Adam Just slow down.

Beat.

Stephanie I wish it was you.

Noah Ok.

Noah picks up his rucksack.

Stephanie I grew up in foster care. *(Beat)* Oi! You listening?!

Wendy Let's not do it like this.

Stephanie No! Shane was right. Why protect him? I spent most my teens bouncing from one foster home to the next.

Noah Right.

Stephanie Mam was committed down the hospital.

Noah Ok.

Stephanie And they sent me all round the place mind, Cardiff, Newport, fucking Port Talbot. Never given time to settle coz if you don't fit straight away they send you back, see.

Adam Stephanie.

Stephanie Mam would be back out, you'd get the phone call, time to come home. And I'd come back and it would be fine for a couple of weeks, then you'd see it all creeping back in. Scratching round the house for breakfast. Kitchen would be a fucking state.

Noah   I can't fix it for you.

Stephanie   Wow. You self-important prick.

Noah   Nobody can, because we're broken.

Adam   You don't need to start with this/

Noah   /Me and you and this family, all fucked/

Adam   /Shut up/

Noah   /Just wreckage, and that's all it's ever gonna be.

Adam   Just shut up!

Stephanie   Speak for yourself mate. We're fine.

Noah   Oh aye. *(Laughs)* Yeah. Love's young dream, you and that animal.

Beat.

Stephanie   Mam's the best she's ever been.

Noah   It's got her by the throat.

Wendy   Not anymore.

Noah   Mam.

Wendy   Not anymore it don't.

Noah *makes his way over to the bookshelf, he pulls out one of the folders.*

Adam   Noah?!

Noah   What's this then?

Adam   Put it back.

Wendy   You wouldn't understand.

Noah   No you're right. I don't. *(Reading)* The body of the local schoolgirl Jean Davis was found at eight-thirty a.m. yesterday, three weeks after her disappearance. You don't even know this girl.

Wendy   I know her son. God help me, I know her.

Noah   Father kills children following divorce. Man found guilty of abduction. It's full of them. Front to back.

Adam   Noah.

Wendy   I know them one by one.

Noah   All these notes you've scribbled down, 'Say goodnight to my boy for me'?

Stephanie   Okay.

Noah   'Tuck him in and stroke his hair'? 'Adam' 'Adam' 'Adam' It's everywhere.

'Adam'!?

Stephanie   Please stop.

Noah   How long has she been doing this? You must know about it? And you just let her hold her hand above the fire.

Wendy   Listen now/

Stephanie   /You're blaming me?

Wendy   Nobody's putting/ blame.

Noah   /Why do you think she's doing this Steph? Why do you think she leaves them in plain view?

Wendy   Listen here/

Stephanie   /What can I do?

Noah   Something, anything, intervene for fuck's sake!

Wendy   Oi! Listen! The pair of you. Oi!. Look at me son! *(Beat)* I won't hide him away under the bed. He spent enough of his time there alive. He's not a dirty little secret. And I won't apologise for how I cope. I won't ask an explanation from you neither, because you couldn't give me one if you wanted to. When your brother passed it was an explosion, son. Look at me. An explosion that threw you half way round the world, and left me and your sister trapped in the rubble.

Stephanie   Mam. Mam.

Wendy   What? What's that?

Stephanie   I don't know. Oh, oh shit. *(Holding her stomach)*

Wendy   What love? What's wrong?

Stephanie   I'm not sure, I … I don't know … Ow!

Wendy   Ok. *(Very calm)* Alright love, no problem, alright. I'll just get your coat. Ok?

Stephanie   Be quick … Oh!

Adam   Steph?

Wendy   Don't you worry now. It's gonna be all fine. Noah, grab my car keys off the hook in the kitchen.

Noah   Okay.

Noah *exits.*

Wendy *exits.*

Stephanie   Oh shit! Oh shit! Oh fuck! Mam, Mam! Mam! Hurry! Quick!

Wendy *enters with two coats.*

Wendy   Ok. I'm here. It's ok. Hold my arm. Noah, keys.

Stephanie   Ohhhh!

Noah *enters.*

Noah   Here.

Wendy   Good boy. Get the door.

Noah *opens the door, the two women walk through it.*

Wendy   Ok now sweetheart. It's all gonna be ok. Shhhhhhhhh.

They exit.

Silence.

The dog starts barking.

Adam   Do you remember her face when we gave her the tickets?
By the time we got down Cwmbran station everyone in the
carriage knew what day it was didn't they? It was our mother's
birthday and her lovely boys were taking her to see the circus.
A tent in a stinking field, just off the dual carriageway, Steph
moaning coz of her brand new trainers. And spade a spade, it
was shit wasn't it? Proper shit. But that night I saw our mam as a
little girl. She gasped, like real, chest going, gasped at the trapeze,
eyes wide at the sight of the tigers, the clowns came out and she
laughed so hard she almost choked. Tears at the corners of her
smiling mouth. She smiled all the way home, and when we got
in the door, she said a thank you so genuine it wrecked me. I lay
in bed that night planning ways to make her smile again, of ways
to make it permanent. *(Beat)* It's the dog barking that always
brings it back for me. Listen. *(Beat)* Do you feel it? That rising
in you? There. Heavy feet past the window. The banging on the
door, mam crossing the hallway to let him in, the chain, the latch.
I can hear the tone of her voice, now. I can hear him looking for
something to latch onto, scouring the house for something to
justify the blistering anger, searching her. It don't take long of
course, then it never did, did it? She turns to pleading, it builds
and builds. See that was all bearable coz you could gauge what
was happening but the silences in it is what I could never stand,
when he was catching his breath, I could hear you crying then,
and you'd always think, he's done it, you know, he's done her in.
(Beat) See I knew you'd never be able to do anything, but I didn't
know that I would, I didn't, honestly, it was one foot following
the other until I was staring at his back and the soles of her feet
lolling. I just thought, it stops tonight. Clear as that. I placed my
hand on his shoulder and it was just like that, it stops tonight.
And he shit himself mind. He did. I think that's why he did me
properly. Because you could see that he shit himself. I just said to
him, I said 'This stops tonight' He pushed me, I said it again 'This

stops tonight.' He punched. I said it again. 'This stops tonight.'
His fingers tightened round my throat, it was just ringing out in
my head. 'This stops tonight, this stops tonight, this stops tonight.'
(Beat) It did though, didn't it?

Beat.

Shane *enters.*

Beat.

Shane   Where are the girls?

Adam   It stops tonight.

Shane   *(Beat)* Going somewhere are we? *(Beat)* Anywhere nice?
(Beat) I hear Thailand's lovely. Here, now don't you worry about
those two while you're away, alright. I'll look after your girls.
(Sniggers) And when you go this time, do us a favour will you,
just stay, stay there for them, for your sister … and for your moth
…

*Without warning **Noah** drives the steak knife into **Shane**'s chest.*
Shane *stumbles back shocked.*

Er?

Shane *stands, blood starts running from the wound, his shirt
becomes soaked in it. He slumps down in the corner of the room
the knife protruding from his chest. Silence, all that can be heard
is **Shane**'s laboured breathing. **Noah** calmly picks up his bag and
slings it over his shoulder.*

Adam   Run.

Noah *exits.*

The lights fade down to black.

End